THE
THOMPSON
INDICTMENT

JAN BONE

PUBLIC INTEREST PRESS

Grateful acknowledgment is made to Random House and Robert Bolt, author of *A Man for All Seasons*. Copyright © 1960, 1962 by Robert Bolt. Reprinted by permission of Random House, Inc.

Grateful acknowledgment is made to F. Lee Bailey and *Newsweek*, Inc., for material on pages xv and xvi, Copyright 1978 by *Newsweek*, Inc. all rights reserved, reprinted by permission.

Grateful acknowledgment is made to John Madigan, whose commentary on the Paul Wigoda case is reprinted through the courtesy of WBBM Radio, Chicago.

Grateful acknowledgment is made to the *Journal of Criminal Law and Criminology* for special permission to reprint the article "Immunity: How It Works in Real Life."

Grateful acknowledgment is made to Herman Schwartz and Bruce Jackson, professors of law and Jurisprudence at the State University of New York at Buffalo — and to *Harper's Magazine* — for permission to quote portions from their *Harper's* article on prosecutorial abuse.

Grateful acknowledgment is made to Judge William J. Campbell of the United States District Court, Northern District of Illinois, for permission to reprint his address "Eliminate the Grand Jury."

Grateful acknowledgment is made to the *American Bar Association Journal* for permission to reprint portions of the article by Superior Court Judge Melvin P. Antell on "The Modern Grand Jury: Beknighted Supergovernment" —from Vol. 51, page 153: February, 1965.

Grateful acknowledgment is made to *Paddock Publications* for permission to reprint photograph of Author Jan Bone on back cover; to Taylor Jones of the *Los Angeles Times Syndicate* for permission to reproduce the drawing on page iii copyright 1978 *Los Angeles Times* reprinted with permission; to *UPI Compix* for permission to reproduce photographs of James Thompson, Otto Kerner, and Edward Barrett; to the *Chicago Tribune* for permission to reproduce photographs of James Thompson, Samuel Skinner, Charles Bonk, Paul Wigoda, and William Rentschler; and to Wide World Photos for permission to reproduce photographs of James Thompson.

My reputation as a prosecutor
is all I have.

JAMES R. THOMPSON,
quoted in the *Chicago Tribune*,
March 7, 1976.

Los Angeles Times
SYNDICATE

Taylor Jones
©The Charleston Gazette 1978

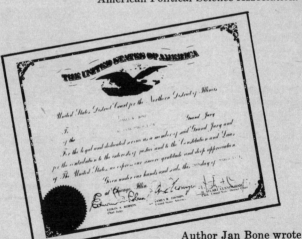

Jan Bone's writing honors
include this award from the
American Political Science Association.

Author Jan Bone wrote
THE THOMPSON INDICTMENT from
a unique vantage point as foreman of a Federal
Grand Jury. U.S. Attorney James R. Thompson
signed the certificate of appreciation she received.

THE THOMPSON INDICTMENT

ABOUT THE AUTHOR

Jan Bone's service as foreman of a Federal Grand Jury in 1974 during James R. Thompson's term as U.S. Attorney led her ultimately to write this important book. The onesidedness of the grand jury process appalled her, and several subsequent free-lance writing assignments further convinced her she should explore the Thompson record as federal prosecutor.

Jan Bone's background and substantial reputation as reporter, free-lance investigative writer, author, and researcher equipped her with unique tools to undertake this demanding and controversial work on the criminal justice system. She devoted hundreds of hours to interviews with the central figures, with judges and lawyers, with other knowledgeable persons, and to the painstaking perusal of court transcripts. trial testimony, and private correspondence.

A graduate of Cornell University at 20 with a B.A. degree in English, Author Bone launched her career as a reporter for the Williamsport (Pa.) *Sun*. She has since won a variety of honors related to her writing. Among these are an American Political Science Association award (1970) for distinguished reporting of public affairs and an Illinois Education Association "School Bell Award" (1968) for best comprehensive coverage of education in Illinois by dailies under 250,000 circulation. She also received a Chicago Working Newsman's scholarship from the Chicago Headline Club, a local chapter of Sigma Delta Chi.

Over the past decade, Mrs. Bone has written more than 500 free-lance articles on assignment for a variety of publications. She is co-author of a widely-used textbook on film study. She has conducted workshops for gifted children and teachers and taught courses in creative writing.

A native Pennsylvanian, she is a longtime resident of Palatine, Illinois, where she lives with her husband. They are parents of four sons.

Contents

Truth forever on the scaffold,
wrong forever on the throne;
yet that scaffold always sways the future
and behind the dim unknown standeth God
within the shadow, keeping watch above
    His own.

          —JAMES RUSSELL LOWELL,
            poet, essayist, and diplomat,
            (1819-1891)

INTRODUCTION

This is a chilling story. It has not previously been told. It was constructed painstakingly by Author Jan Bone over many hundreds of hours from voluminous court records, trial transcripts, sworn testimony, and interviews, mostly taped, with lawyers, defendants, judges, and other knowledgeable figures. Defendants and their families shared with her their files, correspondence, and diaries.

What emerges is a disillusioning tale of arrogance, intrigue, cynicism, blind ambition, and perversion of legal processes by those specifically sworn to uphold the law and seek justice, prosecutors celebrated by the press as idealistic corruption fighters.

This book is a carefully wrought account, through six case histories, of a federal prosecutor's misuse of his office — which one of his recent predecessors describes as "the most powerful office in America, bar none" — to become Governor of Illinois and an eager seeker after the Presidency of the United States in 1980 or later.

The prosecutorial scenario from November 30, 1971, to June 30, 1975, was enacted before the eyes of a normally probing press, which seemingly was rendered "blind" by its own support of, entanglements with, and obligations to James R. Thompson.

THE THOMPSON INDICTMENT is likely to be dismissed by some as a smear, hatchet job, diatribe, political attack. It is none of these. Anyone who takes the trouble to read it will discover a meticulously researched, fully documented, but damning exposé. It has been carefully written by a professional writer with excellent credentials. As a journalistic work, it is as significant as many investigative series which have won Pulitzer awards. It is important as an addition to the body of writing and research on our criminal justice system.

When James R. Thompson, an appointee of Richard Nixon, was named to be United States Attorney for the Northern District of Illinois, he was totally unknown to the public and barely a bit better known to the Illinois political, commercial, labor, and media hierarchies.

At his swearing-in ceremony, the beefy, pale-faced, 6 foot 6 inch Thompson, who soon would be known throughout Illinois as Big Jim, told the assembled dignitaries, among them a host of federal judges and political figures, that he had coveted the Presidency since he was 11, leaving no doubt he regarded this appointment as his first step toward that pinnacle. Then, without pause, he embarked on a carefully plotted path of personal political advancement that would generate maximum media attention and coverage.

During the near-orgy that followed, grand juries were used by Thompson and his staff to obtain virtually automatic indictments of political figures. They were announced with elaborate fanfare at press conferences by Big Jim himself, whose accusatory statements cast a pall of guilt over those who — in our system as it is supposed to work — should still have been presumed innocent. Reputations built over years were destroyed in minutes. Federal building reporters were ethically seduced, cajoled, and virtually added to the prosecutorial team, thus destroying any pretense of objective coverage. In the courtroom, little hard evidence was presented. Thompson and his assistants "proved" their tortured theories of conspiracy, extortion, and other criminal allegations by relying almost totally on the testimony of admitted bribers and other acknowledged wrongdoers, who generally testified under grants of immunity to avoid jail themselves.

Author Jan Bone has chosen six case histories to document her thesis about the unjust policies and improper practices of Thompson as federal prosecutor — policies and practices that made guilty verdicts almost automatic in the poisonous Watergate atmosphere. As CBS commentator Eric Sevareid put it, "Anybody who is hauled up and accused of anything is assumed guilty until proved innocent."

She shows how the processes of justice were misused and the safeguards abused or ignored. She shows how injustice can occur through the promiscuous granting of immunity from prosecution.

She also raises questions that bear directly on the guilt or possible innocence of those convicted.

In this book, the cases of U.S. Appellate Court Judge Otto Kerner, former Illinois Secretary of State and Cook County Clerk Edward J. Barrett, Republican leader and businessman William H. Rentschler, Cook County Commissioner Charles S. Bonk, Chicago Alderman Paul Wigoda, and Lake County (Illinois) Board Chairman Ronald R. Coles are examined in detail by Mrs. Bone.

During his 3½ year tenure as U.S. Attorney, Thompson and his intimate associate and successor, Samuel K. Skinner, were involved in perhaps an equal number of other highly publicized cases.

The sequence and timing of Thompson's political indictments tell something about his plans. Any realistic appraisal of the Chicago political climate gave him little chance against the legendary Daley. But his assaults against the so-called Daley machine, which was anathema to downstate and suburban Republicans, would give him a potent issue in a statewide campaign. Thus he decided to go for Governor of Illinois; and, in apparent violation of the Hatch Act, plotted his campaign from his federal office with the aid of an inner circle of Assistant U.S. Attorneys.

No account of the stewardship of Thompson as U.S. Attorney would be complete without reference to his closest associate, Samuel K. Skinner, who has been said to take considerable pride in his less-than-complimentary nickname, "Sam the Hammer."

Skinner joined the U.S. Attorney's office in the late 1960s, when Thomas A. Foran held that office. Foran assigned Skinner to the Civil Division because, in his words, he felt Skinner at the time was "too-hot-eyed and immature and unstable for criminal stuff."

Skinner's influence expanded greatly when Thompson became U.S. Attorney. No one questioned the fact that Skinner was next in command. He spoke for Thompson in many matters. He was Thompson's crony, alter ego. Thompson as Governor named a dog "Sam" for Skinner.

On June 30, 1975, Thompson resigned as U.S. Attorney to launch his campaign for Governor. He moved smoothly to the big, blue-chip Chicago law firm of Winston & Strawn, taking with him one of his trusted Assistant U.S. Attorneys, Dan Weil. This gave him a $50,000 a year base from which to run his campaign, and also a shrewd, well connected fund-raiser, Thomas A. Reynolds, Jr., a senior partner of the law firm.

When he left, Thompson went all-out to assure that Skinner would succeed him. He strongly urged U.S. Sen. Charles H. Percy (R., Ill.), who originally had proposed Thompson to then-President Richard Nixon, to seek President Gerald Ford's appointment of Skinner. Percy, considered a liberal in matters of individual liberty and human rights, acceded to Thompson's desire and proposed Skinner. This guaranteed that the Thompson record at U.S. Attorney would get no objective scrutiny until after Skinner had completed *his* term in office. Skinner, of course, completed the prosecution of some of the more visible cases launched during Thompson's term, but also sought to leave his own mark as a tough, aggressive prosecutor.

Skinner's style in the office was identical to that of Thompson: high visibility, frequent press conferences, leaks to and close liaison with the media, widespread use of immunity, damaging accusations and comments before trial, selective prosecution in high-visibility cases.

Ultimately, despite a vigorous, media-supported campaign to hold the office after President Jimmy Carter's election, Skinner was "fired" as U.S. Attorney on the strong recommendation of U.S. Sen. Adlai Stevenson III (D., Ill.), who said dryly that he had urged Carter to replace a "politician" with a "professional" as U.S. Attorney for the Northern District of Illinois.

Skinner was succeeded by Thomas P. Sullivan, a low-key rigidly professional former defense attorney whose career with the Chicago law firm of Jenner & Block spanned more than two decades.

Immediately after his swearing-in, Sullivan abolished all extemporaneous shoot-from-the-hip press conferences in connection with indictments or matters of pending litigation, and stated emphatically that he had no political ambitions whatever and intended to return to the private practice of law after completing his tenure as U.S. Attorney. (See Appendix V of this book.)

Clearly, Sullivan's appointment marked the end of an era and a signal change in philosophy in the federal prosecutor's office.

Those defendants whose cases are reviewed in THE THOMPSON INDICTMENT were men of previously unblemished reputation. Several were of substantial stature. Each had made a certain mark through the years. Each strenuously proclaimed his innocence, several unto death. Their losses were incalculable. They and their families suffered untold agonies. They suffered grievous financial punishment, and three went to prison. Terminally ill Edward Barrett was confined to his apartment by judicial order. Three, including Barrett, Kerner, and Bonk, are dead.

If even one was in fact innocent, the scope of the injustice is enormous. But what if two or four or even all were innocent — which seems at least possible on the strength of this record and analysis? That then becomes a shattering indictment of Thompson and the system which convicted them.

It is increasingly clear our criminal justice system works as intended only when each of its components — judge, prosecutor, defense, and jury — functions in good faith and seeks a just outcome. If a judge is inept or corrupt, if a prosecutor hides evidence or badgers witnesses or grants immunity improperly, if a defense attorney permits his client to lie or seeks to deceive, if the jury fails to grasp the subtleties of a case or believes a lying witness, the system almost surely misfires, tainting the result, denying justice, and thus creating human tragedy.

It is the nature of prosecutors under attack, when their tactics and methods are challenged, to point out that guilty verdicts were returned by trial juries and sustained by higher appeals courts. Notwithstanding the American instinct to venerate these institutions, they do not by any means assure that innocent defendants will be found innocent, according to F. Lee Bailey, the prominent defense attorney. He wrote as follows in *Newsweek's* January 2, 1978, issue:

> *A trial by jury . . . is in fact a terrifying experience riddled with uncertainty and often happenstance. Our deification of the notion of a "fair trial" has so far submerged the value of an accurate trial that the latter has no real legal significance. That a trial be "fair" ought to be a minimum standard, not an ultimate objective: someone ought to have the temerity to ask whether the result was correct, not simply whether the rituals were acceptable.*

Laymen are invited to believe that our legal system enshrouds the trial process with an escalating system of checks and safeguards called appellate courts, which will correct affronts to justice. This is unmitigated nonsense, as all seasoned trial lawyers and jurists know, and many unwary litigants have learned painfully . . . Should a jury have erred by believing a lying witness, or by drawing an attractive but misleading inference, there is nothing to appeal. We religiously refuse to make any record of a jury's deliberations . . . and thus forfeit any ability to correct the mistakes we surely know they will make.

. . . An argument to any American appellate court that one's client ought to be granted relief because he was innocent — not that he didn't have a fair trial, but that despite the best efforts of a good trial judge and the earnest intentions of a jury, he was being punished for something he damned well didn't do — would fall on legally deaf appellate ears. Innocence, you see, has at that level no relevance to anything.

Several days before he was nominated for Governor, on March 7, 1976, less than a year after he resigned as U.S. Attorney, Thompson told the *Chicago Tribune:*

"My reputation as a prosecutor is all I have."

THE THOMPSON INDICTMENT is the first searching, serious analysis of that reputation and the record from which it was fashioned.

> *To Dave, with love and gratitude for his patience — and to Jonathan, Chris, Bob, and Dan, who also understood why it was so important that this book be written.*

AUTHOR'S PREFACE

"Janet Bone."

The judge called my name. He looked very imposing in his black robes, sitting on the bench in the high-ceilinged courtroom.

I was a little frightened. I hadn't known what to expect when I answered the summons for federal jury duty. That morning I had watched, not really understanding, as the clerk drew my name from a revolving drum and called it aloud. I was, it seemed, to be part of a *grand* jury. Not the 12-person kind of jury I knew from television shows and movies.

This was a grand jury. And a grand jury is different. In the month ahead, I was to learn just how different it would be from anything I'd imagined. The 23 of us had been escorted to a special room, and told a little about our responsibilities. As grand jurors, we would be listening to the U.S. Attorney and his assistants present evidence against those they believed were involved in federal crimes. If we as grand jurors thought there was sufficient evidence that a crime had been committed, and if at least 16 of the 23 of us felt there was reason to believe a particular person had committed the crime, we had the responsibility to indict. It was not our role to judge whether the person actually had committed the crime. That would be done at trial.

"Janet Bone."

The judge repeated my name, and smiled at me. He looked very big, and I felt very, very small. "You will be the foreman of the March, 1974, grand jury."

It was an education.

Grand jury testimony — by law — is secret, so I cannot describe details of the cases we handled. None of them is reviewed in this book.

A witness called before the grand jury — whether or not he is the subject of an investigation — may not have an attorney with him; in fact, the attorney must wait outside the closed door of the grand jury room, not knowing what his client is being asked or what answers his client is giving. If the witness wants to ask his lawyer whether or not to answer a particular question, the proceedings stop. The witness asks permission from the grand jury foreman, steps down from the witness stand, goes outside the grand jury room to the hallway, talks to his lawyer, opens the door, and returns. Everything stops until he gets back on the stand.

What impression does this make on the grand jury? I know at least what impression it made on me. The impression is negative.

Only the witness, the U.S. Attorney or his assistants, and the grand jurors ever know just what really happens in the grand jury room — what questions are asked in just what way, what evidence is produced. No facts favorable to a prospective defendant ever are presented to the grand jury, which hears only the government's side of the case.

Grand jurors must decide whether or not to follow the recommendation of the prosecutor if he asks for indictment, based solely on whatever the government lawyers and the witnesses have said in the grand jury room. It is possible for a defendant to be indicted without ever having had the chance to appear before a grand jury at all. It is possible for a defendant to take the Fifth Amendment before a grand jury — and many do, feeling the deck is so stacked against them that it is a safer course.

Although individual grand jurors can ask questions, I saw this happen only a handful of times during the time I served. We were walked through an immunity grant — taken through the formality of requesting from Washington that a witness be given immunity as a way of forcing reluctant testimony. In reality, we followed exactly the step-by-step instructions we had been given by the prosecutor. A number of us — including me — did not fully understand what we were doing and why. We were reluctant to question.

At the time, most of us felt we were good, patriotic citizens, helping our government by hearing evidence and voting the indictments the assistant U.S. Attorneys so obviously wanted. Most cases did seem to be pretty clear-cut, and voting "yes" on an indictment was not troubling. And yet — in some of the cases we heard — I and others were disturbed.

Somehow, at least for me, some of the time, I had doubts that the system of justice was working the way I felt ideally it ought to.

And that is why I began the research for this book . . .

Jan Bone

September, 1978

I did not believe Kerner guilty then. I do not believe him guilty now. I tell you this: I believe the jury made a mistake. I expressed my opinion then, and my opinion is still the same. I still consider it a miscarriage of justice. There have been many instances of miscarriage of justice, and I believe this is one of them.

—FEDERAL JUDGE
JOSEPH SAM PERRY,
after Otto Kerner's conviction, in
a private conversation with the
author

•

It's nice of the governor to announce that he will investigate wrongdoing in his own campaign for his own tax proposition. Do you suppose he would have let Otto Kerner investigate himself?

—ROGER SIMON, columnist
Chicago Sun-Times,
September 13, 1978

•

Plea bargaining, at least as administered in the Northern District of Illinois, is the source of great injustice.

—CHARLES A. BANE, Chicago
attorney and former chairman of the
board of editors of the *American
Bar Association Journal*

I

THE
OTTO KERNER
CASE

The widespread granting of immunity inevitably leads to a certain amount of perjury. After all, the prosecutor is in the position of bartering a man's freedom for his testimony, and what is more precious to a man than his freedom? What happens is that some people lie — I suppose you can't blame them — and some innocent people are convicted. That is the height of injustice . . .
—OTTO KERNER

"I was convicted by witnesses who were induced to lie."

That is what Otto Kerner said, from the federal prison where he was confined in Lexington, Kentucky. And that's what he died believing.

There is a compelling case to be made for that charge. For no matter what we may think about Kerner as Governor of Illinois buying stock in a state-regulated Chicago-area horse racing business — and reasonable men can differ in such matters—the well-documented lying of the government witnesses in that trial commands attention.

We know the charge was made by a serious student of the law; a man of wide practical experience; a man who knew the look and feel of lying — in and out of the courtroom.

Subornation of perjury wasn't the only charge Kerner leveled against federal prosecutors and government agents, but it is among the most serious. There were many other questionable liberties taken by the U.S. Department of Justice and IRS in their concerted effort to "get Otto Kerner."

But before trying to reach an impartial assessment of what may really have happened to Kerner — before, during, and after his trial — it is simple justice to acknowledge at the outset that he was a largely good man with a long and solid record of public service. He was a compassionate man. We do not have to say he was perfect in order to say he was good, very good. We do not have to say he had no flaws or made no mistakes in order to say also that he served Illinois and America with distinction. Kerner

2

*himself admitted he "may have been
stupid" to buy the stock — even though
he had a **legal** right to do it—but he was
unyielding in his denial of any criminal
intent in any of his actions.*

If it is our inclination, we can learn much
about the civic virtues of a public man by looking
into Kerner's background; we can learn something
as well about the pitfalls of public service, for we
can learn, too, from his possible error.

And finally we can learn much about the federal law-enforcement practices and temperaments
of U.S. Attorney James R. Thompson and his first
assistant Samuel K. Skinner by taking a close look
at the Kerner case and its aftermath. For Thompson and Skinner were the prosecutors who may
well have suborned, or secretly induced, *whatever*
perjured testimony there was in the Kerner trial.

That gravely serious possibility — that Thompson and Skinner suborned perjury — becomes
more probable than ever in light of their actions
outside the courtroom where Otto Kerner was
tried and found guilty.

*For we do know — and we will here
establish — that Thompson and Skinner
falsely represented their two star witnesses against Kerner. They encouraged
those witnesses to lie about their own alleged roles in the case. They suppressed
what they as federal prosecutors really
thought about their two star witnesses.
They materially helped one of those witnesses cover up her alleged role in the
Kerner case. And in doing all this,*

3

*Thompson and Skinner lied themselves
— by deceiving the court, the trial jury,
the public, and even the grand jury that
brought the indictment against Kerner.*

Big Jim and *Sam the Hammer.* That's how they
were styled — proudly — when Otto Kerner became their first and biggest trophy as crime fighters, their entrée to the spotlight not only in Illinois
but in the nation. They had caught a federal appeals court judge, the only judicial officer of that
magnitude ever to have been convicted of feloni-
ous crime in American history. They had defined the man, moreover, as *venal* and *corrupt.*
Obviously, this made Thompson and Skinner look
good; it made those two aspiring prosecutors feel
they could look *down* on an Otto Kerner.

Kerner's conviction transformed Big Jim
Thompson into Big Jim the Giant Killer. For as
American public servants of the last generation
go, Otto Kerner ranks very high: Governor of
Illinois for seven years, 1961-68; one-star general
in the U.S. Army, two-star general in the National Guard; judge at two levels that took him
to the rung directly below the U.S. Supreme
Court; staunch fighter for civil rights and prison
reform; United States Attorney for Northern Illinois, himself, for eight years; chairman of the
commission that issued the widely acclaimed
Kerner Report on civil disorders.

*The charge Kerner made about wit-
nesses whom the Thompson office induced to lie relates mainly to the two
people whose combined allegations primarily convicted him: William S. Mil-*

4

> *ler and Marjorie L. Everett. Miller and*
> *Everett were wealthy owners of Illinois*
> *racetracks; and Miller had been a mem-*
> *ber of the Illinois Racing Board from*
> *1951 to 1967.*

Marje Everett, *the "queen" of Illinois racing,* found it expedient to begin complaining in 1969 — first to officials of the incoming Republican state administration of newly elected Governor Richard B. Ogilvie, then to federal investigators — that she had been forced to sell racing stock to a number of politicians at prices that amounted to extortion. Bill Miller had forced her to do it, she said, during his tenure as Racing Board chairman.

Mrs. Everett said Otto Kerner and his political associate Theodore Isaacs were two of the beneficiaries of the stock extorted by Miller. Two years later — on December 15, 1971 — Kerner, Isaacs, and three others were indicted. A total of 19 counts charged them with extortion, mail fraud, perjury, conspiracy to bribe, and conspiracy to illegally distribute proceeds of bribery in interstate commerce.

The multiplicity of counts was itself a contrivance to insure indictment and conviction. Jurors were apt to believe that, with so many charges against them, the defendants probably committed at least *some,* if not all, of the acts charged. How else could they incur the government's wrath on so many fronts?

Otto Kerner was named in 17 of the counts:
— a conspiracy that charged 68 overt acts, 32 parts of the conspiracy, and two separate substantive objects of the conspiracy: bribery and mail

5

fraud (all of this in Count I)

— four substantive counts charging the use of facilities in interstate commerce to distribute the proceeds of bribery (Counts II through V)

— eight counts of mail fraud charging fraud on the people of the State of Illinois and certain racing interests (Counts VI through XIII)

— a perjury count charging 18 separate false answers before the federal grand jury relating to questions covering three separate conversations and two distinct subject matters (Count XIV)

— a false-statement count arising out of oral statements made by Kerner to Internal Revenue Service agents Stufflebeam and Campbell (Count XV)

— a tax-evasion count alleging that Kerner's reported capital gains on stock transactions should have been reported as ordinary income from bribery (Count XVI)

— a count charging false statements in a tax return (Count XVII)

Only Theodore Isaacs went to trial with Kerner, even though each of them earlier had unsuccessfully tried to have their cases separated. Isaacs stood trial for the first 13 counts of the Kerner indictment as well as two additional counts of failing to pay enough taxes. By the time the trial opened on January 9, 1973, Miller and his secretary Faith McInturf had been given immunity — and never subsequently stood trial. Nor did Joseph E. Knight, who was terminally ill, ever stand trial.

Isaacs was a long-time friend of Kerner's. Their friendship dated back to their post-World War II National Guard days. Isaacs also had served as Kerner's campaign manager in the 1960 gubernatorial election, as a member of the Governor's cabinet for three years, and as a business associate of Kerner's even after returning to private law practice.

Isaacs' attorney Warren Wolfson says this about the case as it affected his client: "As far as Isaacs is concerned, I did not then and still do not know what crime he committed, because he committed none. I believe that whatever actions he took were completely proper and legal. All he did was buy stock and sell stock. *But the government created the crimes of conspiracy and mail fraud — crimes that didn't really exist.*"

Indeed, Thompson's shotgun indictment launched several new legal theories, in convoluted language that was difficult for even experienced judges and trial lawyers to understand, let alone jurors. But the conspiracy count was most crucial to Thompson's successful prosecution of Kerner, not only because it enabled the Thompson office to imply bribery without directly alleging it, but because as Wolfson put it:

> *Under a conspiracy count, hearsay evidence is permitted. In a conspiracy trial, all sorts of words that are spoken out of the defendant's presence, all kinds of conversations that the defendant had no part in can be used as evidence. It's that much harder for a defendant to convince a jury of his innocence.*

Wolfson's analysis illuminates one of the great ironies of the Kerner-Isaacs case. For everyone involved in the case, including Thompson, Skinner, the jurors, and the judge — Robert Taylor — knew there was a great deal of lying being done

7

by the two star government witnesses. The admissibility in this trial of hearsay evidence, then, is one obvious reason why the jurors chose to overlook all the previous lies Miller and Everett had told — and believe them about Kerner.

Kerner's involvement really came down to one question: did he or did he not accept a *bribe* from Marje Everett in the form of the racetrack stock he bought and in fact paid taxes on? For not a single count in the indictment made any sense at all if Kerner hadn't taken a bribe

> *Jim Thompson had become U.S. Attorney two weeks before Kerner's late-1971 indictment* — **and Thompson made the immediate allegation that, yes, Otto Kerner had accepted a bribe when he and Isaacs each purchased racetrack stock from Mrs. Everett in 1962 for $25,000 and sold the same stock in 1966 for $150,000.**

But Thompson had many problems with this theory, and the problems continue to haunt him to this day. Those problems, moreover, go to the heart of Kerner's claim that he was convicted by witnesses whom the Thompson office induced to lie.

We usually think of the defendants in a criminal prosecution as the only ones with problems, and of course they do have terrible problems. But the problems a conscientious prosecutor faces in those same proceedings can also be massive. It should be pointed out that the problems become especially complex when a prosecutor in good faith attempts to expose a conspiracy-to-break-the-law and attempts to convict the most criminally responsible members of that conspiracy.

It is instructive, on that basis, to put ourselves in the position of a new federal prosecutor who has decided to throw the book at Otto Kerner for allegedly accepting a large bribe while he was Governor of Illinois. Consider the following scenario of thoughts that might go through that new prosecutor's mind:

ASSUMPTION: That Marje Everett bribed Kerner — by selling him stock at a favorable price —so that he would look with favor on her state-regulated racetrack businesses.

FIRST PROBLEM: Although it is not your jurisdiction as federal prosecutor to enforce the Illinois statute on bribery, if you propose to prove Kerner directly violated that statute, you have got to satisfy the elements of that statute in order to prove that Kerner accepted a bribe as Governor of Illinois. Accordingly, you must prove — as set forth in Illinois Revised Statutes Chapter 38, Section 33-1 — all of the following:

1. That Mrs. Everett did tender to Kerner property that was worth far more at the time than the price she asked him to pay.
2. That she did this with the intent to influence Governor Kerner's performance of any act that might harm or help her state-regulated business operations *and that would be related to Kerner's employment and function as Governor.*

9

3. That Kerner did accept the valuable property from Mrs. Everett- *knowing that its tender amounted to her intention of favorably disposing him to her racetrack operations in the performance of his duties as governor.*

4. That for Kerner to accept the favorably priced *property violated Illinois law.*

FIRST FALLBACK POSITION: *Your assumption hold that Kerner was bribed. But since you have neither the jurisdictional authority to enforce a state statute nor all the elements to prove beyond a reasonable doubt that Kerner was indeed bribed* — whether or not his *official* acts as governor *could* help or hurt Mrs. Everett; whether or not Kerner violated state law by owning racetrack stock; whether or not he ever even performed or tried to perform, any overt act to help her businesses — *you can still create other grounds to move against Kerner.* You can charge he *conspired* with others to distribute the proceeds of the bribe you "know" he took, and that he broke various federal laws pertaining to interstate commerce and use of the U.S. mails in furtherance of this "conspiracy."

SECOND PROBLEM: Even on the latter grounds, however, *you have still got to establish the basic elements of a bribe — because the auxiliary violations you are alleging don't make any sense if Kerner wasn't in truth bribed.* You need a source of the bribe, first of all, even if the source happens to be two or more people conspiring to corrupt the judgment of Governor Kerner. You also need to establish Kerner's acceptance of the stock in full knowledge that the stock was tendered him in order to corrupt his judgment.

THIRD PROBLEM: *If the source of the stock bribe is your star witness against Kerner—* ***and if you have chosen not to prosecute her in return for her testimony*** *— you have got to find a way to identify her role in the "bribery conspiracy" that will keep her firmly positioned as generator of the bribe but not name her as a briber and thereby set her ethically apart from the other conspirators.* If you *don't* do this, Marje Everett may:

1. Not testify for you.

2. Testify and be perceived by the jury as just as crooked as you are saying her indicted co-conspirators are — and just as crooked as you also are saying her bribe recipients are.

3. Testify, be believed as someone who was *compelled* to do something she didn't want to do and in fact knew was wrong, but *still* not be able to get the jury to believe — with her testimony alone — that enough basic elements of bribery existed to legally implicate Kerner.

SECOND FALLBACK POSITION: *You "recruit" Bill Miller,* the person you have always claimed to be Mrs. Everett's co-conspirator in arranging the stock transfer to Kerner — the transfer you charge is bribery — *as your second star witness against Kerner.* You do this with a combination of force and rewards. You start out by offering him immunity against incriminating himself before the grand jury. When he declines that offer, you indict him along with

Kerner, Isaacs, and the others. Next, you see to it that Miller's arm is further twisted with a multi-million-dollar tax claim your IRS colleagues in Washington, D.C., may have made even worse for him than his situation realistically warrants. Finally, with full pressure on, you offer him a way out of his troubles: immunity from prosecution, but only if he testifies "truthfully." All you want him to do, after all, is to tell the "truth" about the way he "helped" Marje Everett get the cheap stock to Otto Kerner — and since you are the one who has immunized Miller, you are also the one who will decide whether what he says is "true."

FOURTH PROBLEM: Marje Everett and Bill Miller hate each other for reasons that are of no concern to you except that *you must somehow persuade Everett and Miller to match their sworn testimony on one critical point: the transfer of stock to Kerner.* Even more important — now that you seem to have Kerner pinned by having strengthened the allegation of your first star witness with the allegation of your second star witness — *you have got to collapse the legal, linguistic, and real-life distinctions between being a briber and being the victim of an extortion.* Both Miller and Everett want to come out of this mess with their reputations and their business prospects intact. You can't bluntly accuse either of criminal wrongdoing.

You've got to be especially careful with Mrs. Everett, because you have no criminal prosecution to hold over her head — you probably can't prove she was a briber in the full sense of the

12

Illinois statute any more than you can prove Kerner accepted her stock as a bribe in the full sense of that statute. So you can't force her into accepting an immunity grant, as you have been able to with the former chairman of the Illinois Racing Board, Miller.

FINAL SOLUTION: During the indictment and trial of Kerner, you refer directly to Marjorie L. Everett as little as possible and play down her role as source of the stock that went to Kerner. However, you let *Miller* accuse Everett of bribery — just as you let her accuse him of extortion. In the indictment of Kerner, Isaacs, and the others, you only refer to Mrs. Everett in such oblique phrases as "the principal stockholder of Chicago Thoroughbred Enterprises, Inc. (CTE)," or as an anonymous member of a group you call "other persons." *You never even imply that you really believe she is a briber, not during the trial. You will say that in 1976, when various accounts of the special help you gave this "briber" in California begin to surface; but for the purposes of convicting Otto Kerner, the worst you will say about her is that she was the "unwilling victim" of an extortion by Miller.* Your best hope is that Kerner will be brought down in the crossfire between your two "star" witnesses.

Following the twists and turns of Thompson's tortured theory of guilt in this case does not amount to mere speculation or pseudo psychology. It reflects the concrete facts that Thompson faced when he and Skinner decided to "get Otto Kerner," as they stated their intention in the case on more than one public occasion.

*And the central fact Thompson faced was that he could not make a straight bribery charge against Kerner stick. For no matter how Kerner may have acquired the racetrack stock he owned and profited from, his ownership of that stock in no way constituted a violation of the Illinois statute on bribery. Under state law, Kerner was not even prohibited from owning racetrack stock. Nor was it ever proved in the trial that Governor Kerner did **anything** — either officially or unofficially — that materially benefitted Marje Everett's racetrack business.*

Thompson was therefore working on a theory all along — *not a fact.* He merely *assumed* that Otto Kerner had taken a bribe. That assumption meant that Thompson and Skinner had to smash and twist all the *actual* facts at their disposal in order to make those facts support their assumption. They had to make Marje Everett into a "victim of an extortion" by Miller and a "public-spirited citizen." At the same time, they had to portray Everett's "extorter" as a witness who could tell the truth about *one* thing: that on November, 9, 1962, Miller met with Kerner and Isaacs and conveyed Marje Everett's offer of stock to the two men.

One of the great problems for conspirators — especially conspirators like Thompson and Skinner, who claim they act only in the interests of justice — is that their devious strategies sometimes trip them up.

14

Skinner evidently forgot the game plan on Marje Everett, for example, when at one point in the trial during Miller's testimony, *Skinner said in a "sidebar" conference, out of earshot of the jury, "Miller is a briber, just as Mrs. Everett . . .*

At another point in the trial, Kerner's attorney Paul Connolly exposed Thompson's substantial help to Mrs. Everett with respect to the California racing license she wanted so badly. Connolly was questioning Mrs. Everett:

Q. . . . Mrs. Everett, there came a time when there was some opposition to your getting a California license, is that not so?

A. Well, I have to say —

Q. Justified or unjustified?

A. I would have to say that is a fair statement.

Q. At that time, Mr. Thompson made a public statement concerning your integrity, didn't he?

A. I like to recall it.

Q. What did he say about you?

A. Mr. Thompson made the statement, sir.

Q. What did he say?

A. Well, I don't — I am not too good —I don't want to be inaccurate in a quote.

MR. THOMPSON: I will tell the jury what I said.

MR. CONNOLLY: All right. Go ahead.

MR. THOMPSON: I said that when the indictment of Otto Kerner and Theodore Isaacs was returned, this community owed a great debt of gratitude to Mrs. Everett in coming forward and giving her testimony in this case, and that she was a public-spirited citizen who had the thanks of this entire community for doing that.

MR. CONNOLLY: And that she had never been the

subject of an investigation?

MR. THOMPSON: *She had never been the subject of an investigation nor had she come under indictment.*

MRS. EVERETT: *And I thank you.*

If it hadn't been so serious in its consequences for Kerner, the above courtroom response by Big Jim, followed by Mrs. Everett's simpering expression of gratitude to him — the only think lacking in the exchange is a final "you're welcome" by the federal prosecutor — would be ludicrous. He *thinks* she's a briber — at least in 1976 he says he *always* considered her a briber. But in the courtroom in 1973 he repeats what he had said to the press earlier about her: that she is a *public-spirited citizen.* She's also been named in the indictment, obliquely it is true, as a *co-conspirator;* which makes her a *public-spirited co-conspirator.* She's also been called a briber, by Skinner in the same courtroom; which makes her a *public-spirited co-conspiring briber.* These outrageously tortured descriptions of their first star witness suggest that Thompson and Skinner were bent on destroying the English language as well as Otto Kerner's integrity. But more importantly, the tortured language in the above courtroom exchange once again betrays the tortured theory of Kerner's guilt that Thompson and Skinner had devised for the case.

Who exactly *was* that first star witness on whom the tortured theory turned? *Marjorie Lindheimer Everett,* daughter of racing czar Ben Lindheimer, had become a multi-millionaire in her own right in the "sport of kings." When her father died in 1960, she acquired control of his two race tracks and consolidated them as divisions of a new company: *Chicago Thoroughbred Enterprises (CTE)*. She also owned 11,320 shares of *Balmoral Jockey Club* which, together with CTE's 48,000 shares, constituted a controlling interest in the Balmoral.

But by the time of the indictment Mrs. Everett no longer had stock interests in Illinois racetracks. Her new racing venture was in Hollywood Park Racetrack, in the Los Angeles area. *Her licensing status with respect to Hollywood Park is still to this day crucial to our understanding of Thompson's devious maneuvering in the Kerner trial — and to Kerner's own claim about being convicted by witnesses induced to lie.*

A lifelong Democrat, Marje Everett and her husband, Webb Everett, were prominent fixtures in the Chicago social scene all through the 1960s. She also expanded her father's enterprises by re-modeling her racing plants, adding harness-racing events, and diversifying into real estate and hotel development.

Marje Everett also began offering stock in her racing ventures to "blue-ribbon" people, as she called them — prominent businessmen, well-known socialites, newspaper people, and Illinois politicians. With respect to her stock offerings to Illinois politicians, Thompson claimed she had to do this, that Miller was making her do it — so that her Illinois racetracks would get the most favorable possible dates assigned by the Illinois state government.

In 1968, the IRS had conducted a routine audit of Mrs. Everett's 1966 tax return. By 1969 they were conducting what was termed a "supplemental" audit of that same return. In her 1966 return, Mrs. Everett had claimed a $110,000 tax loss on her sale of racetrack stock to Kerner and Isaacs. That tax loss was based on the difference between the amount paid to her by Kerner and Isaacs in 1966 — the $50,000 total — and what Mrs. Everett claimed was the actual value of the stock in 1966, namely, $160,000.

When Mrs. Everett was approached in 1969 by the newly elected Ogilvie administration's "director of transition" George E. Mahin, she and Mahin began discussing matters that would ultimately surface in the Kerner-Isaacs trial.

"Mahin was also a good friend of Jack Walsh," IRS Agent Oliver P. Stufflebeam's supervisor at the time, according to Stufflebeam. "And that's how Marje ended up talking to the IRS.

"The race track stock probe started in 1969. We were looking at the sale of the stock — who owned what, and so forth."

Like Miller, Everett too was induced to lie — and also like Miller, she was not unwilling to stab her fellow "star" witness in the back as long as she didn't have to incriminate herself in the process. It doesn't make sense that she was the victim of an extortion by Miller, which is the way she portrayed herself and also the way Thompson portrayed her to California racing officials. Nobody could have held a gun at Marje Everett's head and forced her to initiate what Thompson told these officials were payoffs to Illinois politicians.

Nor could Bill Miller have held "the power of life and death" over her business ventures, as she dramatically claimed. Bill Miller, remember, was chairman of the Illinois Racing Board until he resigned from that position in 1967. But he was only one of seven members.

*Furthermore, Bill Miller could **not** have held the "power of life and death" over her racetracks because, logically, any injury to them also would have injured too many other interests. To give Marje Everett her due, she had developed her holdings into well-run businesses that drew great crowds. Arlington Park and Washington Park became, under her stewardship in the 1960s, the two most successful racetracks in the Chicago area. And this of course meant that the State of Illinois received large revenues from Mrs. Everett's racing businesses. It is impossible to imagine a situation in which an Illinois official — even the Chairman of the Racing Board — could drive her out of business without himself being driven out of government by a combination of budget-conscious voters and Cook County racing fans and responsible financial managers in Illinois government and prominent major stockholders in Marje Everett's racetracks. All of which explains why it is so patently absurd for Everett to have alleged under oath in her affidavit and in the Kerner-Isaacs trial — as she did — that*

> *she was extorted by Miller. All of which*
> *also explains that untruthfulness of*
> *Thompson's portrayal of her to the Cali-*
> *fornia racing officials in 1972.*

Marje Everett was also forced to admit — during the trial — that portions of her January, 1971, sworn affidavit were untrue. Defense attorney Wolfson was cross-examining her, at one point in the trial, and the following exchange took place:

MR. WOLFSON: Well, you now feel that the statement you made under oath in January of 1971 was not true, is that right?

MRS. EVERETT: I say, I knowingly did not make a misstatement, but I believe it was a misstatement, sir. I did not lie intentionally.

MR. WOLFSON: You had then from January of 1971 until July of 1971 [the date of her appearance before the grand jury investigating Kerner] to think about it, didn't you? You were interviewed by agents during subsequent times, were you not?

MRS. EVERETT: Yes, I was, sir.

This is the woman, then, who was the first person Thompson chose to "trust" in the Kerner case, his first star government witness. We will have more to say about the Thompson-Skinner trip to California, the trip that virtually assured Marje Everett of getting the racetrack license she needed in that state so that she could continue her business operations in horse racing. We will also have more to say about Richard Ogilvie's actions as governor. For Ogilvie is alleged to have done what Thompson could neither allege nor prove that Kerner ever did: namely, influence the Chairman of the Illinois Racing Board. There is sworn testimony that Ogilvie tried to influence his own Racing Board chairman, Alexander MacArthur, *on behalf of Bill Miller,* an owner of Balmoral Park, south of Chicago.

But before we do those things, let's first look at Miller himself and the relationship between politics and horse racing. Miller was the other person Thompson chose to "trust," remember, after first bludgeoning him with force and then wooing him with rewards — for the very evident purpose of converting Miller into the government's second star witness against Kerner. *And Bill Miller was also the witness Otto Kerner most particularly referred to when he claimed, toward the end of his life, that he'd been convicted with the purchased testimony of people who were induced to lie.*

The courtly, white-haired Miller was a self-made millionaire, a former horse breeder, horse racer, and racetrack owner. He was first appointed to the Illinois Racing Board by Governor Adlai Stevenson on April 26, 1951. He was also a trusted friend of Marje Everett's father, Ben Lindheimer, a friend who promised Lindheimer shortly before the old man's death in 1960 that he, Miller, would do his utmost to keep Lindheimer's racing empire in the Lindheimer family. Bill Miller made that promise while he was a member of the Illinois Racing Board, very possibly an ethical violation of his duty to perform his state regulatory functions in a wholy disinterested and impartial manner.

After Stevenson originally appointed Miller to the Illinois agency that regulates horse racing, two other governors of Illinois followed suit: Republican William G. Stratton and Democrat Otto Kerner. We can surely say, in retrospect, that all three governors made a serious mistake in trusting William S. Miller — although retrospect is always clearer than current vision.

> *If Miller was in Kerner's office on November 9, 1962, to offer racetrack stock to the Governor — and this is what Miller claimed under oath at the trial — he certainly wasn't the caliber of man suited for the position he held.*

And, certainly, Thompson's portrayal of his second star witness as an unprincipled, unreliable, slick influence-peddler raises a serious question about his reliance on the same man, Miller, to establish Kerner's guilt "beyond a reasonable doubt."

But Thompson's second star government witness, Bill Miller, was unquestionably portrayed as more than a manipulator. He was also portrayed as a liar. Thompson himself admitted this during the trial, when he said:

> *The defense was able to impeach Mr. Miller on a number of occasions and on a number of matters, and repeatedly so . . .*
>
> *They say Mr. Miller was impeached in a number of respects. I agree, but that is not so hard to understand, is it?*

Incredibly, after the trial, Thompson sought dismissal of the indictment against Miller. Although Thompson had conditioned Miller's immunity on his testifying truthfully — and had actually admitted in court that Miller's testimony was loaded with lies — he kept his deal with Miller. They both knew that "truthful" testimony could be *any* testimony — so long as it could serve Thompson's overriding purpose of convicting Otto Kerner.

We need not sympathize too much with Miller, then, about the bludgeoning he took from Thompson's efforts to "recruit" him as a government witness against Kerner. Miller got plenty of big rewards. It is instructive, in fact, to look closely at the whole series of inducements Thompson used to create in Bill Miller the witness he needed to support his theory about how Marje Everett's stock was transmitted as a bribe to Kerner.

Listen to what the attorney for Theodore Isaacs, Kerner's co-defendant in the trial, had to say about Miller's slow conversion from the status of indicted co-conspirator to that of immunized informant for Big Jim Thompson. The attorney was Warren Wolfson, now a Circuit Court Judge in Cook County.

Wolfson's closing argument in behalf of Defendant Isaacs explains the reasons why Miller was just as inherently unreliable a government witness as Marje Everett.

> *We could write a handbook about William Miller as a result of this trial. We could call it **The Making of a Witness,** or **How I Made Friends with the Government and Kept My Millions, Too.***
>
> *Look at the remarkable transformation of William Miller. He sets out in January of 1970 by telling lies to IRS agents Stufflebeam and Witkowski. They aren't his friends then. And that's when he says he knows nothing about Illinois Racing Enterprises other than the fact*

that he bought his CHR (Chicago Harness Racing) shares from it. Well, we found out at trial that he was the founding father and an inspiration for Illinois Racing Enterprises.

In 1971, he learns he is under investigation. In May of that year, he appears before a grand jury where he complains he is being blackmailed by the agents, still not his friends. He felt he was being asked to commit perjury so the government could indict somebody.

"I am not going to panic," he said at the time. But apparently later he did.

His efforts to get off the hook continue through 1971. He talks to the prosecutors. He tells them some things, but apparently it wasn't enough, because in December of 1971, he is indicted.

William Miller had learned a valuable lesson. If you want to avoid indictment, you give them what you think they want.

Miller himself feels the government was looking for support for Thompson's theory of guilt. In June, 1978, he says, "The special U.S. Attorney running the grand jury investigation wanted the jurors to hear nothing that conflicted with Mrs. Everett's tale."

Right after the late-1971 indictment, Miller prepared a 68-page statement. That statement was prepared for his lawyer, and it was meant to help his lawyer prepare for trial. **In that statement, *Miller said that he had never discussed racetrack stock with Otto Kerner between 1960 and 1968.***

Defense Attorney Wolfson, in his closing argument at the trial, continued tracing the stages by which Miller "changed" his mind in 1971 and 1972.

"Those were the days," Wolfson said, "when Miller thought the U.S. Attorney was politically motivated . . . he since has changed his mind about that.

> *"Better days were coming for Miller," Wolfson continued. "He got the message and he made peace with the prosecution. Now, I am not saying that they sat down and told him to lie. I don't think they would do that; but with a man as clever and as devious as William Miller, you don't have to tell him. All you have to do is let him know what you are looking for and he will take it from there.*
> *"If it fits the prosecution's theory, they'll use it and leave it up to the jury to decide what the truth is."*

Wolfson's closing argument roared on, tearing Miller's trial testimony to shreds, making it seem altogether likely that Otto Kerner's charge about Miller's perjured testimony was correct.

> *He also told the Racing Board he wasn't a member of that board when he bought any stock. We know that's not true. He bought CHR stock in '64 and held it until December of '66. He did that despite the statute that was passed in August of 1965 that says no member of the Racing Board shall be financially interested in any harness race meets. Well,*

that made no difference to him. He even signed the license for CHR's 1966 dates, knowing that he owned stock in that very same corporation.

He didn't care about the law. He cared about himself. That is all he cared about then, and that is all he cares about now. He has a big investment in Balmoral, in its future. He has a big tax-fraud suit hanging over his head. I can't remember how many millions it is.

And above all, he wants to avoid a criminal trial.

Miller is not completely evil. Nobody is. He is cynical, he is devious, and he is a very selfish man.

Some of the things he said may even be true, just like some of the things Marje Everett said were true.

The problem is, we can't know which. *The prosecution likes to choose those parts of the testimony that fits its theory, or game plan, and ignore the rest. That is the danger in testimony like this.*

*What difference does it make, they say, if you can't believe **both** Marje Everett and Bill Miller? The difference should be clear. **You are being asked to convict people of serious crimes on their word and on their thoughts, as they say they have expressed them.***

With so much at stake, you have a right to demand, not confusion, but clear and reliable evidence.

Defense attorney Wolfson's closing argument well sums up the inherently unreliable quality of the Miller testimony, much of which was perjury.

But Thompson *had* to have that testimony, reliable or not, lies and all, as the linchpin to hold everything together in his case against Kerner. Remember the first fallback position in the earlier analysis? The position was: that even though the federal prosecutor probably did not have all the elements in Otto Kerner's alleged violation of the Illinois bribery statute, he still had to prove the fundamental elements of a bribe: a briber, something of value that the briber gave to a public officer, and the acceptance of that valuable property by the public officer. *Only through Miller could Thompson have his briber: Marje Everett.* But he still did not have the stock-transfer nailed down because 12 days before the trial was scheduled to begin he as yet did not have anyone who could testify that Otto Kerner did indeed indicate his acceptance of the stock *bribe*.

This was the final reason Big Jim needed Miller as a government witness against Kerner. And here is how he got Miller.

A Chicago grand jury was investigating the whole matter in May of 1971, some seven months before Thompson would be appointed U.S. Attorney. Three Washington-based Justice Department attorneys were conducting the grand jury sessions. Bill Miller appeared to testify on May 4, 1971.

Miller told that grand jury and government attorney Victor G. Woorheide, who questioned him, that immunity had been offered to him in November, 1970, on the condition that he corroborate

Marje Everett's story that Kerner was bribed with racetrack stock extorted from her. He testified that he turned down that offer because he believed that he would have to "perjure" himself.

On November 30, 1971, James R. Thompson became the new U.S. Attorney for Northern Illinois, replacing William J. Bauer, elevated to the federal bench. And on December 15, 1971, Thompson rammed through the 19-count indictment against not only Kerner, Isaacs, and wealthy Springfield businessman and Governor Kerner's former Director of Financial Institutions Joseph E. Knight; *but also against William S. Miller and Miller's confidential secretary, Faith McInturf.*

Thompson and U.S. Attorney General John Mitchell made simultaneous public statements, from Chicago and Washington respectively, announcing the indictment, and not only absolving Everett of wrongdoing but pointedly praising her.

On August 15, 1972, only two months before the trial was scheduled to begin, Miller through his attorney, William Barnett, agreed to accept the government's offer of immunity in return for becoming that second star witness Thompson needed to get his theory of Kerner's guilt off the ground.

And did it get off the ground! Thompson wrote Barnett a letter on the same afternoon he'd received Barnett's letter with Miller's acceptance of immunity. Big Jim agreed to sever Miller and Miller's confidential secretary, Faith McInturf, from the prosecution in return for their "complete and truthful cooperation." *Thompson sent that letter at 5:30 p.m., the same day he'd heard from Barnett.*

At 6 p.m. — half an hour later — Miller and a

band of government agents and prosecutors, including Thompson himself, met at the Drake Hotel on the Near North Side of Chicago. Those meetings continued steadily until August 17.

And between August 19 and December 31, according to Miller, he met with the federal agents 27 more times. All the meetings, says Miller now, were "concerned with preparing the case for trial."

If that is true, when did the government produce the special inducements for Miller? *There were at least two big inducements for Miller in the immunity deal he'd received from Thompson* — along with the promise that he wouldn't be prosecuted if Thompson and Skinner "decided" he was telling the "truth."

> *The first inducement had to do with the huge and growing federal tax claim against him. The second had to do with somebody, apparently Thompson-the-aspiring-politician, seeing what he could do for Miller with Governor Ogilvie on racing dates for the racetrack Miller had owned since resigning from the Racing Board in 1967 — Balmoral Park, south of Chicago.*

On April 14, 1972 — months before the immunity agreement — as the screws were being tightened on Miller, the IRS served him with a notice of a tax deficiency totaling $1,845,763, plus 50 per cent fraud charges, for a grand total of $2,768,844. By 1976, however, that total federal tax debt of Miller's was to be settled for a not-so-grand total of $58,552 — only about 2% of the claim. It seems highly probable that the massive tax claim was specious in the first place. Even Miller now admits, "as to this civil tax claim, I feel it was assessed as part of the pressure put upon me to become a government witness."

Thompson needed less time to start producing the other inducement for his new government witness, the one who would help him convict Otto Kerner. This was the inducement that Thompson apparently arranged with Governor Ogilvie and had to do with helping Miller's racetrack get racing dates.

After his indictment and subsequent acceptance of immunity in August, 1972, Miller's Balmoral Park racing dates for the following season were endangered, as can be imagined. Here was a racetrack owner, after all, agreeing to implicate himself as either a briber or an extorter in the Kerner case — and a man who was still under federal indictment himself. Miller obviously sensed this danger, and we can presume he did what negotiating he could with Thompson to avert it. We know nothing of what they may have said to each other about the matter.

But based on the facts, we can draw reasonable conclusions. Let's take a look at the curious sequence of events.

Remember that Miller wrote a 68-page statement shortly after his December,1971, indictment — a memo that said he'd never discussed racetrack stock with Kerner between 1960 and 1968. It took Miller $3\frac{1}{2}$ months, working with his lawyers, to get that statement ready.

Just before Miller was given immunity in August, 1972, Thompson sent him a list of 47 questions. Miller answered them through his attorney, William Barnett. Again, in his answers, Miller said he had never discussed racetrack stock with Kerner between 1960 and 1968.

Miller got his immunity August 15, 1972; met intensively with Thompson, IRS agent Stufflebeam, and other government agents for two days; and continued to meet steadily with them throughout that Fall.

And on November 3, 1972, Miller signed an affidavit with a new fact: he had suddenly found it convenient to "remember" that he had met nearly 10 years previously — on November 9, 1962 — with Kerner and Isaacs in Springfield; and had conveyed Marje Everett's stock offer to Kerner at that meeting. This affidavit contradicted his two previous statements that he'd never discussed racetrack stock with Kerner on any occasion, under any circumstances, anywhere.

We also know that Republican Governor Richard Ogilvie was accused by his former Racing Board Chairman Alex MacArthur of trying to influence MacArthur to give racing dates to Bill Miller's Balmoral Park. And we also know from the sworn testimony of MacArthur that Ogilvie leaned on him in November, 1972, about three months after Thompson had finally been able to immunize Miller.

Ogilvie denied that he did this. But, when the matter publicly surfaced in

> *1974, MacArthur also proudly stated that he resigned the week after Ogilvie asked him to give a special consideration to Miller.*
>
> *And according to Alex MacArthur, the reason Ogilvie gave him for extending special consideration to Miller's race-track dates for 1973 was that Miller was a government witness in an important federal case.*

Judge for yourself whether Alex MacArthur sounds like an honest man, in the sworn testimony below. Remember that in November, 1972, when the conversation MacArthur describes took place, MacArthur was occupying the same important position that Miller himself had held for six years — chairman of the Illinois Racing Board. Imagine if you can how *Miller* might have responded to the words MacArthur will quote Ogilvie as saying. Perhaps you will find a contrast between how Miller might have responded and how MacArthur *did* respond.

The testimony that follows took place in an investigative meeting of the Illinois Racing Board. The time is 1974. The chairman of the Racing Board is Anthony Scariano, appointed by the Walker administration.

MR. MacARTHUR: . . . on Monday, the 23rd of November [1972], I received a telephone call from the Governor in Springfield, and he said he'd like to see me.

CHAIRMAN SCARIANO: Is this the Monday before the Tuesday of the dates?

MR. MacARTHUR: Yes, that is correct, Monday the 23rd before this stormy Tuesday. [The day the Racing Board outvoted its chairman and awarded racing dates to Miller's Balmoral Park racetrack. The day after *that*, MacArthur resigned from the Racing Board.]

MR. OBERMAN: Can you tell us about this conversation with the Governor?

A. The Governor asked to see me on Tuesday.

Q. Did the Governor tell you what he wanted to see you about?

A. No, he didn't.

Q. Was that all of the conversation you had with the Governor?

A. No, sir. The Governor said, "I'll have breakfast with you tomorrow morning in Chicago."

CHAIRMAN SCARIANO: Did he?

MR. MacARTHUR: Yes, sir,

CHAIRMAN SCARIANO: Where?

MR. MacARTHUR: I had coffee and a roll in his office in this building.

Q. Can you tell us what you said and what the Governor said during that breakfast meeting?

A. Well, to the best of my memory the conversation went approximately like this:

He said, *"What's the problem with the Racing Board?"* or *"What's the problem down there?"* And I said, *"We seem to have some disagreement on the awarding of dates. I think we need a little more time. I think we can work it out."*

And he said, *"Why don't you go back to the 19 . . . whatever, '71 or '72 schedule."*

And I said, *"No, no, I don't want to go back in other words to one of the stereotype schedules."*

And I said, *"I don't want to give Mr. Miller any*

33

dates." And the Governor mentioned that Mr. Miller *was soon to be a witness in a Federal trial.*

CHAIRMAN SCARIANO: The Governor mentioned this?

MR. MacARTHUR: (Nodded in the affirmative.)

I said, *"Now, just a minute. You go tell Mr. Thompson that he took an oath of office and I took an oath of office and that's the way it's going to be. You ask me to bend a muscle for you, and I'll do it, because that's called work; you ask me to bend a bone, and I ain't."*

CHAIRMAN SCARIANO How did Mr. Thompson's name get into this?

MR. MacARTHUR: Because *I got the impression in the conversation that one of the considerations I ought to be giving to awarding Mr. Miller dates was so that he'd have a — all I know is that Mr. Miller was going to be a witness.*

CHAIRMAN SCARIANO: Then you drew an inference then that you were being asked to give Mr. Miller dates in return for his cooperation with the U.S. Attorney in connection with the Kerner-Isaacs trial?

MR. MacARTHUR: Well, it wasn't put in that many words, but it was *put* — when I said, *I don't think Mr. Miller ought to get any dates,* it was then said, *"Well, you know, Mr. Miller is going to be an important witness in a trial here."* I believe the Governor said, *"NEED I SAY MORE?"* And it was at that time that I said what I just told you.

MR. OBERMAN: Q. Did the Governor answer what you said about bending a muscle and bending a bone?

A. Well, he looked at me and I said, *"I'm going*

34

to resign. In fact, I'll resign right now."

He said, *"No, no, don't do that, don't resign. That wouldn't solve anything."*

He said — well, then I said, Then you get me some corps artillery, (and I gave him the coordinates. He's an old army tank man. He knows what I'm talking about), and give me some support, fire support.

CHAIRMAN SCARIANO: Did he?

MR. MacARTHUR: No, sir, he didn't. And at noon when I stepped out of the office, and Mr. [Gerald] Fitzgerald [member of Racing Board] was a witness to this conversation, I asked him again for the artillery support. I did not get it.

MR. OBERMAN: Do you recall specifically what he said?

A. He said, "No, I'm not going to do that." And I went upstairs and resigned.

CHAIRMAN SCARIANO: What kind of support did you expect from him specifically?

MR. MacARTHUR: *Well, I just expected him to call down there or have somebody get hold of some of these Commissioners.*

And I thought this was a very serious principle, and this thing of awarding dates to Miller; and I thought that we had worked hard here for a couple or three years, and maybe this was the time when we could really do some restructuring of Illinois racing so it would be meaningful and get rid of these paper associations; and frankly, get rid of some of these people that were running meets that did not make a wholesome contribution to the sport.

MR. OBERMAN: *Q. During this breakfast meeting with the Governor on Tuesday morning did*

35

he refer to any other association that should get dates or shouldn't get dates besides Mr. Miller's?

A. No, sir.

CHAIRMAN SCARIANO: He was just interested in Miller?

MR. MacARTHUR: The Miller matter. The conversation didn't go too far, because when I gave the little bit about bending the muscle or bone, we were on another area of the conversation; namely, my resignation.

The sworn testimony of Alex MacArthur rings true. Governor Ogilvie's denial of his role in that conversation does *not* ring true. MacArthur put his money where his mouth was; he thought a man like Bill Miller was bad for racing, and when he suddenly found after that breakfast meeting that could not convince enough of Ogilvie's other appointees on so fundamental a point as that, he simply resigned. He resigned both as chairman and member of the Racing Board. It was *that* obvious and serious to him that Ogilvie was trying to help Miller.

So Thompson got his witness. Miller got the privilege of not being prosecuted, he got $2 million or so in tax relief, and he got his 1973 racing dates.

Some people may still be under the impression that Marje Everett, the second person Otto Kerner may have had in mind when he spoke about being convicted with perjured testimony, also received immunity from Thompson. She received something even better than immunity. She received Thompson's complete protection *without* having to be immunized. Remember in the Connelly-

Thompson-Everett court conversation quoted earlier that Thompson said he'd never even investigated her questionable practices and operations?

Thompson rendered very substantial service to Mrs. Everett in order to get her to testify and to keep her relatively clean-looking.

She needed a California license so that she could legally assume her position on the board of directors of the Hollywood Park Racetrack, a track in which she had put together the controlling stock interest.

The final solution of Thompson's get-Kerner strategy, remember, was always to keep Marje Everett happy . . . and talking.

When Mrs. Everett wanted to talk to the California licensing officials about authorizing her to operate in that state, Thompson and Skinner really had a problem. They knew she would of course cast herself in the injured-party role as far as her Illinois operations were concerned. That would be to her advantage, since she couldn't expect to get a racetrack license in California if she admitted to being a briber in Illinois.

But what if the California officials didn't believe her injured-party story? What if they asked her if she could *prove* that she was telling the truth? What if they pressed her for details about the alleged transactions with Kerner, with Isaacs, with all the other Illinois politicians she'd dealt with over the years?

Thompson and Skinner personally travelled to California, 22 days after the Kerner indictment, to meet there with California officials. They said they did it to protect their case against Kerner, to protect it by having their star witness Marje Everett not say too much or say the kind of thing that would not square with what she had said and was saying about Otto Kerner and Ted Isaacs.

That's what Jim and Sam said, and there is a certain plausibility about their claim. But it is also reasonable to believe that Jim and Sam may have had private reasons for going.

> *Mrs. Everett has not been known in Illinois racing as a poor negotiator. It is more than possible that she extracted from Thompson and Skinner a commitment to help her get a California racing license. They needed her testimony, after all, if they were going to use Otto Kerner to become famous crime fighters. If she goes out to California and says demurely to the state licensing officials that she can't really say anything about what she's done in Illinois — because saying anything would constitute a breach of good citizenship, and she's currently a star witness in an important official-corruption case — that might cut off further questions.* **It probably wouldn't.**

> **But if Thompson and Skinner go to California and say the same thing, that becomes an even more effective way to: (1) show that they believe she's a good citizen who is telling the truth in their prosecution; and (2) really cut off the questions.**

That's what Thompson and Skinner did. And

it worked, because Marje Everett ended up getting her California license.

That Alice-in-Wonderland courtroom exchange quoted earlier between Kerner's attorney Paul Connolly, Big Jim, and Marje Everett continued a bit further on the California mission of the federal prosecutors. Right after Mrs. Everett had thanked Thompson from the witness stand for his kind words about her, Connolly spoke up.

> *Q. Mrs. Everett, do you think that helped you get your license* [the fact that Thompson had chosen not to ever investigate her operations or bring her under indictment]?
> *A. Well, I appreciated Mr. Thompson's statement. I was sincere in my desire to see racing meet the standards to which I think it should in Illinois, which has provided me with everything I have in the world. I am still very sincere about that.*

Leonard Foote, currently the executive secretary of the California Horse Racing Board, spent more than two years working on the Marje Everett license application. As chief investigator for the Racing Board, he was present at a meeting Thompson and Skinner had on January 7, 1972, with Evelle Younger, the Attorney General of California, in 1978 a candidate for Governor.

Here's how Foote describes the Thompson-Skinner trip, and the events surrounding the issuing of Mrs. Everett's California racing license:

> *For many years, Mrs. Everett had*

been a licensed horse owner in California. As part of her payment for getting out of Illinois racing, she received about 54,000 shares of stock in the Hollywood Turf Club. Webb Everett, her husband, a long-time racing official in California, had previously owned five or six thousand shares of the same stock. Suddenly, then, the Everetts have about 60,000 shares of stock in this major California racetrack — which would entitle Mrs. Everett to sit on the board of directors. But in California, we license all directors of racing associations.

Right at the time the Kerner indictments were being announced, then, we had an applicant for a very important position in California racing. All sorts of good and bad innuendos were floating around about her participation in bribes. The Hollywood Park Board of Directors sued to keep her from her seat on the board, and opposed her application before the California Horse Racing Board for a director's license.

Understandably, the California Horse Racing Board demanded that we have an investigation. Part of it was to find out what happened in Illinois, and her part in it. We wanted to see if she was qualified for a license. California has all kinds of laws related to licensing about people who are not only convicted, but who are engaged in certain kinds of activities.

"The best way to handle such an investigation is to talk with the individual involved," Foote continued. "But although Mrs. Everett expressed her willingness to discuss the subject, she was prohibited from doing so because she had testified in front of the federal grand jury.

"So Evelle Younger, attorney general of California, wrote to John Mitchell, Attorney General of the United States, in Washington. As a partial result of that letter, Thompson and Skinner, his first assistant, made a trip to California. They met in the Los Angeles office of Younger for about 40 minutes on January 7, 1972. Younger was there, of course, and Henry Lewin, our California deputy attorney general, and I were invited to discuss our investigation of Mrs. Everett with Thompson and Skinner.

"Basically, Skinner was saying in effect, 'Please don't write any more letters, because we can't give you the information you want. We will tell you, however, certain things we have deduced from it. One thing is that had there been any overt act on the part of the principals who were indicted — any overt act against Mrs. Everett or her properties such as Arlington Park or Chicago Thoroughbred Enterprises, and so on — that the indictment would have alleged extortion, rather than a conspiracy to use the mail for fraud and to distribute by mail the proceeds of a bribe.'

"Both Thompson and Skinner told us, 'We cannot give you the information you seek. We cannot release the transcript of federal grand jury testimony. The best we can tell you at this point is that we'll keep you informed and advised as to the progress of the trial.'

"But the real purpose of Thompson's and Skinner's 1972 visit to California was that we not press our inquiry at that time. For one thing, the witnesses we were bound to contact could not discuss it. And secondly, if we did come up with anything Thompson didn't have, it would be detrimental to the trial.

"Now I've heard about the statements Thompson made on television [a WBBM-TV interview, in Chicago, by Bill Kurtis] on October 19, 1976, in which he said he told the California Racing Board that Marje Everett was guilty of bribery, and she didn't like that testimony one bit, so the notion that Thompson testified for her in California is diametrically opposite, because he testified against her. That's what he said.

"I got called by the newspapers and asked about this California testimony," Foote says. *"And I said, 'WHAT California testimony?'*

"Later Thompson recanted, and said,

> *'Well, I told them . . . instead of testi-*
> *fying, I told them.'*
>
> "Well, even that was not correct,"
> Foote said. "Basically he didn't tell us
> anything. Skinner was doing the talk-
> ing. **He didn't tell us Marje Everett was**
> **guilty of bribery.**
>
> **"If they did have information that she**
> **was a briber, we were never privy to that**
> **information."**

In an April 7, 1978, story in the *San Diego*
Union newspaper, another Thompson interview
on Marje Everett was quoted — this one, with
WLS-TV, Chicago, on October 24, 1976, " *'I never*
helped her in California,' Thompson said. 'In fact,
I thought I hurt her in California. I was astound-
ed when they gave her a racing license in Califor-
nia, because if I were a member of the California
Racing Board, and the prosecutor told me that his
witness had committed bribery in Chicago, I
wouldn't have given her a racing license.'

"Neither statement is correct," Foote says.
"Thompson neither helped nor hurt. He merely
said, 'We can't give you any information.' "

> *Also contradicting Thompson's tele-*
> *vision statement that he'd told the Cali-*
> *fornia Racing Board Marje Everett was*
> *a briber is Henry Lewin, now in private*
> *practice, but Deputy Attorney General*
> *and Counsel to the California Racing*
> *Board at the time of the Thompson-*
> *Skinner trip.*

"During that period of time, neither Thompson
nor Mr. Skinner nor anyone from Mr. Thompson's

office appeared before the Board and testified one way or the other. I don't care whether Thompson says he testified for her or against her or he rode the fence. The fact of the matter is that he did not testify!

"The posture of Thompson and Skinner in that meeting was that they told us Mrs. Everett was to be a very key witness in the upcoming trial and others. They described a little about the political atmosphere at the time the previous Illinois administration had been in power.

"Their theory was to set the stage that while Kerner was in power, the political atmosphere was such that if you wanted to stay in business, you had to play ball with certain people — that, in essence, Marje Everett was a victim of the type of government that existed then; that in order for her to stay in business, she had to go along and do whatever is necessary.

"But once the administration changed," Lewin continued, *"Thompson and Skinner said that Mrs. Everett stepped forward and laid it on the line as to what had been going on. They said it was extremely important for their case that Mrs. Everett be presented in the proper way and with the proper stage setting so that she comes across as a victim of the type of situation that existed at the time.*

"My impression is that the objective of the presentation by Thompson and Skinner was that Marje Everett was a victim

*of an extortion and not an active partici-
pating briber. We threw him questions:
If you are going to go against Kerner for
receiving a bribe, if he is the bribee, how
can you have a bribe without a briber?*

*"Their strategy was going to be that
she was the victim of an extortion-like
environment — if you want to stay in
business here, you have to make sure that
the right people are taken care of.*

"My impression was that the purpose of the
meeting was *not* to paint her as a criminal," Lewin said, "and at the same time, *to imply to us
that maybe we should not carry on our own independent investigation.*

"We specifically inquired as to whether or not
Mrs. Everett had requested immunity, or whether
a deal had been made that the granting of immunity had been deferred — deferred until after she
testified, Thompson said she had not been given
immunity and had not requested it."

After Thompson and Skinner returned to Illinois, things began looking up for Marje Everett.

"The California Horse Racing Board took the
only avenue they had at that point," says Leonard
Foote. "In our state, we have a provision in the
law which provides that the California Horse Racing Board could issue a temporary license pending investigation. That carries no presumption
that the particular licensee is qualified and fit for
the license, which may be terminated at any time."

On January 24, 1972, at a meeting of the California Racing Board, its chairman John B. New-
man read a letter from Younger saying three options were open: they could take no action on Mrs.

Everett's license until the Illinois matter was resolved; they could grant her a temporary license; or they could grant her a permanent license. "Under normal circumstances," Younger wrote the Board, "you would probably consider it appropriate to hold a public hearing before deciding which of the above options to adopt . . . In that connection, I have been advised that the U.S. Department of Justice, and more particularly, the U.S. Attorney for the Northern District of Illinois, would seek a court order to prevent Mrs. Everett's participation in such a hearing because of the possibility of any statement that she might make which could conceivably be prejudicial insofar as the rest of the defendants in the case are concerned."

Immediately, Attorney Frank Rothman — who represented the Hollywood Park Board in their civil suit to keep Marje Everett off their board of directors — protested. He said he'd petitioned the Los Angeles Superior Court to compel Mrs. Everett to answer the question on whether or not she had offered a bribe. Rothman said, "It seems incongruous to me that this board would consider granting even a temporary license while that question is pending."

Foote's explanation about why the temporary license was granted Marje Everett, however, is this.

"Well, the California Horse Racing Board felt that with so much financial interest in Hollywood Park, she was entitled by the bylaws of the racetrack to hold the position of director. After all, she was only one of 11. Even if she voted against everything, she couldn't harm them that much. So they granted her a temporary license.

"Afterwards, when the Kerner trial was over and an appeal was filed, we were still unable to get everything. I continued the investigation, spending well over 200 hours on it. I talked with former commissioners, people who were named in the Kerner trial who would discuss Mrs. Everett, and interrogated Mrs. Everett on two occasions. As a result of that additional investigative work, in 1972 I recommended to the California Horse Racing Board that *there appeared no grounds under our laws by which we could deny Mrs. Everett the license she had applied for*. Board members adopted that recommendation and affirmed her license on April 9, 1973, thereby in effect, giving her a permanent license," Foote said.

So that's the California story. Did Thompson as he claimed in two October, 1976, television interviews — call Mrs. Everett a briber to the California Horse Racing Board? Foote, Younger, and Lewin say no. And their version of the Thompson-Skinner trip is backed up by the January 10, 1972, letter Thompson himself sent Younger, which says in part: "Unfortunately, while this office would like to respond to your request for the facts of this case, the rules of the United States District Court for the Northern District of Illinois, Rule 6 of the Federal Rules of Criminal Prosecu-

> *tion, the guidelines of the Department of Justice, and the canons of ethics prohibit us from disclosing or commenting on the factual basis of this indictment."*

> **"In addition," Thompson continued, "because of the unusually widespread public interest in this case by the news media and the public, any comments or statements by any persons involved in this lawsuit, including Mrs. Marje L. Everett, could raise questions of prejudice to the right of the defendants to a fair and impartial trial."**

Thompson's concerns about a fair and impartial began, remember, with that shotgun 19-count indictment that was returned on December 15, 1971. Trained lawyers with great perception consider the tortured, obscure language of the 64 pages and more than 10,000 words of that indictment to be legally outrageous.

Moreover, the Kerner case from its very beginnings had distinct political overtones. For it was the Nixon administration, and specifically Nixon's U.S. Attorney General John Mitchell, where the pressure obviously originated to begin the official IRS investigation of Kerner in June, 1970.

Kerner and others believed that Nixon's loss of Illinois in the 1960 presidential election prompted Nixon and Mitchell to bring the full force of the U.S. Justice Department against the Democratic leaders in Illinois, starting with former Governor Kerner, in 1970 — and thus prevent a 1972 repetition of what had happened in 1960.

Kerner himself analyzed those political overtones in a 1973 radio interview with WGN newscaster Frank Beaman. Kerner said: "Mr. Nixon often stated that the 1960 election was stolen from him in Illinois; he continued to make those statements, as reported by the media, for a period of many years, even *after* he was elected President. After his election as President, I would guess about 1969 or 1970, he made some public indication he was going to run for re-election, and he said that in order to win the election, he must win Illinois."

"You think it was anxiety about winning Illinois in 1972 that may have led to some arms of government investigating you?" Beaman asked.

"I have reason to believe that, yes!" Kerner said. Supporting that conclusion is the recollection of a former high-ranking White House aide.

In Chicago, in spring, 1976, promoting his widely heralded book *Born Again,* former White House lawyer Charles Colson described a secret meeting at the Presidential vacation retreat in Key Biscayne, Florida, held the weekend after the 1970 Congressional elections; a meeting whose purpose, according to Colson, was to plan strategy and tactics for the 1972 re-election bid.

Halderman, Erlichman, Mitchell, and several other Presidential aides were there. So was Nixon. So was Charles Colson. They discussed the "Southern strategy," designed by John Mitchell to woo the conservative Democratic vote to the Nixon column. In the North, they were trying to woo the conservative vote away from the Northern Democrats, primarily union voters.

Colson says they finally got around to discussing Illinois. They rehashed 1960, Nixon remembering painfully John F. Kennedy's reed-thin margin of disputed votes which sealed Kennedy's shaky victory that year. During the Illinois discussion, says Colson, Mitchell suddenly stood up and announced they didn't have to be greatly concerned.

"As Mitchell put it," Colson recalls, "when the grand jury got finished with the Democrats in Illinois, there wasn't going to be much left of the Democratic party there."

"It was typical of our attitude about 'getting our enemies,'" Colson said. "Otto Kerner would certainly be included among our enemies . . ."

Mitchell made this menacing remark in a *political* conversation, remember. Nixon's campaign manager in effect thus made the U.S. Department of Justice a political arm of the Nixon reelection effort. And so inappropriate and unethical a remark, by the Attorney General of the United States, lends definite credence to Kerner's belief about the political reasons underlying his prosecution. So does the documented fact that Kerner was the victim of hundreds of damaging leaks, a close "mail cover," possible wiretapping, and other harassments for nearly two years before his indictment.

Lending even further credence to the political overtones of the case was John D. Erlichman's congratulatory phone call to Thompson on behalf of President Nixon, on the heels of Kerner's conviction. The phone call came from Air Force One.

Pre-indictment publicity also damaged Kerner's position, and constituted another serious ethical breach by the government. All through 1970 and into the hot summer of 1971, that publicity had been building, stirred up by the self-styled legal-researcher Sherman Skolnick. Chicago's major daily newspapers were printing story after story that something may happen — that Kerner is in trouble — that there may be a racetrack scandal. Skolnick ran a recorded "hot line" message phone-tape, and just before Thanksgiving, 1971, he put on the message that Kerner was going to be "cooked turkey."

It was Ron Koziol of the *Chicago Tribune* in a copyrighted story on Sunday, November 21, 1971, who broke the major story of the pending indict-ment. Reaction came immediately. That after-noon, Chicago radio stations quoted the Koziol story, adding a comment by outgoing U.S. Attor-ney William J. Bauer that in his opinion, the leak of such information was an irresponsible act. He blamed the Chicago IRS office. The IRS, how-ever, denied responsibility for the leaks.

"As you know," said an internal IRS memo written by Vernon D. Acree, assistant to IRS Commissioner Johnnie M. Walters, "such a meet-ing concerning the Kerner case was held on Fri-day, November 19, at 10 a.m. at the Justice De-partment. It was attended by U.S. Attorney Thompson from Chicago; Henry Petersen [a high-ranking Justice Department official]; Victor Woorheide and Lloyd Williamson of the Criminal Division; and Fred Ugast, Dick Schwartz, Scott Crampton, Darrell McGowan of the Tax Division."

Later broadcasts reported that U.S. Attorney James Thompson, named to the job just days earlier, also said that the stories in the newspaper about Kerner were prematurely leaked by the IRS. Thompson was quoted by radio stations as saying he would indict responsible IRS officials in Chicago for obstruction of justice.

Koziol, concerned that the IRS was being falsely accused, called Thompson to tell him he was barking up the wrong tree.

The IRS internal memo commenting on the leaks said that *Koziol told Thompson he should look to his own department,* "starting in the East and working to the West" — in other words, meaning from Washington to Chicago. Interviewed by the IRS on November 23, 1971, Koziol told their inspector that he had learned of a proposed meeting at the Justice Department in Washington, had come to Washington and checked his sources, written the story of the pending indictment and filed it from there, and then returned to Chicago.

Despite Koziol's advisory report to Thompson — a report that directly contradicted Thompson's own claim about the Justice Department's lack of responsibility for Koziol's pre-indictment story — Thompson *continued* to make the claim. He even said under oath during the Kerner trial that there was no evidence that the government was responsible for any leaks.

Eager to indict Kerner, U.S. Attorney John Mitchell, the man who would make the final decision whether or not to go ahead on the Kerner prosecution, was vitally interested in the sources for the Koziol story. The IRS internal memo was forwarded to Mitchell on November 26, along with a cover letter from Commissioner Walters that read, "Re Chicago news leaks. Knowing of your continuing interest in the matter we are transmitting herewith for your information a copy of the November 24, 1971, memorandum addressed to us by the Assistant Commissioner vis a vis inspection, furnishing us a fairly full report on what IRS has found with respect to the latest leaks.

> *"While no one can be absolutely sure, from what we have learned, it appears that the latest leak in all probability comes from someone in the Department of Justice. We will be pleased to discuss this with you, and we will continue our efforts to identify the source of these leaks."*

In light of all the improper prosecutorial practices in this case, and especially in light of the probable inducement of perjury by Thompson and Skinner, it is not surprising that Kerner and Isaacs were found guilty on all counts.

Under the new system of federal 3-day weekends, it was February 19, 1973, Washington's Birthday: Monday, a clear, crisp day. On the 25th floor of Chicago's Federal Building, the courtroom began to fill. The jury was coming back after only 16 hours of deliberation . . . too long a time, spectators surmise, for acquittal.

Defendants Theodore J. Isaacs and Otto Kerner, Jr. have been summoned by phone and told the jury is on its way back. There was small talk between them and their attorneys, before the arrival of Judge Robert L. Taylor — old, inattentive, a judge who had actually and with some regularity drifted off to sleep during the trial.

Soon the clerk reported the dread verdict,

"United States District Court, Northern District of Illinois, Eastern Division, United States of America vs. Theodore J. Isaacs et al. We, the jury, find the defendant Theodore J. Isaacs guilty as charged in the indictment."

"When they said Mr. Isaacs was guilty, that was it," remembers Helena Kerner Stern, adopted daughter of Otto Kerner. "As far as I was concerned, they didn't have to read any further. I felt the case was so complicated that I didn't really think the jury would be able to distinguish between the two men. If they had been tried separately, as they should have been, it might have been different. But they were really tied together. You might just as well have handcuffed them together and taken them away. I figured the jury thought if one was guilty, the other was, too. I felt crushed. It was really a shock to me, because I had only considered half an hour before that it could possibly happen . . ."

"United States of America vs. Otto Kerner, Jr." The clerk continued. "We the jury, find the defendant Otto Kerner, Jr. guilty as charged in the indictment."

But Judge Taylor, responding to post-trial motions, entered judgments of acquittal for both men on Counts V, VII, X, XI, and XII — one bribery and four mail-fraud counts.

Isaacs was sentenced to three years concurrently on each of the remaining counts, and ordered to pay fines of $10,000 each on Counts I, II, III, IV, and XVIII. Kerner, too, received a three-year concurrent sentence and $50,000 in total fines. (Later, the Appeals Court reversed the travel act counts, but sustained the convictions on the mail-fraud counts.)

"I heard the gasp in the courtroom — a gasp of complete disbelief," remembers the former Governor's adopted son, Tony Kerner, erect and idealistic, deeply loyal and loving.

> *We were completely shocked. The whole courtroom was aghast. I don't think there were a great number of people who believed it, except the prosecution table — and I think even they were a little surprised. Their reaction was one of complete joy.*
>
> *There was no caring . . . no compassion . . . no consideration about what the verdict might have meant.* **I know they regarded Dad as a trophy. It was a big game hunt. Let's go after Kerner. A wild game hunt in the jungle, and a chance for them to bring something home to hang over the fireplace.**
>
> *Even if they truly believed that Otto Kerner was evil, how could they ignore all the positive things he had done? How could they take such pure, unbridled delight in that verdict? Even if they believe that my father was brought down by some tragic flaw, a momentary greed that peeked through and ultimately ly caused his fall, you'd think that anyone who looked at his entire career and what he had done would say to himself,*

"what a terrible tragedy" and would not be sitting over at the prosecution table, gloating over victory . . .

In those few words, spoken by the jury, my father must have felt that his life was completely undone. My sister, Helena, and I asked few questions. You don't want to burden somebody with having to provide answers at a time when they need to have their thoughts. Helena and I understood Dad well enough to keep our distance, to give him breathing room. We understood what was going through his mind. All the conversations we'd had together about the meaning of a reputation, and the hard work that goes into earning it. We knew that many times, the discrediting of a name may also include discrediting the many things that the person who carries the name had tried to do.

I knew that when the verdict was returned, my father felt it wasn't just Otto Kerner who had been found guilty. 'My God,' he must have felt, 'This is discrediting everything my family and I have stood for . . . all the things we've tried to do.'

I know we regarded Jim Thompson and some of the others at the prosecution table with a certain sense of disappointment. They were not people who could possibly have followed their consciences. If what they had done was unintention-

al, I don't think we'd feel that way, but there's a sense of sorrow and disappointment as to what these people are as human beings. It was disillusioning for my father to have given his entire adult life to public service, only to have it undone by people whose consuming interest was putting a trophy up on the wall, whose narrow ambition blinded them to the terrible injury they inflicted."

Tony Kerner's words express eloquently why U.S. Attorney James R. Thompson fell far short of the standards of "a good prosecutor" set down by the late Justice Robert H. Jackson of the United States Supreme Court. For here is how Mr. Justice Jackson sought to define those "elusive" qualities:

The qualities of a good prosecutor are as elusive and as impossible to define as those which mark a gentleman. And those who need to be told would not understand it anyway. A sensitiveness to fair play and sportsmanship is perhaps the best protection against the abuse of power, and the citizen's safety lies in the prosecutor who tempers zeal with human kindness, who seeks truth and not victims, who serves the law and not factional purposes, and who approaches his task with humility.

Almost surely, Thompson and Skinner, from their conduct as prosecutors, "would not understand" the words of Mr. Justice Jackson. Somehow, one cannot conceive Otto Kerner, who clearly understood those words, degrading himself and his high office with such a blatant betrayal of the "fair play and sportsmanship" to which Jackson alluded.

On April 19, 1973, the day he was sentenced to prison — Otto Kerner spoke for the first time since his indictment in December, 1971. In part he said:

> . . . I stand today before the bar of justice, condemned by a jury of twelve citizens for the most terrible crimes which can be charged against a man in public life . . .
>
> Twelve men and women of Illinois have found that I betrayed the public trust . . . that I dishonored the high office of governor . . .
>
> Nevertheless, in my mind and in my heart, I shall always be satisfied that my conscience and my record of loyal and dedicated service as governor of this state were never tarnished or my integrity bought.
>
> In the end, this will bring me peace no matter how disgraced I may stand presently in the public eye . . .
>
> But I do not stand before the Court here today to argue in my own behalf . . . I am neither apologetic nor defensive of my conduct.
>
> The ultimate verdict on me will be

*rendered in future years, and I know that verdict will establish that I was **always** an honest man and a faithful governor.*

Kerner, consumed by cancer, was released from the Federal Correctional Institution at Lexington, Kentucky, after serving seven months of his three-year sentence. Fourteen months later, he was dead.

The words of William Shakespeare, at the end of *Hamlet,* are appropriate.

Now cracks a noble heart.
Good night, sweet prince,
And flights of angels sing thee to thy rest!

Indeed, a volunteered comment by the trial judge on the first day of the trial indicates that even he may have been influenced by the widespread publicity about corruption in local government. During the direct examination of the witness Meyers, who was describing his rental of safe deposit boxes in which he kept funds to bribe public officials, the following occurred:

Q. Now, the box that you maintained with your name on it and your wife's name on it, was that ever changed in any way?

A. Yes, to a larger box.

Q. Now, do you recall the names —

JUDGE AUSTIN: *Was it as big as a shoe-box?*

THE WITNESS: Pardon me, sir?

JUDGE AUSTIN: Next question.

I think we may take judicial notice of the symbolic significance of a shoebox in view of the notoriety which followed discovery of former Secretary of State Paul Powell's cash hoard in such a container.

That a federal district judge would make a gratuitous reference to a shoebox during the bribery trial of another public figure, who may well have been associated with Powell in the minds of some jurors, is, to say the least, distressing. His comment reminds us of how difficult it is to evaluate subtle effects of publicity in the trial of a prominent political figure.

—JOHN PAUL STEVENS, the former federal appeals judge who heard the Barrett case appeal . . . and currently a U.S. Supreme Court Justice

II

THE EDWARD BARRETT CASE

It is doubtful whether separate and distinct felonies, involving different parties, not arising out of the same transaction or dependent upon the same proof, should ever be consolidated. But it should not be permitted where the crimes charged are of such a nature that the jury might regard one as corroborative of the other, when, in fact, no corroboration exists.

—KIDWELL v. UNITED STATES
38 App. D.C. 566, at 570 (1912)

. . . it is the vice of using evidence of one crime to prove the defendant's disposition to commit another.

—JOHN PAUL STEVENS

Noontime at the Civic Center Plaza in downtown Chicago. The sun dapples the wide concrete space in front of the Picasso. It is a bittersweet day in early autumn, with clouds billowing high above the steel-and-glass building — a day in which the lazy stillness of September warmth is suddenly punctuated by a breeze with the sharp, crisp hint of fall.

Two men emerge from the County Building across the street, walking slowly, on their way to lunch. They stop to buy a paper from the little old guy on the corner.

"How're you doing today?"

"Fine," says the vendor, making change. A smile lights his face. "Glad to see you, Ed." As he walks across the Plaza on his way to Toffenetti's, where the restaurant has named a sandwich in his honor, people see him, change direction, and make a point of coming over to shake hands.

Edward J. Barrett was a politician all right — one of the most successful men in the history of Illinois elective politics. Why was that? What were the qualities in Ed Barrett that got him elected to three of the top four positions in Illinois state government — Auditor, Treasurer, and Secretary of State — and then made him a shoo-in every time he ran for Cook County Clerk, the office he held from 1954 until Thompson had him indicted as a corrupt public official in 1972? What had Illinoisans seen in Eddie Barrett, over a period of more than 40 years, that made him so popular?

And what did getting Barrett convicted represent to Big Jim Thompson?

Taking the last question first, you have to understand Thompson's long-standing psychological compulsion to become President of the United

States to understand why he wanted Barrett's scalp so badly. Nor does one need to be an amateur psychologist or a Chicago Democrat to understand Thompson's probable motivations in the Barrett case. For Thompson himself had been blurting out his presidential ambitions clearly and often — with a special candor and crudity, it seems, at his cozy bull sessions with the press.

> *At a Washington breakfast with Capitol Hill reporters last year, for example, Thompson explained simply that he has felt the need to become President since he was 11, an ambition he has shared with others on other public occasions.*

Well, how does convicting Ed Barrett advance such ambitions?

Note the timing of the Barrett indictment, first of all. It came during the trial of Otto Kerner, Jr., the first time in American history that a sitting judge on the U.S. Court of Appeals had ever been accused of such serious crimes. Thompson himself had not initiated the accusations against Kerner, although he deservedly reaped the publicity for having secured Kerner's indictment — barely two weeks after being appointed U.S. Attorney for the Northern District of Illinois. This was late 1971. Millions of Illinoisans were now beginning to take notice of the flamboyant style of the new 36-year-old federal prosecutor.

The style was apparent in the closing rebuttal argument in the Kerner jury trial, an hour-long argument that Thompson himself would deliver in an emotion-choked voice and that would contain these deceptive remarks about his own political ambitions:

> *That's me, a hard-charging vigorous am-*
> *bitious prosecutor, but it won't lead to*
> *political longevity. Because an ambi-*
> *tious prosecutor doesn't indict a federal*
> *judge, particularly in Chicago. He just*
> *goes after the poor, the weak, the friend-*
> *less, the powerless and ends up with a*
> *95% conviction rate.*

The reason the remarks are deceptive, of course, is that a 95% conviction rate of "the poor, the weak, the friendless, the powerless" won't make a *political* name for anybody. But indicting and convicting a federal judge will.

And so will the scalp of an honest-to-God Democratic office holder in Cook County, and in Barrett's case a man who's known and respected throughout Illinois.

Thompson had deliberately set out to become the scourge of corrupt office holders. That was the image he sought; that was the image he was starting to get. Which means he needed what he defined as "corrupt office holders" in order to drive that image home to Illinois voters. He needed a lot of them.

When in 1972 Thompson went after Eddie Barrett, the new U.S. Attorney had never been elected *anything*. And Barrett had exactly the kind of marketable political goods that Thompson knew he himself needed: Barrett had a vast following, people from all walks of life and both political parties, people who by the tens of thousands would vote for Eddie election after election *because they liked and trusted him*.

Barrett was widely perceived as an honorable public man, the very kind of man that Big Jim since age 11 had always wanted to be. But if you can't *be* an Eddie Barrett, the next best thing is to beat an Eddie Barrett. Take away his honor. Transfer it to yourself. And it makes you especially big if you publicly profess scorn for the likes of Eddie Barrett and at the same time — while nobody's looking — try to grab from him the public honors Barrett had fairly earned.

Barrett's record of public service cannot exonerate him if indeed he was guilty of the 16 counts for which he'd been indicted: six counts of extortion, totaling $180,000 in alleged bribes; four counts of failing to pay federal income tax on that $180,000; and six mail-fraud counts. But Barrett's record of service does illuminate the special opportunity that a Barrett conviction would give Thompson.

The Barrett record is essentially this. Over his whole 40 years in public life, Eddie had served in every high state and county office with distinction and without the slightest hint of wrongdoing. Those positions typically gave Barrett vast financial power. He'd been Auditor of the State of Illinois during the Depression of the 1930's, for example, with jurisdiction over nearly 500 banks that were then in receivership. This was before Thompson was born.

So along comes Thompson in 1972, claiming to have invented honesty in public life and with all the naive and boorish jargon that befits a reformer on the make who also wishes to appear street-wise. Here is an example of what Thompson was then saying, as reported in the *Wall Street Journal:*

> *I'd always dreamed of getting into a position of authority to do something about*

> *corruption in Chicago because having
> lived and worked here all my life, I know
> where the bodies are buried. Now that
> I've gotten my chance, I'm not going to
> waste it.*

This would be a fine statement if it were true. But where had Thompson gotten all this inside knowledge about where "the bodies are buried?" Between 1936, when he was born, and the point at which he'd begun undergraduate studies at the University of Illinois? At Northwestern University, where he got his law degree? Out of textbooks? On his summer college breaks? As a *pornography* specialist for the Cook County State's Attorney? During the five years he was a law school teacher at Northwestern? During the year he'd assisted the Illinois Attorney General in matters that never included political crime? *After* he'd been appointed a federal prosecutor on November 30, 1971? *Before* that, in his short apprenticeship in the U.S. Attorney's office?

How, specifically, had Big Jim found out where Eddie Barrett's "bodies" were buried — only several months after becoming federal prosecutor? From whom had he picked up this information about Barrett's "bodies"? From the wholly uncorroborated allegations against Barrett by two convicted felons. That's how. That's where.

And as one of the appeals judges on the Barrett case later correctly pointed out, the fact that Thompson's office introduced into evidence the highly ambiguous personal records of those two convicted felons did not constitute convincing corroboration.

Federal authorities in another part of the country had already caught and convicted one of those felons, Irving Meyers, for stealing $1.5 million from the company he'd "served" as president. That was the same company that had been selling voting machines to Cook County, through the County Clerk, since before Ed Barrett had taken charge of that office in 1954.

And what was the reward the government offered Meyers in return for his help in convicting Barrett and the other governmental officials Meyers *said* he bribed with most of the $1.5 million he stole from his own company? Criminal immunity, of course. But in addition to that, a "total pass" on federal income tax liability for all the stolen money Meyers said he used for bribery purposes.

On the strength of the uncorroborated word of this crook, who with his equally corrupt brother-in-law had everything to gain and nothing to lose by lying that Barrett extorted Meyer's voting-machine company, the Barrett trial jury found Eddie guilty of the six extortion counts and four tax-evasion counts.

To buttress a case that rested only on the words of two well-rewarded crooks, Thompson ingeniously grafted six unrelated counts of mail fraud to the extortion and tax-evasion counts. The majority of the Circuit Court of Appeals judges who subsequently heard Barrett's appeal decided that consolidation was illicit. One of those judges was John Paul Stevens, now a Justice of the U.S. Supreme Court. And the eminent Judge Stevens at the time went so far as to brand this Thompson tactic

the vice of using evidence of one crime to

> *prove the defendant's disposition to commit another.*

Judge Stevens found so many and such flagrant ethical improprieties in the Barrett trial, in fact, that he rendered the opinion that Ed Barrett had been wrongfully convicted and deserved a new trial. He dissented in this finding from his two judicial colleagues on the three-man Barrett appeals panel. But the pattern of gross government irresponsibility that Judge Stevens' opinion exposed — coupled with the unseemly combination of ineptness and hostility towards the accused by his trial judge — makes a highly convincing case that Barrett indeed was railroaded, starting with the artificially inflated 16-count indictment.

Thompson had used the same shotgun approach in getting Kerner indicted. It was a technique Thompson was learning to master, a technique especially designed to confuse laymen jurors.

As lay citizens, it's hard for a jury to remember all the ins-and-outs of a complicated trial. A multiple-count indictment means lengthy and complex instructions to the jury, and a chance for the government to overwhelm jurors with a mix of evidence and innuendo.

The indictment, remember, charged Barrett with six counts of bribery (interstate travel in aid of racketeering enterprises), four counts of income tax evasion, and six counts of mail fraud.

It was the government's theory that Barrett unlawfully, wilfully, and knowingly caused Irving H. Meyers, a Philadelphia businessman, to travel in interstate commerce between Philadelphia and Chicago for the purpose of bribery. Also traveling — allegedly with the knowledge of Mr. Barrett —

and for the same offense, was Anthony Lemisch, Meyer's brother-in-law. Supposedly, said the government, Barrett accepted approximately $180,000 in cash during the period between 1967 and 1970 in a series of six separate bribes for recommending the purchase and rental of approximately 900 voting machines by Cook County from Shoup Voting Machine Corporation.

The government also charged that Barrett and his wife, in filing their joint returns, had understated their income in 1967, 1968, 1969, and 1970. The extra income, said Thompson, came from the alleged bribes paid to Barrett by Meyers and Lemisch. And finally, there were those six unrelated counts of using the mails to scheme and defraud the people of Cook County.

A licensed insurance broker for years, Barrett received insurance commissions from Arthur J. Gallagher and Company — commissions on the premiums Cook County paid for insurance coverage on the voting machines it bought or leased. These premiums were paid to Centennial Insurance Company, a wholly-owned subsidiary of the Atlantic Companies.

Mail fraud happened, said the government, when Barrett's agents mailed premium checks to The Atlantic Companies in Denver, and when the Atlantic Companies, in return, mailed commission checks to Arthur J. Gallagher and Company.

Mail fraud! This was the device Thompson used to bond *everything* together in the Barrett case. He used it to lend credence to the unsubstantiated immunized testimony of two convicted felons and tax cheats in the wholly unrelated — and much more serious — matter of the alleged $180,000 in bribes. Then he reversed field and used the alleged $180,000 in bribes to "prove" Barrett hadn't paid his federal taxes.

But as Judge John Paul Stevens clearly saw, everything finally depended on Thompson being able to prove that Barrett had technically violated the mail-fraud statute — that Eddie had done so by accepting a portion of the legitimate commissions that the taxpayers of Cook County paid annually to have their voting machines insured.

Well, Thompson did prove that. But what he really proved — when all the camouflage is stripped away from the mail fraud statute — is that Eddie Barrett had fallen below the conflict-of-interest standard Big Jim piously proclaimed for other politicians. What Thompson had not — repeat, *not* — proved is that Ed Barrett had violated any state or federal law bearing on the improper use of public funds.

An objective analyst begins to see this distinction when he reads the relevant section of the mail fraud statute (18 U.S.C., Section 1341), which says in part:

> *Whoever, having devised or intending to devise any scheme or artifice to defraud, or for obtaining money or property by means of false or fraudulent pretenses, representations, or promises . . . for the purpose of executing such scheme or artifice or attempting so to do, places in any post office or authorized depository for mail matter, any matter or thing whatever to be sent or delivered by the Postal Service, or takes or receives therefrom, any such matter or thing, or knowingly causes to be delivered by mail according*

> *to the direction thereon, or at the place*
> *at which it is directed to be delivered by*
> *the person to whom it is addressed, any*
> *such matter or thing, shall be fined not*
> *more than $1,000 or imprisoned not*
> *more than five years, or both.*

The language is as obscure as it is menacing. And Thompson's office made it even more frightening and difficult to defend against, according to the *Wall Street Journal*, by nationally spearheading a distorted expansion of the statute's original spirit. WSJ reporter Jonathan R. Laing wrote:

> *his [Thompson's] office has used the fed-*
> *eral mail-fraud statute, a Victorian law*
> *designed to keep lottery tickets out of*
> *the mail, against Otto Kerner and other*
> *officials caught in conflicts of interest*
> *that weren't illegal under Illinois law.*

Nor were Barrett's broker commissions — which he never denied receiving and always paid his full tax on — illegal under *federal* law.

At Barrett's trial, in fact, his attorney Thomas A. Foran called the vice president of the Gallagher Company as a defense witness. That witness testified his company had been receiving a 25% commission on the insurance covering Cook County voting machines since 1961 — and that 15% of *that* commission had gone steadily to Barrett.

Reasonable men can dispute whether Eddie Barrett should have involved himself with this kind of broker's commission — even though the grand total of the six transactions charged by the government netted Barrett only a paltry sum each year. But before rendering too hasty a decision on the matter, reasonable men should listen to what Barrett's defense attorney Tom Foran says about the commissions. Foran tried to have the six points below inserted as one of the instructions to the Barrett trial jury. (The trial judge, Austin, refused to allow this insertion — one of many rulings he made against Foran's reasonable attempts to protect his client's legitimate interests.) Foran's six points were:

1. *The defendant never devised any scheme or artifice to defraud the people of Cook County or anyone else.*

2. *The County received insurance on its voting machines which was obtained at a fair and reasonable rate.*

3. *The only evidence in the case indicates that the insurance was placed at A. J. Gallagher by Mr. Hodgman, and the commissions were not given to Mr. Barrett at his request, or at the request of anyone else on his behalf.*

4. *All commissions received by Mr. Barrett were accurately and fully disclosed on his income tax returns filed with the Internal Revenue Service.*

5. *The people of Cook County were not, in fact, defrauded by anyone with regard to the voting machine insurance.*

6. *The commissions were not secretly received or obtained.*

Eddie Barrett in 40 years of public life never fell below the conflict-of-interest standards of millions of decent, law-abiding Illinoisans who gladly voted for him. Many of these people, probably most, did not expect him to burn his insurance license as long as he did not gouge them or steal from them or force their governmental agencies to pay more for insurance than any other company would charge — and as long as he reported all his income and paid tax on it just like anybody else.

But the question remains, are these distinctions that really decent, really law-abiding people *should* make? Jim Thompson would say *no, they are not.* But Jim Thompson was a "reformer" on the make, a man who in Barrett's own case was capable of collapsing all the moral distinctions between taking bribes from a sewer operator like Irving Meyers and collecting legitimate insurance commissions; capable of collapsing any distinction between these two activities to the point, in fact, that he could and did use the second of the alleged offenses to add credence to the first.

Consider the impact on the jury of this bit of moral vision by one of Thompson's assistants, a government attorney, at the Barrett trial:

> *See, it wasn't enough for Edward Barrett to receive $180,000 in bribes. After he got the machines he got a little hungrier and he wanted some more money, and so he went ahead and worked out an agreement where he could insure the machines, something he was required to do under the terms of his job, and then got a kickback in the form of a broker's commission.*

Did the jury catch the internal inconsistency of this casual speculation, that even though Barrett didn't begin his supposed illicit dealings with Meyers until 1967 he became so hungry *because of them* that he "began" the insurance commission arrangement in 1961? Don't bet they didn't miss it.

One thing is certain about the conflict of interest that politicians are capable of: it can be repulsive. But the person who casts the first stone in this regard had better be sure his own dealings are absolutely clean, as clean and admirable as Eddie Barrett's were for the 40 years he was entrusted with vast sums of money by the citizens of Illinois and of Cook County.

And it is also a matter of record that Thompson increased the cost of the U.S. Attorney's office he ran by *millions of dollars* — ostensibly to straighten out the moral vision of the rest of us. During the whole time Thompson was in that office, and for the 3½ years he headed it, according to the *Wall Street Journal*, the staff of the office tripled in size

> *to 74 lawyers, from 23 lawyers in 1970.*
> *At present, the office has 11 grand juries*
> *running full time compared to just two*
> *under Thompson's predecessors.*

Whether or not Ed Barrett was justified in accepting the small and legitimate insurance commissions, we would all do well to reflect on the wise words of the late Mr. Justice Robert Jackson of the United States Supreme Court. Prior to his Supreme Court service, Mr. Jackson was Attorney General of the United States; and at a meeting of federal prosecutors, he said this:

> *In spite of the temptations to divert our power to local conditions where they have become offensive to our sense of decency, the only long-term policy that will save federal justice from being discredited by entanglements with local politics is that it confine itself to strict and impartial enforcement of federal law, letting the chips fall in the community where they may. Just as there should be no permitting of local considerations to stop federal enforcement, so there should be no striving to enlarge our power over local affairs and no use of federal prosecutions to exert an indirect influence that would be unlawful if exerted directly.*

U.S. Attorney General Robert Jackson spoke these words when James Thompson was still a youngster less than 5 years old. The boy's plan to become our President would not surface for another six years or so, according to Thompson's own account of the matter, when the late Mr. Jackson was encouraging federal prosecutors to use their vast power with restraint — and to especially avoid the temptation to use that federal power to overwhelm what Mr. Jackson called each locality's

> *right under our system of government to fix its own standards of law enforcement and of morals.*

Nor had young Jim Thompson probably yet even dreamed of becoming a "hard charging vigorous ambitious prosecutor."

What was Eddie Barrett doing in 1941, when Attorney General Jackson was counselling federal prosecutors against enlarging federal power in local affairs? Having held high state offices for the preceding 10 years, Barrett was preparing to leave for the Pacific theater of war with the U.S. Marines. This was the second American war he had voluntarily participated in, even though he'd never fully recovered from a World War I lung wound he had received at age 18.

Mentioning these things does not amount to mere flag waving. Nor is it meant to divert attention from Thompson's charges in 1972 that Ed Barrett by then had become a crooked and shabby office holder. The point is not even that Barrett was a pretty good person, just like Illinois voters always perceived him to be, a happy little good-hearted Irishman who didn't hold political grudges but who never walked away from a good war or a good political fight either.

The point is that Eddie Barrett was a real live human being. He was a person who at all times in his life deserved to be treated with at least the minimal human respect that civilized men accord each other. Some rights, after all, are so basic that nobody's ever even bothered to write them down anywhere.

One such right, which even the most contemptible and vicious criminal deserves, is to be treated as a human being. An outrageous number of Eddie Barrett's legal and Constitutional rights were denied him, as will soon be summarized. But at a deeper level even than that, none of Eddie Barrett's prosecutors and other adversaries ever seemed to look at him and see a man with flesh and blood like their own, a man with a good and happy spirit, a creature of God if you will, a man whom little people loved and with very good reason.

On the contrary, Barrett's prosecutors and other adversaries defined him as a human zero, a non-person, a thing, the embodiment of a bad idea in politics, an idea that must and would be held up to public ridicule.

The consequence for Barrett was that he was in a no-win position all the way.

For the record shows that Barrett's Constitutional right to know exactly what he was charged with — exact dates, most importantly, of his six alleged briberies by representatives of the Shoup Voting Machine Corporation — was systematically trampled in letter and spirit.

The record shows that Barrett was thus deprived of the ability to prepare his defense and was forced to approach his trial with absolutely no information concerning *exactly* when he was alleged to have accepted the six separate bribes. And this happened even though the Sixth Amendment to the U.S. Constitution guarantees, among other things, that in all criminal prosecutions the accused has the right

> *to be informed of the nature and cause of the accusation;*

For the record shows that Barrett did not receive — *until the trial was under way* — a government Bill of Particulars precisely stating dates and circumstances of the alleged briberies.

And the record also shows that while Thompson's office may not have decided which of Irving

Meyers' airline and other records to use to "establish" Meyers' allegations of flying to Chicago to bribe Barrett, the government still acted in disregard of Barrett's Constitutional rights by denying him access to *any* part of the complex mass of accusatory data that Thompson's office had been assembling for months in advance of the trial.

> *The record shows that the government financially induced the convicted felon Irving Meyers to provide its key testimony against Barrett by releasing Meyers from his obligation to pay any federal taxes at all on the $180,000 he SAID he gave Barrett and in any case did steal from his own company.*

The record in fact shows that the government's *total* payment to Meyers for his testimony against Barrett and all the other public officials in the country Meyers *said* he bribed amounted to ALL the federal income tax he would otherwise have to pay on $1 million of money he'd stolen.

The record shows that Thompson's own office knew this financial inducement to a convicted felon was so grave a breach of law and ethics — *federal law specifically calls it a crime to pay anyone to induce his testimony* — that a Chicago-based government attorney after the trial was over tried to disclaim responsibility for the Thompson office in so stinking and probably criminal an action.

For the record shows that First Assistant U.S. Attorney Anton R. Valukas tried in 1976 — like Pontius Pilate — to wash his own hands and those of his former boss Thompson by saying that government attorneys in Philadelphia had made the immunity deal that gave Irving Meyers a complete "pass" on paying taxes on $1 million of his stolen money. The *Chicago Daily News* of February 2, 1976, quotes Valukas as saying:

> *Our office in Chicago would never participate in such an arrangement.*

But the record shows that federal prosecutors in the Chicago office *used* that bought-and-paid-for testimony of a convicted felon as the *sole* direct evidence to support its 10 extortion and tax-evasion counts against Barrett. And this makes Valukas' statement no different in character from Pilate's equally weak and hypocritical disclaimer of responsibility.

The record shows that Thompson's office used two elaborate subterfuges to prop up the costly but shaky testimony of Irving Meyers. The first of these subterfuges was using this felon's own personal records to "corroborate" his immunized testimony about the alleged bribes: *his* safe deposit box entries, which Appeals Judge Stevens found irrelevant; *his* records of *his* telephone calls to Barrett, which Judge Stevens found innocuous; *his* airline records indicating when Meyers was in Chicago which, as Judge Stevens saw, told nothing about what Meyers did or whom he met (if anyone) in Chicago; and the price increase on voting machines which *he*, Meyers, imputed in *his* immunized testimony took place because of Barrett's demand for bribe money on Cook County sales but which also, as Judge Stevens pointed out, "was effective throughout the country and arguably justified by legitimate cost factors."

The record shows that the second subterfuge

Thompson used to give Irving Meyers' testimony the look of truth was to illicitly consolidate the six mail-fraud counts to the other 10 counts of bribery and tax evasion. And those other 10 counts, remember, all hinged on the unsupported word and ambiguous personal records of Irving Meyers. Judge Stevens properly called this practice of trying to use one alleged crime to corroborate another a vicious practice.

The record shows that Barrett's trial judge, the late Richard B. Austin, made what Appeals Judge Stevens later branded as "prejudicial and inaccurate comments" from the bench all through the Barrett trial. The tenor of Judge Austin's many casual slurs against Eddie Barrett the man and Barrett's case was so hostile — and some of the comments themselves so obtuse — that Judge Stevens went so far as to claim that Austin's unseemly remarks

> *must have given the jury the impression that the judge fully credited the testimony of the government's key witness [Meyers].*

And finally the record shows that the let's-get-another-crooked-politician bandwagon psychology of Barrett's pre-trial news coverage — coupled with the fact that Barrett's trial happened to open only days after Otto Kerner's conviction — poisoned the public mind against Barrett. It certainly seems to have helped poison Judge Austin's mind against Barrett and his courtroom rights. It probably also poisoned the minds of at least some of Barrett's jurors, who like Judge Austin may reasonably be expected to have read the screaming headline "BARRETT'S TURN NEXT" and accompanying story in the February 19, 1973 *Chicago Daily News*. Barrett's trial opened Wednesday morning, February 21.

So the ground was gone from under Barrett's feet as the trial opened. He had already lost many of his legal and Constitutional rights; and he would lose many more in the poisoned atmosphere of Judge Richard B. Austin's courtroom. He'd not only been judged guilty; he'd been judged as not being of enough human worth to even be accorded the status of a Richard Speck.

But Eddie never did and never would become the human zero that Thompson implied. He never did and never would become a non-person or a thing or a mere idea in Big Jim's head. Eddie Barrett was sad, of course, as the trial opened, and his physical health was terrible; but he was the same old Eddie nevertheless. He never changed.

Barrett was a proud man. He did not wish to gain any courtroom sympathy for his many ills. He and his defense attorney Tom Foran had a signalling system, in fact, so that Foran would call for a court break when the defendant had to take his nitroglycerin pills — which Eddie did not want anyone to see.

Speech-making had never been Eddie's forte. He'd be introduced, tell a story or two, smile, and sit down — all in less than five minutes. Eddie always ran on his record, rather than on his speeches. His vote-getting strength came from the man in the street — the little guy who recognized Eddie and supported him. "In every big crowd or political meeting," one man recalls, "Barrett wouldn't stay long on the podium. He'd be down on the floor, shaking hands and talking to two or three people in a small group.

"When he talked to you, his face would light up and he'd get a sparkle in his eye. No matter how mad he was at somebody, if you'd come up to him and shake hands, a smile would spread over his face."

Now, in 1972, in the autumn of his career as a public official, Eddie Barrett walks a little more slowly across the Civic Center Plaza. Dapper and sharply dressed as ever, at 73 years old — and always with the Purple Heart bar in his lapel. His World War I wound has been bothering him, ever since his lung was aspirated to remove fluid. The lung is back in working order again, but the wound still drains through the hole that had to be made in Eddie's back during his World War II Marine service. The vest he wears has been carefully sewed to conceal the drainage pad.

Count I of the indictment alleged that Barrett had caused Irving H. Meyers to travel in furtherance of the bribery scheme "in or about November, 1967." Other charges were similar. "In or about August, 1968" in Count II. "In or about August, 1968" in Count III, except that this time, the alleged briber was Anthony Lemisch. "In or about February or March, 1969" in Count IV. "In or about March, 1970" in Count V. And "in or about August and September, 1970" in Count VI.

Because the prosecution would not supply specific dates and locations before the trial, Barrett was totally without the necessary information which would have enabled him to prepare his defense. Before the trial started, he was told only that each of the offenses occurred "in Chicago." *It was not until his trial was actually in progress — and the government was introducing its evidence — that Barrett learned that Thompson intended to rely specifically on the following dates to support the bribery charges:* November 14, 1967, in Count I; August 9, 1968, in Count II; August 21, 1968, in Count III; February 13, 1969, in Count IV; March 23, 1970, in Count V; and August 30, 1970, in Count VI.

As County Clerk of one of the largest counties in the United States, and as a man who traveled frequently, Barrett should not — in justice — have been expected to prepare a defense to such general charges, or to be confronted — for the first time — at his trial with such specific dates. A criminal case such as this one is not some sort of game between the government and the defendant, with each trying to outsmart the other. What it should be is a serious search for truth. If the prosecutor has the ability to provide important information as to when and where — exactly — the defendant is believed to have committed crimes, then he should give the accused that information. That is what the Sixth Amendment to our Constitution says a prosecutor should and must do. That is what a decent prosecutor does.

It was not that the government did not have specific times and places for the alleged bribery events. Quite the contrary. Thompson knew. But the government chose not to disclose this information until the trial. And, amazingly, Judge Austin approved of this tactic. One can reasonably argue that, by depriving him of *advance* knowledge of the dates on which he was accused of accepting bribes, Thompson had reversed the terms of the proposition that a man is presumed to be innocent until he is proved guilty beyond a reasonable doubt. Thompson's formula was that a man is presumed guilty until he proves himself innocent.

Pre-trial publicity became an issue in the Barrett case when Judge Austin denied the defense motion for a continuance.

On Monday, Feb. 19, 1973, a Federal District Court jury returned "guilty" verdicts for all 17 counts on which Otto Kerner, a United States Court of Appeals Judge, had been indicted the previous December.

Front page news stories carried the Kerner conviction publicity. Like Barrett, Kerner's charges involved bribery, income tax evasion, and mail fraud. While no person could have predicted the Kerner verdict would have been reached literally on the eve of the Barrett trial, the prejudicial effect of the sensational publicity damaged the County Clerk's credibility. That *Chicago Daily News* headline "BARRETT'S TURN NEXT" helped to inflame the atmosphere and to raise a presumption of guilt in the general public.

In addition, there had been substantial Chicago publicity in the months before Barrett's trial which alleged misconduct of many prominent public office holders in Cook County. And only weeks before, there had been major publicity concerning insurance commissions received by many prominent politicians in Cook County. Barrett, of course, had been charged with mail fraud in conjunction with insurance commissions he had received — and the public linked the two.

Even a brief continuance — a reasonable delay of the trial — would have allowed some of the sensational publicity to die down, and would have permitted community feelings to simmer slowly down in intensity. Yet Judge Austin denied the defense motion for a continuance.

He stated that he did not believe Barrett had sufficiently demonstrated a connection between the series of events about the publicity and the Barrett trial. Judge Austin then went ahead with jury selection.

During the *voir dire* examination (a preliminary examination to determine the competence of a juror), Judge Austin refused to allow Defense Attorney Foran to ask a number of questions relating to the possible bias of jurors. These questions were particularly important in view of the type of widespread publicity then occurring about politicians. Many persons have feelings of prejudice against public officials, and in fact distrust them; and since these feelings had been seriously aggravated by the widespread publicity regarding political misconduct, the defense wanted the prospective jurors to be interrogated with respect to their possible prejudices against politicians and public office holders.

This refusal by Judge Austin to let Barrett defend himself from the mob psychology of inflamed people was part of the judicial pattern Appeals Judge Stevens later would find so appalling. Stevens specifically cited many of Austin's comments from the bench.

One such conversation concerned the subject of

Irving Meyers renting a larger safe deposit box at some point in his seamy career. Judge Stevens quoted the exchange between Judge Austin (referred to as "The Court") and Barrett's defense attorney as follows:

> *The Court: And when did they open the joint box?*
> *Mr. Foran: Not until 1967, your Honor.*
> *The Court: Well, they didn't need to open one because they hadn't met Mr. Barrett yet. Maybe the boxes that they had were sufficient, but when they met him they needed bigger boxes.*

Then Stevens said in his appeals finding that he considered this casual slur on Barrett's character by the trial judge

> *so manifestly improper that I would presume that it was prejudicial. Certainly it makes me wonder if it is appropriate to construe other ambiguous comments made in the presence of the jury as having been harmless.*

As far as the six bribery charges were concerned, the government charged that Barrett "unlawfully, wilfully, and knowingly did cause Irving H. Meyers to travel in interstate commerce between Philadelphia and Chicago, with intent to promote, manage, carry on, and facilitate the promotion, management, and carrying on of an unlawful activity — namely bribery — in violation of the laws of the state of Illinois, and that thereafter, Barrett did perform and cause to be performed acts to promote, carry on, and facilitate the promotion and carrying on of said unlawful activity."

Five counts of the indictment said that Irving H. Meyers had done the interstate traveling; the sixth count said that Anthony Lemisch had.

Who were these men? What connection did they have with Eddie Barrett?

Irving H. Meyers was a 10 per cent owner and president of Shoup Voting Machine Corporation, of Philadelphia, which sold voting machines to Cook County. As County Clerk, Barrett was responsible for buying and insuring voting machines.

Since the early 1950s, the Shoup Voting Machine Corporation had sold its machines to Cook County. In 1954, the State's Attorney of Cook County had given the opinion that competitive bidding was not required in the purchase of voting machines, since it was important to maintain uniformity in all of Cook County's precincts.

Between 1967 and 1970, Cook County had purchased and rented approximately 900 machines from the Shoup Corporation. Since no one other than Shoup sold comparable machines, competitive biddings was not practical. In fact, the State's Attorney's opinion said that "you may request a bid from the Shoup Voting Machine Corp. only," though bids for machines needed the approval of the County Clerk, and then of the County Board.

At the trial, Meyers testified that he had proposed to sell 250 voting machines to Cook County in 1965 at $1,791 each. Meyers described a meeting Meyers said he had with Barrett in Barrett's County office:

I said to Mr. Barrett that any dealings between the Shoup Corporation and the County of Cook in the future would be between he and I. I hold Mr. Barrett that I was committed to pay him five per cent cash on all voting machines sales to Cook County.

Mr. Barrett said to me that he was getting more money than that before. I said to Mr. Barrett that this was a new ball game, and that is all the money that I was committed to pay.

Mr. Barrett said that he wanted $200 per machine.

I hesitated for a moment, and then I said to Mr. Barrett that the only way I could pay him $200 per machine would be to raise the price of the voting machine by $100 to the County of Cook, and that I felt he could vindicate the $100 increase in price, because Cook County had a bastard type voting machine.

He asked me what I meant by that.

I told him that we made two standard models of machine, and it had been the Shoup policy, whether or not we sold a county one machine or a thousand, the price was always the same. But Cook County had a machine like no other county in the United States. So therefore, there was nothing to compare Cook County's price against any other price.

Mr. Barrett said that he could take care of the increase.

Mr. Barrett asked me when he would

> *get the money.*
>
> *I told him naturally, I would pay him the money after Shoup received the money from the County for the purchase of the voting equipment.*

Trial testimony brought out the fact that Barrett had requested a bid for 300 voting machines. The proposal by Shoup, sent on Oct. 20, 1967, set the price at $1,890—$99 above the 1965 bid. On November 7, 1967, the Cook County Board unanimously approved the bid.

Meyers testified that he flew to Chicago on November 14, 1967, with a blue plastic valise containing $30,000 in cash. He and Barrett met at O'Hare and had lunch together at the restaurant. Meyers said that after lunch, Barrett picked up the valise with the money and left.

As "proof" that this event had actually happened, the government introduced travel records to show Meyers' flight from Philadelphia to Chicago, which arrived at 12:17 p.m. — and the return flight, which left O'Hare at 2:10 p.m. Phone records showed a call from Shoup's office to Barrett's home. And safe deposit company records showed a visit on November 13 to one of two safe deposit boxes in which Meyers kept cash to make payments.

Throughout his testimony, Meyers told similar stories of other meetings with Barrett — a $30,000 payment in cash on August 9, 1968, "confirmed" with plane tickets, a phone call, and a visit by Meyers to his safe deposit box.

Meyers testified that on August 20, 1968, he gave $15,000 to his brother-in-law Anthony Lemisch in a sealed envelope. Lemisch testified that he had gone to Chicago that day and delivered the envelope to Barrett in his County Clerk's office. Records introduced by the government show a safe deposit entry on August 16, and phone calls to Barrett on August 20 and 22.

The next payment to Barrett, said Meyers, was for $45,000 on February 13, 1969. Meyers testified that he was on his way to Las Vegas for his daughter's wedding; took a plane with his family to O'Hare; met Barrett at the gate, while his family remained on the plane; gave the blue valise to Barrett; and then continued on to Las Vegas.

A similar pattern, said Meyers, happened with other payoffs — one for $30,000 on March 23, 1970, and one for $30,000 on August 30, 1970. Safe deposit box entry records and airline tickets were introduced by the government in support of Meyers' testimony.

Meyers said:

> *I paid this money to Mr. Barrett to insure getting the business, the voting machine business in Cook County. I felt that with Mr. Barrett's recommendation on the purchase of the Shoup voting machines that there would be no problem in passing the board.*

Translated into plain English, in other words, this convicted felon Irving Meyers says he paid Barrett $180,000 in bribes so Cook County would keep buying his company's voting machines — *machines that, by 1967, the County had been buying since before Barrett had become County Clerk and which were mechanically unique in the United*

States.

Trial evidence demonstrated that Irving H. Meyers, without the knowledge of anyone in the Shoup Voting Machine Corporation, embezzled almost $1,600,000 from Shoup — then deposited about $1 million of that amount in various safe deposit boxes. Meyers claimed he gave the money to various public officials to secure business for the corporation.

Trial evidence also brought out that Meyers kept no records of the money that was deposited in the safe deposit boxes; that no record was kept of any disbursements from the safe deposit boxes; that no stockholder or superior in the corporation was even aware of the money in the safe deposit boxes; that the money in the safe deposit boxes was under his total control; and that the only disbursements of the money were within the sole discretion of Meyers.

What did Meyers say himself about where he got the cash he allegedly paid Barrett?

> *In 1965 when I became president of Shoup, I devised a method of raising cash where there might be purposes of obtaining business where I did not have a legitimate representative, and paying cash was the only way to get the business.*
>
> *The method I devised was to pay different persons checks to represent Shoup in certain areas where I did not have representation, or to pay by check different professional people, lawyers, or so forth for professional fees for services that were not rendered.*
>
> *When I paid these checks to these peo-*

ple, they would pay their income tax, and then return to me 40 or 50 per cent in cash. At the end of each year, I would send out a 1099 form to all these people so that they could report — make sure they would report this money on their income tax.

This is the way or the method that I used to raise cash.

At Barrett's trial, there was a stipulation about the method Meyers used to generate the million dollars in cash allegedly used in the bribes of Barrett and other public officials in other areas of the country. The stipulation involved the reading of the statements of 11 witnesses who had submitted false vouchers for fictitious services to the Shoup Voting Machine Corporation.

Meyers had the Shoup Voting Machine Corporation pay the false bills. The witnesses would pay the income taxes on the illicit money received, and then return half of the balance to Meyers in cash. All 11 of these phony purveyors were immunized in exchange for their testimony. The testimony and fact of immunity appeared in the Barrett record, by the reading of the stipulation into the record by the Assistant U.S. Attorney.

None of the 11 witnesses who had been immunized knew Barrett or had ever spoken to Barrett. All of their dealings had been with Meyers.

And what of Meyers?

The government's promise of immunity was one of the terms of a plea bargaining deal negotiated with Meyers in his earlier criminal trial in Philadelphia. Meyers and Lemisch pleaded guilty to several counts of conspiracy and mail fraud, and to counts of filing false income tax returns which did not report as taxable income portions of a $700,000 fund. Meyers also agreed to testify in other proceedings about what happened to the $700,000.

In return, the government recommended a sentence on all counts of one year and a day, to be imposed under a statute which made Meyers immediately eligible for parole, and the sentence was to be served at the detention facility at Eglin Air Force Base, Florida.

The government also granted Meyers and Lemisch transactional immunity to preclude state prosecutions. In addition, the Pennsylvania prosecutor recommended to the Internal Revenue Service that it exempt Meyers and Lemisch from *civil* tax liability on any part of the money which they would testify under oath they had paid as bribes or political contributions to public officials.

Transactional immunity is the immunity that tells a man that he cannot be prosecuted for any events that he testifies about — that is, he cannot be charged. *Use* immunity, on the other hand, says he can be charged, but the government cannot use directly or indirectly what he says against him. Transactional immunity, clearly, is the greater protection.

However, under the Immunized Crime Control Act of 1970, within the federal system, use immunity became the *only* kind of statutory immunity permitted — that is, there was no longer any kind of transactional immunity that could legitimately be granted by the time the government made its deal with Meyers.

Knowing this, the agreement with Meyers and

Lemisch seems even more unbelievable! If Meyers and Lemisch were indicted and convicted for failing to report some of the safe-deposit box cash as taxable income to themselves, how can the government contradict itself by excusing his *civil* tax liability on that income?

Let's take a close look at the Pennsylvania agreement:

The agreement itself was made in the United States District Court, Eastern District of Pennsylvania, in February, 1972. Irving H. Meyers, Murray Hirshon, and Anthony Lemisch were part of a group of defendants — as well as Shoup Voting Machine Corporation. The U.S. Attorney recommended to the Court that total punishment for all counts of the indictment to which the men pleaded should be one year imprisonment without additional fine or a period of probation; for Lemisch, the government recommended a six months stay in prison without any additional fine or imprisonment.

The U.S. Attorney also recommended that the U.S. Parole Board consider the defendants eligible for parole at the beginning of their sentence. Here's the pertinent part of the immunity grant that Anton R. Valukas said Thompson's office would not have entered into, but did in fact *use* to protect the key witness against Ed Barrett:

> *In the cases of Meyers and Lemisch, we have indicated to the defendants and have advised that it is our understanding that after consultation with the appropriate officials of the Internal Revenue Service in this district that the position of the Internal Revenue Service relating*

to civil liability is that regardless of the pleas that are entered, regardless of the precise charges that are the subject of the indictment, IRS will assess for civil purposes as income only moneys that have been received and retained as income money given defendants.

To the extent that the defendants have received moneys and have not kept it as income, and have passed it on to other persons, either lawfully or unlawfully, this will not be considered income, and will not be assessed against them as income. The government will accept their testimony in this regard.

It will not be necessary that the persons to whom the defendants testified they gave money acknowledge receipt of that money, and it will not even be necessary that such persons in every case be charged or convicted of obtaining or receiving that money, but if the defendants have testified under oath and have identified the persons to whom they transacted the money, and if the government has accepted their testimony, on the basis of their full cooperation, then their testimony in that regard will be accepted, and it's our understanding that it will be considered in that light by the Internal Revenue Service for civil purposes. They are not immunized for perjury.

The government justified its granting civil tax-relief liability on the grounds that Meyers was a mere conduit and not the beneficial recipient of the cash; and, therefore, that the cash was not taxable income to him. But there is difficulty in squaring this explanation with the fact that Meyers was convicted.

Was the money income to Meyers?

On the one hand, he could be considered an agent of Shoup Voting Machine Corporation in raising cash through false vouchers to the company, and in using the cash to bribe public officials to buy Shoup voting machines. On the other hand, he could also be considered as embezzling the cash from Shoup, taking complete control of it, and using the money.

In a similar trial in the Eastern District of Pennsylvania, (*United States v. Osser*) held in fall, 1972, both Meyers and Lemisch testified on behalf of the prosecution that they had given money to a public official — but the jury returned a verdict of not guilty. In the *Osser* trial, Meyers testified that he did not know if the government had accepted his word (and therefore if his civil tax liability had been reduced).

Since Thompson advised Barrett's lawyers on the morning the trial began that the government had accepted Meyer's word, and since Meyers testified that he would not have been on the witness stand against Barrett if he had not been so advised, the defense should have been entitled to ask if the "not guilty" verdict in the Osser case had been discussed by Meyers and the prosecution, and what effect that discussion had on the importance of his testimony in the Barrett trial.

Lemisch, on the other hand, testified in the Barrett case that he did not know whether or not the government had accepted his word.

> *The civil tax liability of Meyers and Lemisch, by their own testimony, was one of vital interest and importance to them. It was the most important element contained in their plea agreements, and they so testified.*

In short, for all the money they testified they gave to public officials, they reduced their civil tax liability — and the acceptance of this agreement and even the *use* of their testimony against Barrett clearly and blatantly is improper conduct on the part of the prosecutor.

Obviously, in a trial of this nature, the financial status of the witness Meyers was extremely important. At a time when he reported comparatively minimal net income, Meyers spent money with extraordinary freedom. Various records of safe deposit boxes in the names of Murray Hirshorn and Anthony Lemisch were excluded from the trial by the Court. Yet Meyers testified that both men periodically were sent by him to get money out of safe deposit boxes. He further testified that when he did not accompany them to the boxes, he would not know which safe deposit box they entered — and that they would partially withdraw these moneys through and including 1970.

The prosecution, however, objected — and its objection was sustained — saying that these exhibits should not be admitted into evidence. Because some of this evidence was excluded, the defense could not show the jury the incredible frequency with which these witnesses were using the safe deposit boxes.

So the government used certain dates the safe

deposit boxes were entered to "corroborate" the testimony of both Meyers and Lemisch — testimony that they had bribed Barrett on certain dates.

Ledger sheets for the apartment occupied by Irving H. Meyers in Philadelphia between 1965 and 1971 were also excluded from the trial. Barrett's lawyers charged that rather than bribing public officials with the money he had stolen from the Shoup Voting Machine Corporation, Meyers had kept the money for his own use and benefit. The evidence of the ledger sheets was offered to demonstrate that Meyers was living far beyond his legitimate sources of income.

Also excluded: a letter signed by Meyers in which he said that he had paid $20,000 to renovate his apartment. At first, on cross-examination, Meyers denied he had spent that much money on his apartment, but then conceded that he had written the letter and identified his signature. The evidence would have demonstrated that Meyers had lived far beyond his means, and had stolen the money from Shoup for his own use and benefit.

Bank statements of Irving H. Meyers from 1967 through 1971 at three different banks were also excluded by the Court's decision — on the grounds that the government objected, because the defense was unable to demonstrate precisely that Meyers' excessive personal expenditures equalled the whole $1 million he had embezzled.

Certainly, however, Meyers had access to substantially more money than his income would indicate. This is evidence which could have been used to support the position that Meyers was using the "slush fund" for his home repairs and other excessive personal expenses, which included heavy gambling. And by sustaining the government's objection and excluding the evidence, here again Barrett was hurt.

Defense investigation had also established that personal checks totaling $47,230 were written by Irving Meyers and made payable to Ash Resnick, the man who runs the Casino at Las Vegas Caesar's Palace. Though Meyers admitted having done extensive gambling at Caesar's Palace — he was not charged fees for his daughter's wedding there, and frequently received complimentary accommodations — he said he had written these particular checks to repay Resnick for a loan. These checks, again, showed the amount of money available to Meyers, and supported Barrett's contention that the slush fund money found its way into Meyers' pocket, since this amount of money was far beyond Meyers' reported sources of income.

Though defense attorney Tom Foran tried repeatedly to question Meyers and Lemisch on their personal finances, and to have access to those records, the Court felt otherwise. In fact, even before the trial had started, the defense had been denied access to income tax returns for Lemisch and Meyers — it was not able to have the Meyers returns till the first day of the trial. Though obviously Meyers' financial condition was relevant and important to Barrett's defense, the prosecution objected vigorously when the defense tried to admit Meyers' returns into evidence — and Judge Austin once again went along with the government. He felt that the defense had insufficient supporting documentation which "was necessary to give meaning to the income tax returns." Yet the fact that Barrett's attorneys could not even get the returns till the first day of the trial shut them out from a proper investigation about underlying documentation.

Bank statements of Meyers, also, were ruled inadmissible as evidence — because, said Judge Austin, the defense was unable to complete a net worth analysis of Meyers which would explain the bank statements and income tax returns. Much of the information Barrett's attorneys needed, however, was sitting in the Justice Department files — denied to the defense.

In addition, defense attorneys were denied access to statements that the government had in its files — statements which told what Meyers claimed he gave other public officials. During cross-examination, Meyers repeatedly said he did not know how much he gave to these other officials, and did not know how many others he had accused. Since the theory behind Barrett's defense was that Meyers had been recklessly accusing public officials across the country of taking bribes from him so that he would be in a position to reduce his own civil tax liability, these facts were clearly relevant.

Other evidence, too, was excluded by Judge Austin. Important, but never allowed, was a letter signed and identified by Meyers, about a general four per cent rise in the cost of Shoup voting machines. Judge Austin kept the letter out on the basis that Meyers testified the price rise applied everywhere in the country "except Cook County." And yet the price rise was consistent almost to the last cent with the price that Meyers sold voting machines to Cook County!

Could Barrett — who did not testify in the trial — get his defense theory over to the jurors?

Could his attorneys convince a jury which may well have been influenced, even subconsciously, by the widely-publicized Kerner-Isaacs guilty verdict, that being a politician was not automatically synonymous with corruption?

No, they couldn't. The jury found Barrett guilty.

Eddie Barrett and his wife, Jeanne, take the verdict hard. Both were sure he would have been exonerated. Barrett is shocked . . . astounded. The smile is subdued; the twinkle disappears. Oh, there are moments — flashes of Eddie the veteran campaigner — like the day he asks a friend, "Lend me $2, will you."

"Sure, Eddie. Here you are."

"I just want to tip the shoeshine boy." And Barrett does.

The legal battles to keep Barrett out of jail continue. There is an appeal to the Seventh Circuit Court. But on Nov. 8, 1974, the majority of the 3-man appeals court panel affrms his conviction — with that strong dissent, of course, by Circuit Judge John Paul Stevens. The day after Christmas, Barrett's petition for rehearing *en banc* is denied. In January, 1975, the 7th Circuit mandate is stayed, pending a petition for *certiorari*.

By this time, however, Barrett is ill and confined to his home. When the United States Supreme Court denies his petition for the writ of certiorari, and Attorney Tom Foran files a petition for the re-hearing. It is now June, 1975. Eddie is almost completely immobilized, and only able to move from his bed to his chair.

His doctor for nearly 35 years tells the court *Mr. Barrett is totally and permanently*

incapacitated. Diagnosis includes ar-
rested pulmonary tuberculosis, broncho-
pleural fistula, diabetes mellitus, myo-
cardial ischemia, congestive heart fail-
ure, and severe disseminated osteoarthri-
tis. Needless to say, incarceration of this
patient would be devastating.

The Court, however, is firm. Judge Austin says this:

Well, I assume that he could go out if
he left in an ambulance. I will stay the
incarceration until the 22nd of January,
at which time he is to be incarcerated.

Fortunately, both lawyers work out an arrangement whereby a dying man need not be taken off to prison in an ambulance, Barrett is paroled in his own home, and he never leaves it till he dies on April 4, 1977.

The government strangled Eddie Barrett's rights in so many ways that the list staggers the imagination of an impartial and fair-minded observer. Probably the government's worst single overt action in the entire case, however, was to induce Irving Meyers to testify by granting that convicted felon tax relief on a million dollars he'd stolen.

It is instructive in this regard to compare what Thompson did and what Thompson's first assistant and successor on one occasion *said* about the immunity policy of the office. For Samuel Skinner on November 25, 1975, told the Chicago Bar Association:

Only when we are convinced of the val-
idity of the proffered evidence are we

> *willing to enter into an agreement . . . in*
> *almost all of these successful cases there*
> *has been corroboration through addition-*
> *al evidence which was checked before the*
> *grant of immunity.*

Since there was no convincing outside evidence with which Thompson and Skinner could validate the accusations of Irving Meyers, how then *did* they validate those accusations? The answer is they didn't. They just took the word of a convicted felon.

But bad as that uncorroborated, bought-and-paid-for testimony was, even worse was the government's fixed and quite obvious determination to find *some legal means or other* of convicting Eddie Barrett. So legalistic and amoral and vindictive was this concentration by the Thompson prosecutor's office — and so little concerned with achieving justice in any but the narrowest possible technical sense — that the recent words of Aleksandr Solzhenitsyn are relevant. This great Russian freedom fighter, intellectual giant, and writer — in a June, 1978, commencement speech at Harvard University — analyzed with surgical precision the moral blindness that afflicts so many in our society. He said:

> *I have spent all my life under a com-*
> *munist regime and I will tell you that a*
> *society without any objective legal scale*
> *is a terrible one indeed. But a society*
> *with no other scale but the legal one is*
> *not quite worthy of man either.*
> *People in the West have acquired con-*
> *siderable skill in using, interpreting, and*
> *manipulating law, even though laws tend*

to be too complicated for an average person to understand without the help of an expert.

Any conflict is solved according to the letter of the law and this is considered to be the supreme solution. If one is right from a legal point of view, nothing more is required, nobody may mention that one could still not be entirely right, and urge self-restraint, a willingness to renounce such legal rights, sacrifice and selfless risk; it would sound simply absurd. One almost never sees voluntary self-restraint. Everybody operates at the extreme limit of those legal frames.

Mr. Solzhenitsyn was obviously not referring to Big Jim Thompson in these remarks. But Thompson's record in the Barrett case makes Big Jim a perfect epitome of what Aleksandr Solzhenitsyn convincingly claims is partly responsible for the moral rot in Western society.

Eddie Barrett had his faults, and taking the small kickback insurance commissions may well have been one of them. But he was never morally blind, and he also knew how to die well.

Only hours before he dies, he tells his wife of 29 years, Jeanne:

Darling, I just want you to know that I'm absolutely innocent. I don't want you to be bitter towards anyone, Jeanne. I know I'm all right with the Lord.

III

THE WILLIAM RENTSCHLER CASE

It is impossible for a visible political figure at this time in this part of America under these prosecutors to get a fair trial . . .
> —THOMAS A. FORAN, senior partner, Foran and Wiss, and former U.S. Attorney, Northern District of Illinois.

A man may be visionary in his plans and believe they will succeed, and yet, in spite of their ultimate failure, be incapable of committing conscious fraud. Human credulity may include among its victims even the supposed imposter. Under our system of laws men are not punished criminally for mere mistakes, mere mismanagement, or mere errors of judgment.
> —UNITED STATES v. PORTER, 441F.2d 1204, 1208 (8th Cir. 1971).

Feeling his oats after a series of high-visibility prosecutions and the flattering attention of the media, Big Jim Thompson laid bare his prosecutorial philosophy:

We have a saying among prosecutors.
It's, "Don't 'pink' the dragon." You
either kill him or you leave him alone.

Cold. Clinical. Win no matter what you have to do. Then the victim can't come back to haunt you. That's how Thompson put it to a free-lance writer in a Chicago *Sun Times* piece that ran on February 23, 1975.

And that's how Jim Thompson set out to dispose of Bill Rentschler.

In the grey days of early November, 1973, Federal prosecutor Thompson moved further into the half light between personal political advancement and law enforcement — when he introduced a variation on his official-corruption theme. That was when he decided to finish up a job that one-term Republican Governor Richard B. Ogilvie began in 1969.

The job was burying Bill Rentschler.

Rentschler, a prominent Republican "citizen-politician" from Lake Forest, had mainly been engaged in acquiring, launching, and running a succession of entrepreneurial businesses since the late 1950s. All through the same period he'd taken active, highly visible roles in public affairs and his party's campaigns, including major state-wide leadership roles for Sen. Charles Percy, Attorney General William Scott, and former President Richard Nixon. Rentschler also campaigned twice for the U.S. Senate on his own behalf. The second of these senatorial runs came in late 1969 and early 1970, when he conducted a strong but losing bid — against Governor Ogilvie's picked candidate and express wishes — to replace the late, legendary Everett McKinley Dirksen.

What made Rentschler a peculiarly difficult kind of troublemaker for Ogilvie and some other professional politicians were his consistent efforts to revitalize and "open up" the clubby Illinois GOP and thus wrest a share of party leadership from them. He spoke out on a wide range of public issues and made a point of resisting all attempts to control and box him out of the Republican club. Rentschler's substantial constituency, especially in downstate Illinois, gave his political thrusts an unpredictable but real substance.

So in the course of that 1970 campaign Ogilvie heaved what he may have thought was the last shovelful of sod on the upstart by unleashing against him the state GOP's entire massive array of organizational and financial resources — and also by having Bill threatened with financial disaster. But instead of leaving Rentschler's corpse on the political battlefield, Ogilvie only managed with such tactics to help bury his own chances for reelection as governor in 1972.

Then, on November 8, 1973, Big Jim, whose early political tutelage came from Ogilvie and his operatives, heaved another and much heavier shovelful of sod on Rentschler: a 23-count grand jury indictment charging him with issuing a false financial statement to federally insured lending institutions. With the government still unprepared to bring its highly complex financial case to trial a year and a half later — and with their case therefore slipping away according to the "speedy trial" mandate contained in the 6th Amendment to the U.S. Constitution — Thompson indicted Rentschler again on March 24, 1975. This time, there were 17 counts charging "conspiracy" and "stock fraud" — all of them having to do with an entrepreneurial, high-risk timber venture in which Rentschler was the first, last, and largest investor — as well as by far the largest loser, financially and otherwise, when the dust finally settled.

Two indictments, the second growing out of and clearly designed to reinforce — possibly even salvage — the first. A second 17-count indictment also obviously meant to fragment Rentschler's resources, sap his will to resist, and guarantee his conviction. A total of 40 counts charging financial wrongdoing. Federal investigations apparently inspired at the outset by Richard Ogilvie's influence with the Nixon Justice Department — for that was the clear implication of the threat Ogilvie's operatives transmitted to Rentschler through one of his 1970 campaign consultants, who will be quoted. Investigations that Thompson's immediate predecessor as U.S. Attorney, William J. Bauer, now a federal appelate judge, did not choose to pursue. A target, however, that presented Thompson with a superb opportunity to rebut the growing clamor that his main aim was to dismantle the Daley machine and become Mayor of Chicago.

Although Rentschler was found guilty in the Malaysian timber company case, his part in the "conspiracy" was considered so tenuous that the trial judge, highly regarded Hubert J. Will, handed him a "slap-on-the-wrist" sentence of 90 days on work release and fined him $5,000; Judge Will later vacated the fine.

The first and more serious indictment — the one charging that Rentschler intended to defraud a number of banks where he had obtained personal and business loans — was not to be finally disposed of, however, until April 19, 1976. That was an incredible 30 months after the indictment, a clear violation of Rentschler's Sixth Amendment right to a "speedy trial" — especially in a district where criminal trials were being disposed of either by trial or plea in a median time of less than six months. And the only reason it was disposed of even then was that Rentschler, his funds and energies finally dissipated, pleaded guilty to one of the 23 counts.

And what was that one bank "fraud" count? He pleaded guilty to submitting a false financial statement to a New York bank in connection with a $150,000 loan he'd received. A loan on which $127,000 of the principal had been repaid well before he was indicted! A loan on which interest in excess of $30,000 already had been paid! A loan from a bank that held collateral adequate to cover most of the modest unpaid balance!

And for that plea of guilty, Rentschler spent almost nine months in a federal prison. Which goes to show, among other things, what Richard Ogilvie and James Thompson had always known to be true, and which Big Jim himself neatly put into words, as reported in the March 21, 1975, Waukegan *News-Sun:*

The power to indict is almost like the power to destroy regardless of the verdict. You may change a life that may never change back.

For reasons that will become clear, however, the efforts to bury Bill Rentschler first by Ogilvie and then with greater finality by Thompson — efforts that may well have been deliberately coordinated — still by 1978 have not been able to leave Rentschler for dead. He is very much alive.

Before reviewing Thompson's massive 2-stage marshalling of federal forces against Rentschler — and prosecutorial tactics that including fishing expeditions and pressures on potential grand-jury witnesses, the probable inducement of various bankers to demand from Rentschler immediate payment of all loans outstanding, and the government's stalling and evasive tactics in providing specific accusatory data to Rentschler — it is instructive to look at the kind of man who was accused of cutting all the corners in the financial-integrity book. We will take such a look, here.

And it is even more instructive to contrast that man's character — not in general terms, but in very specific terms having to do with the 40 counts of financial wrongdoing that Big Jim brought against him — with the character of Thompson himself. We will make that contrast as well.

First, the man himself, William H. Rentschler. Most of his first 48 years were good ones. He was the first of three sons of successful, intelligent, financially well-fixed people in the heart of the nation — Hamilton, Ohio, not far from Cincinnati, not far either from the Kentucky and Indiana borders — and descended from staunch

German stock. Bill's boyhood was typically Mid-western.

Whatever deficiencies there may have been in Rentschler's business judgment in the specific situations involved in his indictments, in his political skills, and in his acknowledged potential in both arenas — and as Chicago Attorney Tom Foran rightly says, "Nobody alive's a striped-ass saint" —style and drive were never among those deficiencies. Rentschler's self-description, that from his childhood on he won grades and friends and acclaim easily, perhaps too easily, he admits, rings true to the many friends and dedicated election supporters he was later to acquire in his maturity in Illinois.

Rentschler's business and political contacts with people in Illinois and elsewhere have always been fresh, easy, casual. His personality, voice, and manner carry the irresistibly captivating force and effervescent zeal of a leader and great sales-man who believes in himself. Even those who critically analyze that product in greater depth than Rentschler himself does are generally very impressed by the product. Republican strategist and writer-teacher John H. Cleland — a sworn witness on two occasions during the timber trial — recalls being told privately by one of the several young assistants who prosecuted the Malaysian timber case, for example, that

> *Rentschler could easily make $100,000 a year or more as a salesman for a big corporation, like IBM.*

Based on that same conversation with Assistant U.S. Attorney Michael Higgins, Cleland also puts his finger on the reason why the layman jurors in

Rentschler's two trials could easily have misconstrued Rentschler's core motives to be fraudulent:

> *Higgins himself could not seem to understand how a man with as much talent as he knew Bill had could possibly involve himself in so speculative a venture as cutting virgin mahogany in Southeast Asia. He just couldn't grasp the possibility that a man can be honest — not consciously set out to cheat anybody out of a dime — and still be involved in a shoot-the-rapids entrepreneurial business.*

> *While I respect Michael Higgins' motives in this case, I was amazed at Higgin's apparent feeling that the only legitimate outlet for great business and selling talents is in a big staid company.*

Judge Hubert Will, who presided in the Malaysian timber case, made the same specific distinctions — between conscious fraud and a businessman's sometimes-uncritical faith in his product and ability — for the benefit of the three young federal prosecutors and the untutored jury.

On one occasion in the trial, the following court-transcribed conversation took place. It was a "sidebar" conversation — one not meant for the jury's ears — and involved the inadmissibility of some government "evidence."

> *JUDGE WILL: As a matter of fact, you can say from the evidence in this case anything you like. One, that the corporation* [Corporation Mid-America, the timber company] *never was worth a tinker's dam; two, that it had great poten-*

tial and would be worth $15 million if they just could have carried it off. You can say anything between those two, and the jury will have to decide what, in fact, the evidence shows. But I am certainly not going to operate on the assumption that all evidence is admissible in which one defendant said the corporation was worth something, just because I now happen to know it was worth nothing: No such thing. [The company's option on an exclusive concession to a vast tract of virgin timber from the government of Malaysia was exercised only in part, and Corporation Mid-America subsequently went out of business.]

Later in the same conversation, another of the government prosecutors, Guy Seaberg, laboriously attempted to "sell" Judge Will the government's tortured theory of Rentschler's fraudulent intent.

MR. SEABERG: One of the things that the evidence has established, to the government's way of thinking, is that these victims [individual investors who bought Corporation Mid-America shares from co-defendant Hardesty] *were told that those shares of stock were worth money. That they were worth something. That they were worth investing in, and that that statement was made intentionally.*
JUDGE WILL: The defense is, not only was it made, but it was believed. It was an honest belief at the time. You know, what fascinates me is the theory Mr. Rentschler told the bank it was worth

$300,000 proves it was a fraud.

It proves, if anything, he believed they were worth something at the time. I don't understand how it proves anything with respect to fraud. If you had a statement in which he said, you know, "flush these down the toilet, they are worthless" while at the same time he was telling somebody that they were worth money I would say you bet, the flush-these-down-the-toilet statement is admissible because it is relevant to the representations which were being made inconsistent therewith, to people whom he knew were being talked to . . . But to say he told somebody else . . . what Hardesty [an officer of Corporation Mid-America, and one of Rentschler's two co-defendants in the trial] *was telling these people, sure doesn't prove there was a fraud.*

It proves, if anything, they really believed the stock had value.

You see, you get yourself in the position where you think the corporation was worthless because on hindsight it turned out to be worthless, and we all know now that everybody lost money. But even some of the people who lost money don't feel badly about it. Mr. Ferrell says, well, you know, that is the way it goes sometimes.

I have got to tell you, you sit up here and listen to these people and you think well, the world is full of incalculably op-

114

timistic Pollyannas . . . what is absolutely fascinating, is what people believe. This is, I suppose, part of the philosophy of a free enterprise society . . .

MR. SEABERG: *. . . the government believes it has introduced evidence that establishes that these shares were not worth a great deal of money, and Mr. Buehrer* [another of Rentschler's co-defendants in the case and the man who persuaded Bill in the first place to become involved in the speculative venture] *himself testified, in his opinion, the book value of these shares was nothing.*

JUDGE WILL: *The evidence does not establish they* [the representations of stock value] *were false. I have been around that track with you . . .*

You conclude that they were worthless. On hindsight they were, but at the time it was arguable, certainly, that they had real value.

MR. SEABERG: *Either way, the only evidence I am arguing to introduce, is the evidence that Mr. Rentschler valued the shares at $300,000* [from Rentschler's statement to a Chicago bank].

JUDGE WILL: *And that you are not entitled to introduce with respect to a transaction which is not here involved; and which is no evidence there was a misrepresentation of any kind.* [Judge Will correctly saw that Thompson's office was desperately trying to tie the two indictments against Rentschler together].

MR. SEABERG: *But it does nothing to the state of mind of the defendant?*

JUDGE WILL: *I guess I don't reach you. I said, there is no reason why he couldn't honestly have had a state of mind [that told him] they were worth $300,000.*

MR. SEABERG: *Then it might work to his advantage.*

JUDGE WILL: *Might very well. Certainly would not be inconsistent with his contention at this stage of the game in these dates — in the fall of '69 — he thought 500,000 shares of Corporation Mid-America were worth $300,000, because at that stage of the game the pie was still in the sky . . .*

Once you have concluded that somebody was engaged in a fraud, then every statement he made is fraudulent, if in hindsight it turns out not to have been realized. But I have got to tell you I have seen an awful lot of fantastic statements which turned out to be true. I have seen a lot more which turned out not to be true, but it doesn't prove that they were knowingly misrepresenting at the time of making them because they turned out not to be true.

MR. SEABERG: *Your honor, could you explain your thinking on why that statement does not go toward the defendant Rentschler's intent? That is the only thing that is troubling me.*

JUDGE WILL: *Certainly. Because the*

fact that he told the bank they are worth $300,000, and he tells a prospective purchaser they are worth $300,000, doesn't prove that he doesn't believe they are worth $300,000.

In order for him to engage in the fraud, he has to be telling a knowing falsehood, a material misrepresentation of a fact, knowing it to be a material misrepresentation of a fact. And, if he tells everybody on the face of the earth this stock is worth $300,000, it sure doesn't prove he didn't believe it.

MR. SEABERG: That is correct. I don't disagree with you on that; but there is no other evidence in the case.

Listening to his colleague floundering in an argument with a judge who obviously knew far more about business than the young prosecutors — and, consequently, more about what really constitutes fraudulent intent — Higgins then jumped in.

MR. HIGGINS: Your honor, may I add one thing? You state the company might be worth $15 million.

JUDGE WILL: That is the testimony.

MR. HIGGINS: The testimony was that the concession was worth $15 million. The evidence shows they didn't even have the concession.

JUDGE WILL: The company might have been worth more. You see, Mr. Higgins, you can argue to the jury that the company was worthless, and they can argue that it wasn't.

MR. HIGGINS: *But they didn't have the concession.*

JUDGE WILL: *They had, on the basis of the evidence before us, a right to complete and get the concession.*

MR. HIGGINS: *That is different than having the concession.*

JUDGE WILL: *And they had, if Mr. [Hashim] Hamid [attorney from Malaysia] is to be believed, even beyond the period in which they were selling stock into '71 and '72 —*

MR. HIGGINS: *He did testify the concession was never transferred from the Malaysian government to Corporation Mid-America because the company wasn't formed in Mayalsia, and the money wasn't paid.*

JUDGE WILL: *There isn't any question they never formally acquired the concession, but there is equally no question they signed a contract to acquire it, and they paid $27,000 [Rentschler's own money] down on that contract, and if that contract had been completed, if the concession had been exploited to its maximum, might have been worth $15 million . . .*

Is it any wonder that the jury, which was not privy to the lengthy "sidebar" conversation quoted above, found Rentschler and his two business associates in Corporation Mid-America guilty as charged on all 17 counts of "conspiracy" and "stock fraud?" Not even three bright, well educated, presumably well motivated young government attorneys could follow what Judge Will was telling them about the real world of business hopes and dreams. When it came to an honest well-intentioned salesman's sometimes uncritical but always abounding faith in himself and his product, they simply couldn't do it. They and Judge Will, as the above conversation amply bears out, were like ships passing in the night. They didn't see what the Judge was saying; they couldn't even imagine what he was talking about.

How then could the untrained jurors in Rentschler's timber trial — most or perhaps all of whom were less well educated and less sophisticated than the government prosecutors, and with as little real-life exposure to the thin line that divides fraud from reaching for the stars — do what the government attorneys couldn't do? The jurors couldn't do it. So they decided Bill Rentschler conspired to defraud some investors he never met.

The same young government prosecutors quoted earlier used highly questionable tactics throughout the trial to destroy Rentschler's credibility in the eyes of those jurors. They referred incessantly to peripheral matters to create an illusion of wrongdoing, saying

• that Corporation Mid-America didn't really have the concession from the Malaysian government, even though the corporation's attorney had assured Rentschler that the option to get that concession was tightly contracted for;

• that Rentschler was preying on "small and unsophisticated investors," even though the government never even tried to establish that he, personally, had sold even one share of stock in the venture, which he had not done;

- that — during the white heat of Rentschler's 1970 Senate campaign — he personally appeared in somebody's living room in Oak Brook to talk about the company's prospects, even though Rentschler flatly denied this in his sworn testimony and his co-defendant Buehrer admitted that it was he, Buehrer, who was in that living room doing the talking and that Rentschler was not present and had absolutely no knowledge of the meeting. Since the testimony that Rentschler was present came from five people who, by their own admission under oath, had never before that "meeting" laid eyes on *anyone* from Corporation Mid-America — and since both Buehrer and Rentschler are both about 6' 3" and rangy — it is evident they either collectively erred in their identification, which is improbable, or, and this is more likely, they were "convinced" by the prosecutors that Rentschler was indeed the one who made an appearance. The Oak Brook "five" were "sprung" on the defense in a slippery ploy by the prosecutors, thus denying Rentschler's lawyer a chance to interrogate them in advance, as he was entitled to do. One of those witnesses under oath during cross-examination acknowledged that Assistant U.S. Attorney Guy Seaberg had "reviewed" his testimony with him the night before he testified, and twice within the prior week. This was one more evidence of the get-Rentschler-at-all-costs philosophy which motivated the prosecutors during his long ordeal.

Looking back on all the trivial incidents and peripheral people the government had to rely on to undermine that credibility, the case looks threadbare of substance. Judge Will's slap-on-the-wrist sentence clearly indicates that he personally did not believe Rentschler had fraudulent intent.

Judge Will was not taken in, as apparently the timber-trial jurors were, by all the references to "small and unsophisticated investors." For he knew that Rentschler himself made the first investment in the corporation: $27,000. The judge understood and the evidence clearly affirmed that Rentschler's total loss when the company finally expired — $49,000 — represented considerably more than half of the $79,000 which the government charged was lost as a result of the so-called "fraudulent scheme."

This, of course, means that the government *in effect* was accusing Rentschler of "defrauding" himself of nearly $50,000. Rentschler's jurors evidently failed to note or failed to understand the absurdity of this logical deduction. ***And on that basis alone, an impartial observer can call their guilty-finding outrageously wrong.***

So was the *Chicago Tribune* story that appeared on Friday, November 21, 1975 — the day after Rentschler had been found guilty in that timber-company trial. The story's front-page banner headline read: "RENTSCHLER CONVICTED IN $79,000 SWINDLE." And here is the way *Tribune* reporter Richard Phillips wrote the opening paragraph verbatim of course:

> *William Rentschler, 50, former candy manufacturer and prominent figure in Republican politics, was convicted Thursday for his role in a Malaysian timber swindle **in which small investors lost $79,000.***

So not only did Rentschler's jurors manage to hear only what the Thompson prosecutors wanted them to hear, but even an experienced federal building reporter managed to hear only what those prosecutors wanted him to hear. Not becoming embittered and discouraged by such pitifully poor understanding of a plain fact amounts to the kind of moral courage which most successful men have never been compelled to show.

Rentschler's own explanation of what the prosecutors turned into a complex and diabolical scheme is both simple and logical:

> *There's no mystery really about Corporation Mid-America. It was brought to me by a man I'd never previously met but who was introduced through a trusted mutual friend. I saw it strictly as an investment opportunity, potentially one of the best I'd ever been offered. It involved an exclusive opportunity to cut mahogany on a 40,000-acre tract of virgin forest in Malaysia. The Malaysian government was seeking to attract American dollars and jobs for Malaysians. The total investment required initially to obtain concession rights was $27,000, with another $26,000 to come later. That was a modest outlay for rights to cut timber with an estimated market value of $15,000,000. That potential seemed incredible, but I checked it out meticulously. We met in Chicago with a Malaysian attorney, Hashim Hamid, who also was chairman of a Malay-*

sian development company; he later testified at my trial and confirmed the validity of the concession. My attorney and personal friend, Bob Chatz, checked every fact and all legal documents and gave me the green light to proceed. We sent another attorney to Washington to meet with government agencies and determine the stability and reliability of the Malaysian government. I felt I was prudent before investing. I wouldn't have gone forward without what I presumed was competent legal advice.

But I made it clear from Day One I was an investor, not an operator or manager of the business. I was involved in a Senate race which took about 110 per cent of my time, and later I accepted a job as chief executive officer of a company in the Washington, D.C., area. The government's case was dishonest in the extreme. They were interested only in getting me. Those prosecutors ought to be ashamed for the rest of their lives for their scandalous misuse of the processes of justice.

I was the first to invest, and the last. I put in far more money than everybody else put together — and I lost far more. I took no salary. I invested because it looked like one hell of an opportunity. Like any investor, my sole aim was to make money, even though I admit I was intrigued by the idea of investing in an exotic land and in a small way maybe

123

helping an underdeveloped country. Obviously, if I made money, everybody else would make money.

I never sold a single share of stock, never met or had any sort of contact with any of the small investors who put in money later on. I didn't even get to know Lloyd Hardesty, the fellow who sold some stock, until after he'd sold it, mainly to his own friends and acquaintances.

No responsible prosecutor ever would have indicted me in that case. I not only had no intent whatever to defraud anybody but I did not defraud anybody of a dime. I will never understand how this could happen in a nation which prides itself on justice under law.

Judge Will knew that a crucial element in the case, as far as Rentschler's culpability was concerned, was whether Rentschler's confidence in the timber company's prospects was: (1) genuine; or (2) knowingly false.

Judge Will tried to help the jurors understand this by delivering to them the following passage, as part of the judicial instructions to them prior to their final deliberations, instructions which seemed to reflect his faith in Rentschler's story:

A man may be visionary in his plans and believe they will succeed, and yet, in spite of their ultimate failure, be incapable of committing conscious fraud. Hu-

man credulity may include among its victims even the supposed imposter.

Under our system of laws men are not punished criminally for mere mistakes, mere mismanagement, or mere errors of judgment. They are punished only for intentional wrongdoing.

*(from **United States v. Porter**)*

And now, in the formal language of the law, comes James Thompson, United States Attorney for the Northern District of Illinois, whose actions and statements in that official capacity will be examined for internal consistency and honesty with as much scrutiny and patience as Judge Will used in examining Bill Rentschler's valuations of his timber company's stock.

If we can believe Judge Hubert Will, we have seen how there can be an internal consistency in the oft-dashed, sometimes uncritical, but always abounding faith of a man like Bill Rentschler — in himself, in his high-risk business enterprises, in his own ability to ultimately pay his debts. That may not be prudence by the standards of most people; and it may on occasion amount to bad judgment. But Thompson was having Rentschler tried on 40 counts of defrauding small investors and big banks. And there are no laws in this country against either bad judgment or risky ventures.

It seems so simple — if it serves his purpose — for a self-proclaimed moral extremist like Big Jim, however, to equate crime and bad judgment as exactly equal terms. He seems to have done it in the Otto Kerner trial. He did it in the Barrett trial. And he did it, perhaps working hand in hand with Richard Ogilvie, in the two Rentschler trials.

Former U.S. Senator J. William Fulbright of Arkansas gained great respect with a huge segment of American public opinion, by way of analogy, for being the earliest and fiercest opponent of what he considered "President Johnson's war in Vietnam." But Fulbright was charitable, saying that Johnson

was guilty of nothing more than bad judgment, and he probably deceived himself.

One cannot fail to see the fairness and balance and good will of Fulbright's statement. That is the sort of fairness and balance and good will that Big Jim Thompson characteristically lacked in his $3\frac{1}{2}$ years as federal prosecutor, and which he specifically did not exhibit in his direction of the long and tortuous stringing out of Bill Rentschler. In the same Waukegan *News-Sun* story quoted earlier, the one where Big Jim with some glee says that the power to indict is almost like the power to destroy, he added — probably to justify the casual tone of so menacing a statement — that that's the reason his office works slowly, methodically, and thoroughly. He emphasized that

It's a long, tortuous course that these proceedings take.

But this is not a candid statement, considering

that the Thompson office didn't even call Rentschler before the grand jury when it had him
indicted the first time in 1973. Big Jim just
hustled through the 23-count indictment, and only
then started putting *all* the pieces together so
that they might reasonably appear to be the massive conspiracy he was charging. For 30 months
between indictment and trial are just too many
months — too much total elapsed time — by the
standards of the Sixth Amendment mandate for
a "speedy trial."

That 23-count indictment, returned in early November of 1973, charged Rentschler with a scheme
to defraud 30 banks or financial institutions. According to Thompson, Rentschler in his entrepreneurial activities presented false and fraudulent
financial statements to obtain loans for himself
and for various business ventures. Rentschler,
they said, understated his personal liabilities and
overstated his assets in seeking the loans.

Counts 1 through 12 charged that Rentschler
used the mails, a consistent Thompson ploy, in
furtherance of the scheme to defraud the banks.
Counts 13 through 23 charged him with specific
violations of a federal statute which makes it a
crime to submit a false financial statement to a
federally-insured institution.

That first indictment was "a whopper," says
Rentschler.

> *Sure, I had a lot of loans, but I was
> involved in a lot of companies. I'm a
> risk-taker by nature. The government
> made no attempt to understand the na-
> ture of my financial dealings. I had a
> reputation for candor, and I tried always*

> *to operate on a high ethical plane. Those*
> *young U.S. Attorneys were callow and*
> *righteous, and they saw evil lurking in*
> *every corner. Most of 'em couldn't run*
> *a lemonade stand.*

Jim Thompson issued his usual publicity release and held his usual accusatory press conference, crowning the previously-unsullied Rentschler with the strong presumption of guilt.

When word of the indictment hit the headlines and newscasts, many who knew or knew of Rentschler were stunned. CBS-TV commentator Walter Jacobson referred to him that night as "the Mr. Clean of Illinois Republican politics."

"A lot of people sympathized," Rentschler remembers. "Some of the more knowledgeable types, especially old friends in the media, told me Thompson needed a Republican to offset all the Daley Democrats. I was his "showcase" Republican. I heard that explanation over and over again. I still hear it today, five years later."

What was it like to be charged with a crime after all the good years, all the acclaim and success? Rentschler says this:

> *There is an awful unreality about*
> *something like this. You can't believe*
> *it's happening to you. Especially if*
> *you're not a lawyer and don't under-*
> *stand the devious workings of the legal*
> *world and the criminal-justice system.*
>
> *I knew I'd done nothing wrong and all*
> *I'd have to do would be explain things*
> *to the U.S. Attorney. That's what I'd*
> *always believed: justice will prevail. I*

> *grew up in a good midwestern home*
> *where Dad's heroes were Senator Rob-*
> *ert A. Taft and J. Edgar Hoover. What*
> *a shock! What a naive boob I was.*
>
> *When I first heard the rumblings, I*
> *went right to Bert (Albert E.) Jenner*
> *(Jr.), a friend I regarded as the best*
> *lawyer in Chicago. He set me straight*
> *in a hurry. He told me I was in big*
> *trouble, that there was nothing he or I*
> *could do to prevent an indictment, and*
> *that 85-90 per cent of all indictments in*
> *federal court result in a guilty plea or*
> *guilty verdict. He said word was out*
> *that Thompson wanted to indict a Repub-*
> *lican, and he reminded me the govern-*
> *ment has all the firepower. Bert was 100*
> *per cent right. Boy, was he ever right!*

For more than a year prior to that indictment, remember, Bill Rentschler's financial affairs had been under investigation. "The first I knew of anything was when I got a call from Charles Kidd of the First National Bank of Highland Park, a banker I had borrowed money from through the years," Rentschler says.

" 'What's going on, Bill?' he asked. 'We've just gotten a subpoena for your loan records at our bank!'

"I talked to another banker with whom I'd also had a close relationship — Dick Newland of the Bank of Waukegan — and he told me, 'We've had some postal inspectors asking questions about you. They wanted to see your loan file.

"That gave me pretty much of a shock. Especially when I remembered how I'd been warned several years earlier that I could be in trouble because of my political activities."

Those political activities included bucking incumbent Republican Governors — twice — to run for the GOP nomination for U.S. Senator. William G. Stratton, a seasoned pro, took Bill's 1960 challenge with good grace, even though Rentschler, a political novice at 34, came close to winning the nomination.

But Richard B. Ogilvie, nominated narrowly over John Henry Altorfer and then elected over former Lieutenant Governor Sam Shapiro in another close race in 1968, reacted with cold fury. After the death of Senator Everett McKinley Dirksen, Ogilvie chose as a replacement the late Ralph Tyler Smith, a colorless political veteran from Alton, across the river from St. Louis — a man with obviously dim prospects for attaining the stature of a U.S. Senator, as his landslide loss to Adlai Stevenson would soon prove. Smith had served as speaker of the Illinois General Assembly, but his chief claim to fame was his early support of Ogilvie's gubernatorial ambitions when the former Cook County Sheriff had few backers in downstate Illinois.

When Rentschler decided to run in the Republican primary against Smith, Ogilvie was enraged. At a Republican fundraising dinner, Ogilvie summoned Rentschler from the audience and delivered a pointed ultimatum. Rentschler recalls that ultimatum vividly. Ogilvie told him:

"Bill, you continue with this race and you're running against me. Don't ever

forget that."

Rentschler continued, however, running harder than ever. Rentschler had entered that race on October 16, 1969, with considerable citizen support but virtually no backing from the Republican political organization or high level Chicago businessmen, who were effectively "turned off" by Ogilvie and his operatives.

> *The word was out that Ogilvie meant to "destroy" Rentschler, and Rentschler got the message from more sources than the governor himself. First it came through John Sears, a strategist who had a key role in the 1968 presidential victory of Richard Nixon. Sears would surface again in 1976, as Ronald Reagan's chief political brain truster. Sears assisted Rentschler for awhile, on a consulting basis, in putting together his 1970 campaign.*
>
> *Sears was close to some of the Ogilvie political operatives; and in December, 1969, delivered this chilling message to Rentschler: "You've got loans outstanding, haven't you, Bill? Is there any way you can pay them all back right now?"*
>
> *Rentschler's answer: "No way."*
>
> *"Well, Ogilvie 's guys are going to put pressure on those banks and try to get them to call your loans all at once. And maybe put you into bankruptcy." Rentschler, obviously concerned, nonetheless shrugged it off.*
>
> *"I don't see why the banks should buy*

those tactics," he told Sears. "My relations are generally pretty good with the banks and I'm guessing they'll stand behind me."

"Don't bet on it, Bill. The governor's got a lot of clout."

Similar pointed messages from Ogilvie — implied threats, really — reached Rentschler from other sources during that 1969-70 Senatorial campaign. And Dick Ogilvie by this time was in a good position to back up the veiled threats he was conveying. For as the Republican governor of Illinois, his influence was growing with John Mitchell's Justice Department in Washington.

And the federal investigation of Rentschler's financial dealings did begin, remember, in 1971. Either Ogilvie's people or the government leaked word of those investigations. An article appeared in *Chicago Today*, leaked from the usual "reliable sources."

Rentschler called William J. Bauer, Thompson's immediate predecessor as U.S. Attorney for Northern Illinois. Bauer professed to know nothing but said he would "check around the office" to see what the nature of the investigation was. "Give me a week," he told Rentschler.

When Rentschler called back, Bauer told him, "Yeah, we got some stuff here," but suggested Rentschler forget about it, saying his office had files on all sorts of people.

Rentschler was not satisfied: "What if some hot-eyed young guy in your office decides he might make some nickels by indicting me?"

"I'm the U.S. Attorney, and I sign every indictment personally," Bauer responded, "and I'm telling you to forget it."

Bauer soon ascended to the federal bench, however, and the Thompson era began. Prosecutorial restraint went out the window. Big name Democrats were indicted, and before long there were dark mutterings about Thompson's crusade to dismantle the Daley machine in a bid to make himself Mayor of Chicago.

Politically-sensitive, Big Jim quickly realized he needed a Republican to counter increasing charges of partisanship.

So in early November of 1973 the 23-count bankfraud indictment came through, even though the government obviously had not prepared its case.

A month later, December 7, 1973. Rentschler's indictment had been assigned to Judge Philip Tone, and Assistant U.S. Attorney Steven Mora was handling the case. Rentschler pleaded not guilty, and the trial was scheduled for April 29, 1974.

Two weeks later, however, at the government request, the trial date was vacated. New trial date: May 28, 1974 — the first of many delays, largely, in one way or another, the fault of the government.

On February 1, 1974, George J. Cotsirilos, Rentschler's attorney, asked for a 4-day extension to file numerous pre-trial motions. The brief length of this extension was typical of the few short delays that were attributable directly to the defense.

On February 22, 1974, the government requested — and was given — an additional two weeks to answer Rentschler's motions. About this time, Prosecutor Mora resigned from the U.S. Attorney's office. Rentschler's case was reassigned to a new team of prosecutors headed by Assistant U.S.

Attorney Jeffrey Cole.

The dates rolled onward.

Finally, on May 10, 1974, Judge Tone entered an order which granted substantial portions of Rentschler's pre-trial discovery motions.

Judge Tone, however — the original judge assigned to Rentschler's bank-fraud case — was soon elevated to the federal appellate bench. Ailing Judge William Lynch, Mayor Daley's former law partner, took over, but after a period of illness and inactivity, he died. A third judge, Alfred Y. Kirkland, recently appointed to the federal bench, was assigned by the U.S. District Court's executive committee.

But unbeknown to Rentschler, a *second* grand jury had by early 1975 begun to investigate his relationship with Corporation Mid-America, a company formed to cut and market Malaysian timber in which Rentschler had been by far the largest investor. No documents are subpoened from him nor is he called before the grand jury. In fact, despite his 1973 indictment, he has *never* up to this point been called before the grand jury.

Though the government has been aware of Rentschler's relationship with Corporation Mid-America as early as spring, 1973, there were no steps to initiate charges against Rentschler until more than a year after the bank loan fraud charges had been made.

Early in March of 1975, Rentschler was invited to discuss the grand jury system on a talk show hosted by CBS-TV personality Warner Saunders, a longtime friend. The panel included Elmer Gertz, noted Constitutional lawyer; George Crowley, vet-

eran defense attorney, and the late Ralph Berko-
witz, first assistant to Cook County States Attorney Bernard Carey.

> *Saunders launched the program by
> noting that since Rentschler had been
> indicted, he ought to be able to offer
> some first-hand insights on the grand
> jury.*
>
> *Not so, replied Rentschler, he'd never
> been called before a grand jury, never
> been given a chance to tell his story and
> perhaps head off his indictment.*
>
> *Maybe the prosecutors were afraid
> you'd sway the jury in your favor, one
> of the panelists volunteered.*
>
> *Two days later, George Cotsirilos,
> Rentschler's attorney, obviously nettled,
> called him:*
>
> *"What the hell were you doing on TV?
> I've got a grand jury subpoena here for
> you."*

So Rentschler had the audacity to tell a TV audience that Jim Thompson and Sam Skinner
hadn't given him a fair shake! We'll teach that
wise-guy a lesson — was the apparent message of
the subpoena.

So Rentschler would have his chance to appear
before the grand jury and tell all — after the
fact, of course — at the risk of having his words
twisted into a perjury charge, a technique the
prosecutors used against Otto Kerner and Cook
County Commissioner Floyd Fulle. A perjury
charge tells the trial jury they're listening to an
accused liar, which makes suspect every word of

testimony the defendant utters. It further lengthens the already long odds against him.

In Rentschler's case, the subpoena amounted to nothing more or less than sheer intimidation, a crude, arrogant, and empty gesture, since the prosecutors knew neither Cotsirilos nor any other competent defense attorney would permit his client, an obvious target, to testify in such perilous circumstances.

"At the time I was subpoenaed," said Rentschler, "I wasn't even aware the Malaysian timber matter was under investigation. I thought that had long since been laid to rest. It came as a terrible blow."

With Cotsirilos, he walked down one of those long, grey, faceless halls in the Federal Building to the assigned grand jury room. Then he went in, alone, since witnesses are not permitted to be accompanied by counsel, still another way the system is stacked against the defendant.

Assistant U.S. Attorney Cole was inside. The grand jurors were seated randomly on metal folding chairs.

The preliminaries over, Cole, his voice heavy with sarcasm, confronted Rentschler. The words as Rentschler remembers them were:

"I understand, Mr. Rentschler, you complained to the news media that you never had an opportunity to tell your story before a grand jury. Well, now I'm giving you that opportunity . . ."

Rentschler had no choice.

"My lawyers had told me, under the circumstances, that if the government asked me any questions at all — even which way it is to Lake Michigan — I should claim my Fifth Amendment rights. So that's what I did. I'd have welcomed the chance to tell my story. But I was clearly in a 'no win' situation.

"Very shortly afterwards, I was indicted."

The *new* indictment — returned March 21, 1975 — came from the February 1975 grand jury. This time Rentschler had co-defendants: Lloyd David Hardesty and Calvin Buehrer. All were charged with being part of a conspiracy in the complicated stock fraud case referred to earlier — the timber company Corporation Mid-America. In addition, Hardesty was accused of making false declarations before the grand jury.

What did swaggering Jeffrey Cole, now in charge of both of Rentschler's prosecutions, say to Hardesty?

> *"Deliver me Rentschler's head on a platter, and you'll go free."*

> *Those were Cole's exact words, says Hardesty.*

> *Chilling words, and tempting, too, especially when spoken by a federal prosecutor to a potential defendant in a criminal trial.*

> *Jeffrey R. Cole was one of the bright young men Jim Thompson bragged about. The "offer" to Hardesty, which he and his lawyer understandably interpreted as an offer of immunity, was flatly turned down. He was one of a lonely few who refused to bargain their way free from prosecution during the Thompson era when immunity was dished out like peanuts to anyone willing to testify*

against a targeted "big name."

The government's two cases against Rentschler moved along in fits and starts but reinforced each other in highly important ways; their cumulative effect was enormous. Alarmed lenders began to tighten the screws or cut off credit, the lifeblood of the small companies he owned.

The two cases were even to affect each other in court. The timber case, remember, came at a point in early 1975 when the prosecutors thought Rentschler might be slipping from their grasp. Some 27 months — two long years and a quarter of a third — after the government began nosing into Rentschler's financial affairs, and 15 months after his first indictment, little progress had been made in stitching together a credible case against him, a case that made any sense whatever, a case that would stick.

Jeffrey Cole's vindictive, accusatory tone in his pre-indictment interviews with possible timber-case witnesses — along with that revealing offer of immunity to Lloyd Hardesty — left no doubt that Rentschler was the key target for the Thompson office. Former GOP committeeman John Cleland, for example, remembers such a conference.

> *Jeffrey Cole, in a general, rambling conversation, invited me to speculate to Rentschler's detriment on several personal matters that had absolutely no relevance to Malaysian timber or bank loans, which is what they were supposedly investigating. Cole was trying to dig around in the dark corners in order to come up with something, anything.*

On his wall, about three feet from his desk, Cole even had a newspaper picture of Rentschler taped up. Every once in a while, he would shift his eyes to the right and look at Rentschler's picture with a kind of a leer. It was a shabby and tasteless fishing expedition, pure and simple.

Sharee C. Kapsh, Rentschler's personal secretary from 1969-72, related her grim experiences with the prosecutors and her feelings about the verdict in a letter to Judge Will after Rentschler's conviction:

*Although I was a government witness, I feel a great deal of my side of the story was not brought out. I also feel the federal prosecutors were only interested in obtaining a conviction no matter what damage was done to truth and justice. I would like to give you a little background of my experience with the federal prosecutors. I was not called in front of the grand jury, but **on at least six different occasions** I voluntarily talked with each of the prosecutors. The first time I went in I was kept there for five hours. And, although I had come in voluntarily, **I was badgered to the point of becoming physically ill.** I was job hunting at the time and the day after being there I was so ill I was forced to cancel two appointments. **False accusations were made, words were put into my mouth** — finally when I was in tears they let up a bit — but **I'll always remember that experience*** *as being one of the worst in my life. In fairness to the prosecutors after my first bad experience they were more considerate of my feelings. But, I also feel that I was not called in front of the grand jury because I was not saying what they wanted me to say.*

I was there during Corporation Mid-America — I know what happened. There was no conspiracy — Corporation Mid-America was a viable corporation — it just didn't make it. Mr. Rentschler is not capable of "ripping off" small investors. He never sold a share of stock and never met or had contact with any investor. I thoroughly enjoyed working for him and found him to be very honest and straightforward in all respects. He is a man who is simply not capable of doing what he has been convicted of.

I am firmly convinced the verdict was unjust.

Among the dozens subpoenaed in the so-called bank fraud case was W. Eugene Danneberg, president of the Mid-West National Bank of Lake Forest, from whom Rentschler had borrowed off and on over a decade in amounts ranging up to $50,000.

On several occasions, Danneberg trudged down to the Dirksen Federal Building by "invitation" to meet informally, like John Cleland and Sharee Kapsh, with the prosecutors prior to any possible grand jury appearance.

Big Jim Thompson and his crew left nothing to chance. They wanted the script carefully rehearsed before witnesses went before the grand jury, lest a recalcitrant witness upset the apple-cart or raise doubts with the jurors, whose only purpose, in the minds of the prosecutors, is to follow, sheep-like, their bidding and return indictments on signal.

Danneberg, with Rentschler's loan file in hand, spent considerable time in those informal sessions. He kept telling them that Rentschler paid his loans, met his obligations, and was a good customer of the bank. Oh, sure, he was late with some payments, occasionally tight for funds, but he kept his word and paid off.

Even today, Danneberg speaks warmly of Rentschler. He says, "Rentschler never defaulted. He never was — or is — in trouble with the Mid-West Bank of Lake Forest."

They finally figured Gene Danneberg was a total loss by their strange standards and sent him home again. And they denied him, too, the "honor" of appearing before the grand jury to recite "their" version of how Bill Rentschler had attempted to "defraud" the Mid-West Bank.

By any impartial standards, such prosecutorial handling of witnesses clearly is improper. It may be illegal. It violates standards set down through the years by leading jurists.

Yet when federal prosecutors blatantly ignore their obligations, they get away with it. This is what Herman Schwartz and Bruce Jackson, professors of law at the State University of New York at Buffalo, say in an article from *Harper's:*

> *Since prosecutors claim to act in the interest of public morality and safety,*

*there are few restraints on those who de-
cide to abuse their extraordinary powers.
Such abuse, which occurs in both political and criminal cases, has increased significantly in the past decade. Worse yet,
many prosecutors engage in illegal acts
not because they are concerned with the
justness of the case, but because they
want to win. Even if they are found out,
the police and the courts seldom do anything about it . . .*

Such conduct by prosecutors makes an unequal
contest almost impossible from a defendant's
standpoint. Listen again to Schwartz and Jackson:

*In recognition of the enormous power
wielded by the prosecutor against any defendant, and because the prosecutor represents all of us in enforcing the community's moral code with its most dras-
tic sanctions, the prosecutor's responsibility is not victory but justice. When he
refuses to disclose or hides evidence of
innocence, or introduces false testimony,
the already heavy advantage enjoyed by
the prosecution is magnified. What was
only an unequal contest becomes a corrupt one, with the possible result of years
in prison for a person who is presumed
to be innocent.*

Further evidence of Thompson's and Skinner's
desire to get Rentschler at all costs was the fact
that their prize witness against him was a twice
convicted felon and unemployed international ad-

venturer called Dr. Edward von Rothkirch, who admitted under oath he was called "Doctor" because he had been "awarded" such a degree by a defunct institution named "Midwestern U." The prosecutors moved that von Rothkirch's two prior convictions, one for larceny, the other for "impersonating a federal officer," be withheld from the jury. Their motion was granted over vigorous defense objections that such knowledge was vital to the jury's evaluation of the witness's credibility.

On October 2, 1975, Judge Kirkland issued a significant order — one which favored Rentschler. The government was ordered to set forth dates and names (in the bank loan case) which relate specifically to each institution named in the indictment, and to file a clear, complete and unevasive bill of particulars — all within 20 days.

Kirkland's order helped Rentschler, who was still trying to discover specific dates and transactions referred to and to comprehend specifically the charges against him in the bank loan case — now nearly two years old.

According to Kirkland, defendant "sought disclosure of the dates of the alleged fraudulent transactions and the names and addresses of the persons with whom each was made." The government's response, Judge Kirkland pointed out coldly,

> *is evasive, wholly inadequate, and obviously not a good faith attempt to comply with the order previously entered herein by Judge Tone. Twenty-eight financial institutions are listed in the indictment as victims of fraudulent transactions.*

This list was later supplemented by two others. There is no possible way the Court or defendant could relate 14 dates and names to 30 institutions.

The government is ordered to set forth dates and names which relate specifically to each institution named in the indictment . . .

The government is ordered to inform defendant, with respect to each of the 23 counts, specifically what liabilities defendant omitted in each allegedly fraudulent loan application, what liabilities were understated, and the dollar amounts of each.

Then Judge Kirkland — in his October 2, 1975, order — severely criticized what had by then become the Skinner office.

The government's bill of particulars, he wrote, indicates a clear intention by the government not to comply fully with Judge Tone's order. Time of counsel and the Court should not have to be spent in remedying obvious attempts to evade full compliance with a Court order.

The government is ordered to file a clear, complete and unevasive bill of particulars, as ordered, within 20 days from this date.

The sort of foot-dragging and confusion by the government that Judge Kirkland castigated makes apparent, once again, how little candor there was in Thompson's previously quoted statement about the care his office took in preparing cases. The preparation of Rentschler's bank-loan case *lacked* proper care and even the slightest concern for the defendant's rights.

At a time when the waiting and wondering was sheer torture, Rentschler read a small news item in the *New York Times*. A federal judge in Florida, it said, had dismissed an indictment against F. Lee Bailey, the superman of defense attorneys, in an alleged franchise fraud. Bailey claimed he had been denied his Constitutional right to a speedy trial because 22 months had elapsed since his indictment. The judge concurred.

At that very moment, 21 months had passed since Rentschler was first indicted in 1973. No trial date had been set. None was in prospect.

If Bailey's indictment was dismissed, why not mine, reasoned Rentschler.

The Constitution was clear; the Sixth Amendment starts this way:

> *In all criminal prosecutions, the accused shall enjoy the right to a speedy and public trial . . .*

Rentschler broached the idea to his attorneys, George Cotsirilos and James Chapman, who initially brushed it aside. Cotsirilos estimated the odds as at least 100 to 1 against it. Rentschler persisted.

> *Have we reached the point where we just ignore the Constitution, he wanted to know?*

Rentschler would not back down. Finally, he obtained lawbooks from his lawyers to read for himself the "speedy trial" law. He felt his case was overwhelming. He wrote a long memo to Cotsirilos and Chapman, and, even though he is not a lawyer, tried his hand at a brief. With the aid of a young associate, Gerald Murray, they produced a scholarly, compelling, 40-page argument asserting that Rentscher had indeed been denied his Constitutional right to a speedy trial.

The vast majority of the delay had been directly attributable to acts of the government . . . the delay had been highly prejudicial to his right to obtain a fair trial . . . the delay had been highly destructive to Rentschler's personal and professional life.

Rentschler argued that the loan transactions in the indictment all took place years earlier, at least one as far back as 1969. The transactions were complicated, sophisticated business dealings. They involved some 13 corporations in which Rentschler had an interest. The government's indictment combined personal and corporate loans, loans on which Rentschler was a direct obligor or co-signer, and loans on which he was merely a guarantor, often one of several.

The net effect was to make Rentschler's direct liabilities appear substantially greater than in fact was the case, or than he acknowledged in his personal financial statement.

The government's interest clearly was not in "protecting" the banks or in recovering their loans, because Rentschler and/or his companies had repaid in full — or were repaying — the loans in question. He also had established through the years a consistent record of meeting his obligations, even when one of the companies was in difficulty. Furthermore, the Thompson-Skinner office, pushing a clumsy, noisy investigation, effectively destroyed the companies which Rentschler depended on to generate funds to pay off the remaining loans.

It is highly revealing that most banks, once the investigation started and apparently under pressure, real or implied, from federal agencies, simply decided to make guarantor Rentschler solely responsible for all the loans still outstanding, by obtaining judgments against him alone. They asked nothing of the other corporate-loan guarantors, and Thompson's office simply decided those others were not worth the trouble of pursuit.

> *It took 17 months after Judge Tone's order for the government to answer a substantial portion of Rentschler's requests for amplification on its bill of particulars.*

Now, more than two years after indictment — and in some cases, nearly nine years after the particular loan — Rentschler must review each disputed asset and liability, a task well nigh impossible in view of the inevitable dimming and distorting of memories . . . the inability to locate witnesses . . . the difficulty in accurately reconstructing details of the complex transactions . . . the transfer, retirement, or change of bank personnel, and Rentschler's seriously deteriorating financial condition.

Most important, all the charges in the bank-loan indictment had been based on the fact that Rentschler allegedly overstated assets in his personal financial statement. The primary item in dispute

147

was the status of an item valued at $750,000; the government claimed Rentschler put down — falsely — that he *owned* stock worth that amount in a family company. But Rentschler's statement carried the stock as an "expectancy" of inheritance. What Rentschler had really told lenders was that he expected to inherit the stock — yet did not own it outright at the time of the loan, that he had every reason to presume he and his two brothers each would own ultimately one-third of their parents' stock in a long-established foundry in Hamilton, Ohio.

He says the bankers would invariably ask him to pledge those family foundry shares as loan collateral — but always understood his explanation why that was impossible: the stock was not then in his name and would not be until the death of his parents, then both well into their 70s. The bankers Rentschler dealt with obviously believed him in this matter, for those who granted loans did so even *without* getting the shares they'd asked him to pledge. They simply took his word about his family expectation. And bankers are not noted for being gullible people.

Rentschler acknowledges his financial statement was "undoubtedly imperfect, since I've never taken an accounting course, even in high school." But he maintains vigorously it was "generally an accurate reflection of my financial situation at the time it was presented."

He is convinced the "green" assistants who attempted to put the case together had little understanding of financial practices, accounting, or the practical aspects of business.

I am convinced those zealots could ut-

terly confuse any jury and convict any businessman, especially those involved in entrepreneurial ventures, by using the tactics they used against me. The only ones who have a chance against such tactics are the officers of big public companies, who are effectively surrounded by lawyers, lobbyists, and unlimited lucre. Thompson gave that type a break, because he felt he'd be seeking their financial support later when he ran for office. But the small business guy, like myself, stood naked against their storm trooper tactics. The strategy, plain and simple, was to bleed me, dissipate my resources, destroy my reputation before the fact, put cruel pressure on my family, and utterly destroy my will and ability to resist. They had no interest whatever in a just result.

They deal in illusions, not truth. If they have no case, they manufacture one. More than anything, I found it a sad commentary on the way the system works, thoroughly disillusioning, even though I am certain all prosecutors don't operate that way.

Rentschler's father died unexpectedly on January 25, 1976. If Rentschler had been brought to trial even within a two-year period, his father would have been available to testify with certainty that his first son would indeed inherit the family stock or other assets of comparable value.

Because of the long delay in bringing the case to trial, Bill Rentschler could not defend himself

149

properly. All but one of the companies cited as borrowers in the indictment and/or the bill of particulars were defunct, some destroyed by the loss of credit and shock of Rentschler's troubles. Essential books and records no longer were available. Important witnesses could not be located, had retired, or could not reasonably be expected to remember details of such long-ago transactions.

In addition, the time delay caused by the switch in three judges, three sets of prosecutors, and two postal inspectors can hardly be Rentschler's fault, for as the Supreme Court has noted, it is not a defendant's obligation *to bring himself to trial*. Yet, his potential defense was critically penalized by the delay.

Rentschler's attorneys argued that the man's promising political career had been devastated, that he had suffered through several years of unfavorable publicity, that his reputation had been sullied, his family and good friends subjected to months of agony, that he could not hope to get a salaried job . . . all because he had been denied his right to a speedy trial.

By the time they submitted their motion to Judge Alfred Y. Kirkland, the third judge assigned to the bank fraud case, the lawyers were showing little signs of optimism, Rentschler recalls.

> *Cotsirilos even told me the odds were down to 5 to 1.*

Kirkland, trim and brisk, with close-cropped pepper-and-salt hair, was a rookie federal judge newly thrust into the cauldron of criminal law in a case heavy with political overtones and media interest. A decent man who climbed the ladder to become president of the Illinois Bar Association, Kirkland, a conventional corporate lawyer from Elgin in suburban Kane County, was no boat-rocker.

In retrospect, there was no way, notwithstanding the power of the Constitutional argument, that the careful new judge, faced with almost frenzied opposition from the prosecutors, would throw out the Rentschler indictment.

He didn't. With no hearing or explanation, he brusquely denied the motion.

That was it for Bill Rentschler. Cotsirilos called in Bill and Martha Rentschler . . . bluntly told them it would cost $100,000 or so in legal fees to take the case to trial . . . that he would need a good share of the money first . . . and advised negotiations with the government. What choice? Bill was shaken, Martha in tears.

So Rentschler pleaded guilty to that one count of the bank-loan indictment, and agreed to drop his appeal in the Corporation Mid-America Malaysian timber case — a conviction he had always considered unjust, despite Judge Will's slap-on-the-wrist sentence of 90 days on work release. In return, the government agreed to drop all other counts of the bank loan indictment. He was sentenced to a year and a day. The sentence ran concurrently with his 90 days in the timber case. Hoping for an early parole, or placement in the work release program, Bill Rentschler achieved neither. He served the maximum 8 months and 21 days in Chicago's Metropolitan Correctional Center. He remembers being told more than once by prison officials that the U.S. Attorney would not look kindly on anything less than the full measure of punishment.

Let's now return to that examination in detail, promised earlier, of the internal consistency and honesty of Big Jim Thompson's actions as United States Attorney for Northern Illinois. Compare that internal consistency and honesty, as we go along, against the internal consistency and honesty that Judge Hubert Will found in Bill Rentschler's oft-dashed, sometimes uncritical, but always abounding faith in his entrepreneurial ventures and in himself.

Most of the specific standards we'll use in sifting Big Jim's record can be derived from the enlightened counsel of the eminent U.S. Supreme Court Justice Robert H. Jackson, counsel the late Mr. Justice Jackson gave to all U.S. federal prosecutors when he was still Attorney General of the United States. After advising the prosecutors to rededicate themselves to the spirit of *fair play* and *decency,* Jackson said this:

> *Your positions are of such independence and importance that while you are being diligent, strict, and vigorous in law enforcement, you can also afford to be just. Although the government technically loses its case, it has really won if justice has been done.*
>
> *Any prosecutor who risks his day-to-day professional name for fair dealing to build up statistics of success has a perverted sense of practical values, as well as defects of character.*

Based on that counsel, then, we will concentrate on the professional and ethical *quality* of Big Jim's record as federal prosecutor.

And we'll also analyze the quality of Thompson's own published statements about his record, again in terms of internal consistency and honesty.

Thompson's twisted interpretation of immunity figured strongly in his convictions of Otto Kerner and Eddie Barrett. It was not a factor in Bill Rentschler's conviction for his allegedly fraudulent actions with respect to the Malaysian timber case. But remember the crude and unethical invitation to one of Rentschler's co-defendants, Lloyd Hardesty, in that case?

"Deliver me Rentschler's head on a platter, and you'll go free."

That's what Jeffrey Cole said, and Cole's invitation perfectly epitomizes the abusive, irresponsible purposes for which the Thompson office used immunity grants. That invitation abused justice and fair play by showing exactly how selective the Malaysian timber case prosecution was — a prosecution that was meant to "get" Rentschler. And it also abused the standard of prosecutorial responsibility, for Cole wanted to relieve himself of the prosecutor's responsibility for proving wrongdoing beyond a reasonable doubt. He wanted to win his case the easy way.

Thompson has been saying for years, remember, that the *only* reason he made such heavy use of immunity as a federal prosecutor was to catch crooked public officials extorting money and accepting bribes. The speciousness of this apparently plausible justification becomes apparent in the crude invitation of Thompson's assistant Jeffrey Cole in the Rentschler timber-company case — a case in which three businessmen were said to have made misrepresentations about the value of their company's stock.

Now let's look at some of the other internal contradictions in Big Jim Thompson. Internal contradictions between his words and his actions. Internal contradictions between different statements he has made at different times and under different circumstances. Internal contradictions between a characteristic personality pose of exaggerated public swaggering about his accomplishments and the possible inner feelings that swaggering may obscure, even to himself.

These internal contradictions in Thompson relate to several of the growing public criticisms against him that he has dealt with over the years.

Those growing public criticisms charge not only that the quality of Thompson's federal prosecutor work wasn't fair but wasn't even as statistically effective as his Chicago press boosters have led the public to think.

Those growing public criticisms charge that Thompson used his prosecutor's office for personal political gain at the expense of high-profile public figures with strong records of public service.

Those growing public criticisms charge that Thompson frequently grandstanded for the press and that unsophisticated portion of the public which believes everything printed in a newspaper or seen on a television set.

In *qualitative* terms of fairness, then, the Thompson record is very poor. We have seen how the shotgun indictment technique works to thoroughly confuse layman jurors, to throw sand in their eyes, to say in effect that anyone charged with so many "different" crimes must be guilty of *something*. There were 17 indictment counts against Otto Kerner, 16 against Eddie Barrett, and a total of 40 hurled against Bill Rentschler.

Do you know how many indictment counts Tom Foran thought it fair to use when he was U.S. Attorney for Northern Illinois? The *maximum* number of counts, in other words, that Foran thought should not be exceeded even when prosecuting the worst of defendants? *Eight*. Anything more than an 8-count indictment, Foran judged, did not give the defendant both arms to fight with, in other words, a fair chance to prevail.

Read Foran's closing argument in the Bonk case, Appendix III of this book, to see how formidable a fighter Tom Foran is. But he's a good fighter, a fair fighter; a fighter who expects to be hit once in a while himself by an opponent who does not have one arm tied behind his back, by an opponent who is not in effect drugged before the fight begins with more charges than he can *reasonably* defend himself against.

Thompson himself made a very revealing statement that underscored his lack of fair play and decency, as a federal prosecutor, in the month before he was elected governor of Illinois. Walter Jacobson, political expert for the CBS television outlet in Chicago, was interviewing Big Jim for the October, 1976, *Chicago Independent*. Toward the end of the interview, Jacobson brought up the subject of the use of immunity by the Thompson U.S. Attorney's office. Jacobson was suggesting, in his question, that Thompson had let some criminals get away in order to get politically bigger fish. Thompson answered:

> *I didn't let them get away. All I did was obtain evidence* **in whatever fashion I could** *in criminal offenses. And I established rules for the use of immunity and we followed them. The juries were always there to correct our mistakes, because the jury's got the power. If they believe that a prosecutor made a bad immunity deal, they merely say "not guilty, Mr. Prosecutor, you have the wrong fellow in the witness chair and the wrong fellow in the defendant's dock." And they did that once. We once made a* **bad** *immunity deal and we got a* **not guilty.** *But only once in five years and that's not bad.*

The Thompson statement above is both false and specious. It is false because as federal prosecutor he never in fact did establish any rules for the use of immunity. He once said he was going to have the question studied by someone on his staff, under pressure from a critical editorial in a Chicago newspaper. But there were never any rules. He immunized every sleazy crook he could find who would help him convict what he defined as a "corrupt office holder."

But the statement also shows Thompson to be well below the line of prosecutorial fair play and decency, the line that Supreme Court Justice Robert Jackson advised federal prosecutors to meet. Jackson, remember, said a prosecutor should dedicate himself to a spirit of justice.

Thompson's answer about immunity in the *Chicago Independent* interview with Walter Jacobson shows how far Thompson was from the spirit of justice, even in his *understanding* of the spirit of justice. He said he made a bad immunity deal only once, obviously referring to the government's two immunized star witnesses in the Bonk trial — Robert Haskins and John Daley — which will be examined in the next chapter.

Thompson said he made a "bad immunity deal" with Haskins and this Daley *because the jury found Bonk not guilty.* In other words, Thompson's two sleazy immunized witnesses were not believed by the Bonk jury and that makes Thompson's immunity deal "bad." But Justice Jackson said that what really determines justice doesn't have anything to do with whether a defendant is convicted or not. Juries do the best they can, and sometimes they *follow* the principles of justice; but juries do not *define* the principles that make an action just or not.

This quotation from the *Chicago Independent,* on the contrary, shows that Thompson consistently defined justice and the principles of justice by whether or not the juries believed his assistant prosecutors and immunized witnesses. And this in turn shows that courtroom victory, not the achievement of justice, was always the guiding principle for Jim Thompson the crimefighter.

This is so basic to understanding him. Victory. Not justice. Big Jim's use of the same Robert Haskins in the Paul Wigoda conviction (which a later chapter of this book deals with) was a "good" immunity deal, because it worked. It was a "bad" immunity deal in the Charley Bonk exoneration, because it didn't work.

A decent prosecutor could be expected to look at the background of John Daley and Robert Haskins and say:

> *No. I'm not going to make a deal with these men. I'm not going to protect them from all criminal recourse in order to add Charley Bonk or Paul Wigoda to my conviction list, much as I suspect both Bonk and Wigoda of official wrongdoing.*

But Big Jim didn't do that. He looked at Haskins and Daley and saw in them the clubs he needed to add Charley Bonk and Paul Wigoda to his list of courtroom victories. Then he turned around a year or two later and said he made a bad deal with Daley and Haskins. *Not an unjust deal. A bad deal.*

But the *Chicago Independent* quotation from Thompson goes even further to convict him in the only court he now cares about — the court of public opinion. For he implies that as federal prosecutor he was held in check by the jury system, not only in the courtroom trials but in the pre-trial grand jury proceedings. *But he was never restrained by those juries, neither grand jury nor trial jury, as he well knows, because jurors just aren't equipped to restrain the abusive potential of an abusive federal prosecutor.*

And Superior Court Judge Melvin P. Antell of New Jersey, undoubtedly one of this country's chief opponents of the grand-jury system, knows why Thompson's statement is false. In 1965, Judge Antell put the reasons in an article that appeared in the *American Bar Association Journal.*

It simply is not true that the grand-jury system protects the individual from oppression; indeed, it has a far greater potentiality as an instrument of oppression. And if there is anything more grotesque than the thought of a grand jury competently policing the affairs of government and the morals of public officials, it is that this belief can be seriously entertained.

Later in the same article, Judge Antell explains why the prosecutor can ram literally anything he wants through a grand jury:

Though free to take part in the interrogation, the grand jurors must place enormous trust in the prosecutor's guidance. It is he, after all, who tells them what the charge is, who selects the facts for them to hear, who shapes the tone and feel of the entire case. It is the prosecutor alone who has the technical training to understand the legal principles upon which the prosecution rests, where individual liberty begins and ends, the evidential value of available facts and the extent to which notice may be taken of proposed evidence.

In short, the only person who has a clear idea of what is happening in the grand jury room is the public official whom the 23 novices are expected to check. So that even if a grand jury were disposed to assert its historic independence in the interest of an individual's lib-

> *erty, it must, paradoxically, look to the*
> *very person whose misconduct they are*
> *supposed to guard against for guidance*
> *as to when he is acting oppressively.*

No, Big Jim was never restrained by a jury, either trial or grand. Yet he has said time and again that he really wasn't as one-sided a prosecutor as people were saying. In the *Lerner Newspapers* issue of September 15, 1974, for example, Big Jim said:

> *I'm not a scalp hunter. I'm not interested*
> *in turning this to political gain. We just*
> *go after the crooks, no matter who they*
> *are.*

All of which goes to show the inconsistency between his words and actions.

Toward the end of his tenure as federal prosecutor, one of Big Jim's sorest points was the growing criticism that he was a political scalp hunter, which he obviously was; but which he just as obviously did not want anyone to see him translating into personal political gain.

At one point, *Tribune* reporter Robert Enstad asked Thompson what accounted for his poor conviction-rate showing compared to his three predecessors. Reporter Enstad said Thompson told him, in this regard, that

> *he never kept track of his overall con-*
> *viction record, but that "I am sure the*
> *court records are right." He said he only*
> *kept track of his official-corruption cases.*
> *And in those cases, Thompson stated, he*
> *had a 100 per cent conviction record on*

state and local officials until Bonk's ac-
quittal."

*"I suppose now that rate is about 99
per cent," said Thompson.*

It begins to become clearer, after an examination like this, that Bill Rentschler and Jim Thompson are indeed different. But they are *not* different in the same way that first suggests itself.

*The person who does not know Bill
Rentschler — or anything about his record except that he served almost nine
months in a federal prison for allegedly
cheating people out of money — has some
right to think he is inconsistent. Says
one thing, does another. Lies. Is inter-
nally inconsistent. Is dishonest.*

*But we have heard Judge Hubert Will
on that matter. And he tells us there can
be an internal consistency in a great
salesman's oft-dashed, sometimes uncritical, but always abounding faith in his
ventures and himself. And his slap-on-
the-wrist sentence to Bill Rentschler tells
us that he believed Bill was just such a
man.*

*And then we look at Thompson and see,
for all outward appearances, a perfect
marble statue of a successful crime fighter, a man all of a piece, perfectly consistent and even candid, without internal
contradictions. Big Jim gives the show
away with his exaggerated public swaggering, which a man who has inner con-*

161

fidence in what people think of him, does not do; which a man who has confidence in what his professional colleagues in the law think of him, does not do.

Jim Thompson fails by many standards of internal consistency and honesty. Bill Rentschler seems to fail by those standards, but the only place he really comes up short — on a close examination of both his life and the massive two-stage bludgeoning he took from Thompson's office for five years — is in his business judgment. And that, only occasionally.

Bill Rentschler's father died at 78, not long after Bill's conviction on the Malaysian timber case, shortly before the resolution of the bank matter, never fully comprehending how things could have turned out this way for his eldest son.

Rentschler's mother, devastated by the loss of her spouse of 53 years, weak and soon to die, didn't understand either. In a rare act of kindness, Gerald M. Werksman, the tough but obviously tender attorney who represented her son, wrote her this poignant letter to ease her pain little more than two months before her own death:

May 17, 1976

Mrs. Peter E. Rentschler
510 South D Street
Hamilton, Ohio 45013

Dear Mrs. Rentschler:
As you know, I represented your son Bill in the trial that took place last fall as a result of the failure of Corporation Mid-America in 1970. I had never met Bill until he was referred to me by a mutual friend after his indictment in the Mid-America matter early in 1975. When I saw Bill last week he told me that he had been to see

you and one of his brothers in Ohio over Mother's Day, and that there are still nagging doubts and uncertainties as to the extent of his involvement.

It has always been my opinion, based on twelve years of experience in criminal law (as both prosecutor and defense lawyer) and based on my thorough investigation, that Bill was guilty of no more than misjudgment and inattention to the company's affairs. I am confident there was nothing criminal in his actions or intent.

As you know, Bill lost a great deal of his own money in this venture, far beyond that of any other investor. It was established at the trial by a Malaysian attorney that Corporation Mid-Amerca had made a $27,000 down payment and had timber-cutting rights on a 40,000 acre mahogany forest in Malaysia. One of the reasons that the venture failed, in my estimation, was that just when it had begun, Bill had the opportunity to run for the vacant seat of Senator Dirksen and this demanded his full attention. The timber project was thus left in the hands of an associate who turned out to be just plain inept.

Testimony and other evidence during the trial showed conclusively that Bill never sold any stock or attempted to sell any stock, and that he never met or had any contact with any of the purchasers of stock, including the barber who was played up by the press in some of their sensational stories. Sadly, Bill relied on associates who probably were badly chosen and who clearly let him down.

One of the risks in any trial is that if there is a finding of guilty the judge will be severe in imposing a sentence. The opposite was true in Bill's case. As you know, he received a minimal sentence. I believe this occurred because Judge Will, who sat through the six-week trial, felt that although he could not throw out the jury's verdict, it would not be fair to penalize Bill harshly for the actions of others and for his minimal involvement in the actual running of the company. I think Bill's candid, open personality, his straightforward testimony, his obvious belief in his innocence of any criminal wrongdoing, and his attempts to salvage the situation struck a responsive chord in Judge Will.

For myself, I shall always believe that Bill was guilty of mismanagement and inattention rather than a purposeful desire to defraud anyone. In short, I do not believe he did anything that was criminal in nature.

I might add that it is rare for a criminal lawyer to engage in, or desire the friendship of a client once a case is terminated. However, I have been so impressed with Bill's resilience, good nature and basic decency that I am happy to consider him a friend. Nobody was more crushed than I that he was not acquitted.

Through all of his adversity, Bill has never been a cry-baby. He has constantly sought to protect his family and his reputation. He has borne up well under all these pressures; he is looking to the future and it would be a tragedy if you and his brothers did not understand the circumstances surrounding this case. If I can help in any way to explain further for you, please do not hesitate to call me.

Very truly yours,
S / Gerald M. Werksman

For Bill Rentschler, it had been the most agonizing period of his life. But he was fortunate; he endured. By nature strong-willed, resilient, optimistic, buoyed by his devoted wife Martha and 10 children (including five stepchildren), he served 8 months and 21 days in a high-rise federal prison in Chicago.

He shared a short handwritten letter he received two days after he entered prison from his friend, Lawrence B. Perkins, a distinguished Chicago architect, now over 70, who founded the world-famous firm of Perkins & Will:

Dear Bill —

I believe Job asked the same question — Why? When you emerge from this bit of purgatory you will find your same friends waiting to greet you and cheer for you. It may someday be that to have been a political prisoner will become a proof of honor and courage as it is in Germany, France and many other countries . . .

s / Larry

Rentschler emerged, as he puts it, "with a deeper faith, a certain humility, strong ideas on the shame and hypocrisy of the criminal justice system, and a determination to make things better in the world."

Or, as Bill says . . .

I was put on this earth to do more than ignore injustice and lead a life of frictionless ease. God willing, I'll be back.

Clockwise from upper left: U.S. Attorney James Thompson announces on December 15, 1971 — two weeks after he was appointed to the position — the indictment of Federal Appeals Court Judge Otto Kerner. Thompson studies "opportunities" in Illinois state government. Two of Thompson's assistant federal prosecutors — Steve Kadison, and Thompson's first assistant Samuel Skinner — listen attentively as their boss announces the Kerner indictment. *(Photos courtesy of UPI)*

JUNE 30, 1975:
Thompson resigns as
U.S. Attorney and,
according to the
Associated Press, says
"nothing about his
future political plans."

JULY 1, 1975:
Thompson announces
that he will run for
Governor of Illinois
in 1976.

(Wide World Photos)

Clockwise from upper left: Otto Kerner talks to newsmen on July 9, 1974, after his sentence-reduction plea was denied in federal court. Kerner meets in Chicago with former President Johnson, Johnson's daughter Luci, and the late U.S. Senator Paul Douglas of Illinois. Kerner leaves the Federal Building in Chicago with his daughter Helena. Kerner walks past newsmen as he enters the Federal Correctional Institution at Lexington, Ky., to begin a three-year sentence.

(Photos courtesy of UPI)

The lionization of James Thompson, left, and Samuel Skinner, as political crime-fighters begins the same afternoon Otto Kerner is found guilty — in early 1973. Thompson and Skinner were not slow to seize the opportunity, as their same-day press conference shown here indicates. They knew the world would now begin to pay attention to them, spurred by rave notices about them in the newspapers and on the broadcast media.

(Photo courtesy Chicago Tribune)

"Do you solemnly swear to tell the truth, the whole truth, and nothing but the truth in exchange for immunity?"

The Press as Perverter of Justice

The inherent limitations of the press that pervert the ends of criminal justice: hastiness, superficiality, sensationalism, and power without moral responsibility.

The press too, of course, enjoys the widest freedom . . . But what sort of use does it make of this freedom?

Here again, the main concern is not to infringe the letter of the law. There is no moral responsibility for deformation or disproportion . . .

Because instant and credible information has to be given, it becomes necessary to resort to guesswork, rumors, and suppositions to fill the voids, and none of them will ever be rectified, they will stay on in the readers' memory. How many hasty, immature, superficial, and misleading judgments are expressed every day, confusing readers, without any verification. The press can both simulate public opinion and miseducate it . . .

Hastiness and superficiality are the psychic disease of the 20th century and more than anywhere else this disease is reflected in the press. In-depth analysis of a problem is anathema to the press. It stops at sensational formulas.

Such as it is, however, the press has become the greatest power within the Western countries, more powerful than the legislature, the executive, and the judiciary. One would then like to ask: by what law has it been elected and to whom is it responsible? In the communist East, a journalist is frankly appointed as a state official. But who has granted Western journalists their power, for how long a time and with what prerogatives?

—ALEKSANDR SOLZHENITSYN,
in a 1978 Harvard University
commencement address

. . . perfectly clear that the publicity did not help the defendant's cause, and may well have tended to develop a "bandwagon" psychology that would make his conviction more likely.

—JOHN PAUL STEVENS,
Associate Justice of the U.S.
Supreme Court, referring in an
appeals court opinion to the
conviction of Edward J. Barrett

170

Thompson as Perverter of the Press

Thompson on the fine art of "leaking" information about pending prosecutions to his powerful, hasty, superficial, sensational, and morally irresponsible ally: the press.

I am the last person in the world who ever would leak a story that he [William S. Miller, a star government witness Thompson "recruited" to convict Otto Kerner] now agreed to become a government witness, because it simply doesn't suit my purpose.

Let's make no bones about it. Nobody leaks anything to a newspaper reporter unless it serves some purpose that he has in mind . . .

When you leak something to a reporter, he is supposed to protect you. Otherwise, you are a one-time source and a one-time source only, and that is not how the game works. Any reporter I ever told anything to — and he identified me as the source — would never get another leak . . .

If you leak, it is most often for the purpose of having them glorify you in the press.

> —JAMES R. THOMPSON, page 175 of the court trial transcript of the Kerner case

Judge Philip W. Tone, presiding in the mail fraud trial of Earl Bush, former press aide to Mayor Daley, in another courtroom, promptly issued an order forbidding James R. Thompson from holding a press conference on the Wigoda case, expressing fear this would affect Bush's trial. But Thompson already had told a reporter he was pleased with the result, and he congratulated the jurors for their courage and the prosecutors, Joel Flaum and Dan K. Webb for their handling of the [Wigoda] case . . .

> —THOMAS POWERS, *Chicago Tribune*, October 11, 1974

I wasn't a headline prosecutor just as I won't be a headline governor.

> —JAMES R. THOMPSON in an October, 1975, interview in *Chicago Life*

NOTE WELL the contradiction between the statement immediately above — about not using his position as federal prosecutor to grandstand for his political future — and Thompson's remarkable knowledge about the art of leaking self-serving "news" to the press. Measure that statement also against Thompson's pre-indictment and pretrial publicity adventures documented in this book: in the Kerner, Barrett, Rentschler, Wigoda, and Coles cases.

Republican William Rentschler, left and lower right, represents another of the political scalps Big Jim Thompson got as federal prosecutor. The upper picture shows Rentschler in 1968, with the late U.S. Senator Everett McKinley Dirksen, at the Republican National Convention in Miami Beach, Florida. The lower picture of Rentschler shows him after his conviction involving a Malaysian timber venture.

Former Cook County Commissioner Charles Bonk, lower left, is shown walking out of the Chicago Federal Building after being found not guilty of the charges Thompson had placed against him — BEFORE Thompson subjected him, however, to double jeopardy.

(Lower photos courtesy Chicago Tribune)

Former Cook County Clerk Edward J. Barrett, 73, a power in Illinois politics for 40 years, enters car outside the Federal Building in Chicago on April 17, 1973 — he had just been sentenced to three years and fined $15,000 for taking bribes from a voting machine company.

(Photo courtesy of UPI Compix)

. . . good gimmick or bad, I don't have any.

—BIG JIM THOMPSON in the
October, 1975, *Chicago Life*

Once on the campaign trail, however, Big Jim learned all about gimmicks. Before long, according to Chicago Tribune columnist Michael Kilian in the May, 1978, issue of Inquiry Magazine, Thompson "was going about in what became a uniform of cowboy boots, jeans, and checkered sports shirt, which he even wore to formal Italian-American testimonial political dinners. He also acquired a dog — an Irish setter he named 'Guv.' This investment was instantly and amply rewarded with front page newspaper pictures. Similarly generous press treatment was accorded his later acquisitions of a second and yet a third dog."

Having discovered dogs for the first time in his life at age 40, Thompson knew a good thing when he saw it. The above picture shows him "treating" one of his dogs, Little Mo, to a giant slide at the 1978 Illinois State Fair. *(Wide World Photos)*

Even long into his term as governor, Thompson continued the gimmicks and stunts, the caps and special T-shirts, and all the other flukey public relations efforts. One such stunt had him "stampeding" media and photographic interest by bringing a horse — *on an elevator* — to the second floor of the State Capitol rotunda in Springfield. There, in suitcoat and tie, and only a few feet from the guard rail, Thompson mounted the creature and posed for newspaper photographs. The AP wirephoto of this "media event" shows the horse with his head almost touching the floor, giving the appearance of shame.

The above photo shows Thompson at a hog auction at the 1978 Illinois State Fair. *(UPI Photo)*

My reputation as a prosecutor is all I have.
—JAMES R. THOMPSON,
quoted in the *Chicago Tribune*,
March 7, 1976.

As federal prosecutor, Thompson's overall conviction record was lower than the records of the three men who immediately preceded in the U.S. Attorney's office.

Records of the federal district court in Chicago show that Thompson's 1973 conviction rate in *contested* criminal cases, for example, was only 66.6 per cent — a 10-year low for the U.S. Attorney's office in Chicago.

The records also show, according to the *Chicago Tribune* of July 20, 1975, that Big Jim achieved an overall conviction rate in his 3½ years as federal prosecutor of 94 per cent. The *Tribune* is quick to add this important qualification to the figure:

However, the great bulk of those convictions was based on guilty pleas by criminal defendants.

Defendants often plead guilty rather than go to trial . . . in hopes they will receive lighter sentences. In fiscal 1974, some 83 per cent of defendants pleaded guilty before a federal district court judge.

In a detailed tabular comparison, the same story compared Thompson's overall conviction rate for his whole tenure with those of his three predecessors: Edward V. Hanrahan, Thomas A. Foran, and William J. Bauer. All three men achieved annual conviction rates that were from 1 to 3 percentage points higher than Thompson's 94 per cent.

Far more importantly, however, Hanrahan, Foran, and Bauer were more well-rounded prosecutors than Thompson. Their cases included more hard crime — heroin, Mafia, union racketeering, the infiltration of organized crime into legitimate businesses.

Thompson also fell below his predecessors in contested cases that actually went to court. Here's what the *Tribune* story said:

> *Thompson did poorest when his office had to take a defendant to trial and put all the evidence of guilt before a judge or jury for decision. In those contested cases, Thompson's conviction rates were 66.6 per cent in 1973 and 73.4 per cent in 1974.*

> *By contrast, Hanrahan obtained convictions in more than 88 per cent of the bench and jury trials in 1967 and 1968. Foran had an 85.7 per cent rate in 1969 and 78.6 per cent in 1970. Bauer's rate in contested cases was 81.4 per cent in 1971.*

Former Chicago Alderman Paul T. Wigoda, shown here talking with newsmen after his conviction for accepting an alleged bribe, is obviously depressed by the jury's finding.

(Photo courtesy Chicago Tribune)

Republican Ron Coles of Lake County, Illinois, became a key downstate GOP scalp federal prosecutor Thompson needed to advance his "qualifications" for statewide office in Illinois.

IV

THE
CHARLES BONK
CASE

. . . nor shall any person be subject for
the same offense to be twice put in jeopardy
of life or limb.
—from the Fifth Amendment
to the U.S. Constitution

He was heavy-set, Polish and proud of it, with a twinkle in his eye, like a roly-poly Santa Claus. They called him a martyr, the saint that Thompson killed . . . a quiet, unassuming nice guy who didn't try to bargain his way out of trouble.

He was Charley Bonk from 18th Street. And that's the way he referred to himself — Charley Bonk from 18th Street who grew up there, brought his bride to the old neighborhood, raised his family, and lived all his life in the same house on 18th Street where he had been born. And he was the same Charley Bonk whom Thompson indicted on a total of 17 counts. Twelve of the counts charged Bonk with affecting the movement of building materials, articles, and supplies in interstate commerce through extortion under color of official right. Five other counts charged him with filing false and fraudulent income tax returns — for 1968, 1969, 1970, 1971, and 1972.

He was Charley Bonk, member of the Cook County Board of Commissioners. And after his trial jury had acquitted Bonk on all 17 counts, Thompson seven weeks later threw him back into the lion's den by imposing on him an immunity that forced him to testify before the very same grand jury which originally indicted him —*and on the same issues that were settled in his trial.*

That action of putting Bonk back through the grand jury-immunity process after he had been exonerated amounted to much more than a bizarre — and apparently unprecedented — legal tactic by Thompson and his crew of zealots. A number of expert judicial observers see in the action, for one thing, the definite appearance of a vengeful striking back by Thompson at one of the only men he ever indicted who was found innocent.

Judge Warren D. Wolfson of the Circuit Court of Cook County said at the time:

> *It looks and feels as if Bonk is being punished for being acquitted. It looks and feels as if he is being set up for a perjury charge, since the government has committed itself to the credibility of Haskins and Daley.*

Robert Haskins and John Daley were two of the *self-confessed* "zoning fixers," unscrupulous lawyers, and tax cheats who testified at the Bonk trial and who escaped all consequences for their many admitted crimes because Thompson had immunized them in order to convict Bonk.

But Thompson's peculiar tactic of compelling Bonk to answer under oath questions *concerning the matters upon which he had already been tried and acquitted* went beyond the palpable vindictiveness of a frustrated federal prosecutor. The issue goes beyond Bonk and takes on a constitutional magnitude in light of the Fifth Amendment to the U. S. Constitution, which reads in part:

> *. . . nor shall any person be subject for the same offense to be twice put in jeopardy of life or limb.*

The self-evident result of what Thompson did in this case was to put Charley Bonk in double jeopardy, in violation of his constitutional rights.

As usual, Thompson twisted the Fifth Amendment guarantee that nobody can be compelled to testify against himself in a criminal case, but this time he reached new creative heights with his twisted interpretation of the immunity doctrine. For his interpretation clearly violated the double-jeopardy clause of the same Fifth Amendment.

Charley Bonk served on the Cook County Board from August 14, 1962, till his death on April 20, 1976. He had been the Democratic ward committeeman of Chicago's 21st Ward and had served as a Chicago alderman. His political career began with his election to the Illinois General Assembly in 1952.

To everyone who knew him, Charley Bonk was a friend. "I don't think the man had any enemies," one of the county workers said. "I have nothing but good words for him."

Another remembers Charley's golf days and dinners. "He'd be saying hello to everybody. He'd smile. He'd be very warm. He wasn't aloof. Though he wasn't a particularly brilliant conversationalist, he was a very good host. He made everybody feel comfortable. Charley was a great fellow — everybody loved him."

As a Chicago alderman, Charley cared greatly about the housekeeping chores of his ward. No one remembers him making many speeches. No one remembers him introducing legislation during the nine years he served on the City Council. But Charley took care of the human needs of his ward. He cared about getting stop signs, about having good schools, about watching out for traffic problems and garbage pickups and keeping a good clean ward. He was persistent about getting these kinds of things done—the routine jobs that go along with being an alderman and that aren't listed in political science books.

Charley contributed to the organization. He went along with it. And when the time came, through seniority and loyalty, to work himself up the ladder and go on the County Board, Charley was there.

As a county commissioner, Charley Bonk served as the chairman of the Zoning and Building committee; County Hospital committee; the Tax Delinquency committee; and served as vice-chairman of the Finance committee.

In 1973, he was one of five outstanding community leaders named at the "Man of the Year-Woman of the Year" testimonial dinner for the benefit of the Marshall Square Chicago Boys Club.

Like Eddie Barrett, Charley Bonk was a Purple Heart veteran — Charley had served in the 2nd Infantry Division during World War II. He was a joiner throughout the years . . . Theodore Roosevelt Post of the Veterans of Foreign Wars, Pilson Post of American Legion, and the Wilson Post of the Polish Legion of American Veterans. He was also a member of the Polish National Alliance and the Polish Roman Catholic Union of America.

Honored at the 1973 testimonial dinner, less than 16 months later Charley Bonk was indicted by the Special March 1974 Grand Jury. The income tax counts where straightforward; they charged that in the years 1968 through 1972, Charles S. Bonk has willfully and unlawfully made false and fraudulent returns and had substantially understated his income.

In other words, he didn't report the money Thompson charged he got from extortion, or pay tax on it.

And just what did the original indictment charge that Charley Bonk was supposed to have extorted?

—$10,000 from Arthur R. Kiney and Ronald A. Reichert, and Attorney John Daley, in connection with the rezoning of a 66.65-acre tract for a mobile-home-trailer park;

—$500 from John Daley for the rezoning of a ¾-acre tract;

—$500 from John Daley for the rezoning of 1.2-acre tract for a Standard Oil gas station;

—$500 from John Daley in connection with the rezoning of a 1-acre tract for a Payless Stations, Incorporated, gas station;

—$500 from John Daley in connection with the rezoning of 9/10 of an acre as a Cities Service Oil Company gas service station;

—$500 from John Daley in connection with the rezoning of ½ acre as a Marathon Oil Company gas service station;

—$5,000 from John Daley in connection with the rezoning of a 36-acre tract as a Shell Oil Company gas service station;

—$5,000 from John Daley in connection with the rezoning of 144 acres belonging to Eugene R. Corley Builders, as a multi-family residential development;

—not more than $2,500 from John Daley in connection with the rezoning of a 4.2-acre tract belonging to William Zino and David Haller, doing business as the R & S Development Company, for a multi-family residential planned unit development;

—not more than $2,500 from John Daley in connection with the rezoning of a 1¾-acre tract belonging to Dorothy Santucci, for a restaurant;

—$15,000 from Thomas J. Origer, Origer Builders, and Robert Haskins, in connection with the rezoning of a 96-acre tract for use as a multi-family planned unit development;

—and $10,000 from Melvin Isenstein and Robert Haskins in connection with the rezoning of a 42-acre tract for a multi-family planned unit development.

Clearly, if the government was right, Charley Bonk had been a rather busy man.

So had John Daley.

An attorney versed in zoning matters, Daley was a cousin of the late Mayor Richard Daley and 18th Ward Democratic committeeman. Later in the trial, he testified that he had made 17 payoffs to Bonk between 1969 and 1971.

This is the same John Daley whom Bonk's feisty defense attorney, Thomas A. Foran, hammered away at all through the trial. Tom Foran, himself the former United States District Attorney for Northern Illinois, effectively undermined John Daley's credibility in the minds of Bonk's jurors. Foran in his closing argument characterized Daley as "handsome, talented, born with a golden spoon in his mouth, clever, and capable.

"You saw him," Foran told the jury. "Smooth as glass.

"He wouldn't talk at all. His buddy Haskins was talking at the time, but he wouldn't talk at all, not a word, *until they got him immunity*. Then after he was home free, he left his clients abandoned and alone.

"Remember? He hadn't talked to them for four years. The last thing he said was that if the government comes to talk to you, don't talk because if I get in trouble on this I will put you into it.

"Boy, he did that all right, didn't he?" Foran told the jury. "All of them who testified, DiFranco, Kiney, Reichert, his clients. These men, by the way, were given no immunity. They are sitting up there testifying under oath to crimes . . ."

Haskins, another zoning expert, had testified under a grant of immunity less than a year earlier, in the Paul Wigoda trial, as a star witness. He will take the stand in Charley Bonk's trial, and again tell of payoffs — this time, to encourage quick action by County Board Democrats on zoning charges.

And again, Haskins is under an immunity grant from the United States Attorney's office.

Two additional men get immunity in Charley Bonk's trial: Melvin Isenstein, millionaire developer, in connection with Palatine Township rezoning; and Thomas Origer, millionaire and former owner of the defunct Chicago Fire professional football team, in connection with a 96-acre tract rezoning in Northbrook Township.

Let's look at John Daley's immunity grant, because it contains a piece of extra action — action that's controversial enough for the *Loyola University Law Journal* to later analyze in a 20-page article. Here's what the immunity order said in pertinent part:

IT IS FURTHER ORDERED that no testimony of the witness, JOHN DALEY, compelled under this order (or any information directly or indirectly derived from such testimony or other information) may be used against him in any criminal case, except for a prosecution for perjury, giving a false statement, or otherwise failing to comply with this order in accordance with the provisions of Section 6002, Title 18, United States Code.

IT IS FURTHER ORDERED that no testimony of the witness, JOHN DALEY, compelled under this order as above, may be used against him in any administrative proceeding, disciplinary committee, any bar association or state Supreme Court, in conjunction with any professional disciplinary proceeding or disbarment.

Enter:
Edwin A. Robson (signed)
U.S. DISTRICT COURT JUDGE
Dated at Chicago, Illinois this 18th day of July, 1974.

Had the federal government gone too far?

In his zeal for another conviction, had Thompson and his assistants granted an immunity protection they could not legally give?

Disbarment proceedings constitute a civil, non-criminal action . . . an action in which Illinois exercises control over the members of the bar. The right to do so comes from the reserved powers which are vested in the states . . . powers which the United States Constitution expressly protects from federal intervention.

The *Loyola University Law Journal* article says this about Daley's questionable immunity grant:

> Perhaps this additional incentive of protection from disbarment or state disciplinary action is needed to obtain full cooperation from attorneys involved in criminal conduct. It might well be true that society will tolerate the continued practice of some of these attorneys in exchange for the removal from public office of officials involved in the same criminal dealings. *It is, however, beyond the discretionary powers of the federal prosecutors to make these value judgments when Congress has not given them the power to grant immunity from disbarment.* The state's interest in the matter remains paramount and unimpaired by this attempted exertion of federal control over disbarment proceedings. Such immunity orders stand in the way of the state's power to determine an attorney's fitness to remain a member of its bar.

The U.S. Court of Appeals used even stronger language when it finally struck down — on February 11, 1977 — Thompson's attempt to shield John Daley not only from *criminal* prosecution but from

State of Illinois disbarment proceedings, which are *civil* proceedings. Circuit Court Judge Sprecher said in his carefully drawn finding that

> *The United States Attorney acted outside the scope of his jurisdiction and **utterly without authorization of law**. His actions are therefore **bereft of validity**.*

And just what *did* John Daley testify to?

He said that he had passed along $46,500 in bribes to Bonk from his clients between 1966 and 1971.

Neither Daley nor Haskins are "choirboys," said Assistant United States Attorney Howard Hoffmann in his closing argument, but instead are "a part of the system that condones shakedowns . . . a system in which Bonk was an integral part." But since people go to jail, not systems, Hoffmann's conclusion — *that Bonk should THEREFORE be convicted and sent to prison* — violated logic and twisted what may be a general truth into a specific falsehood.

Haskins, of course, had already been in trouble with the government on his income taxes. Under a grant of immunity in the 1974 trial of Chicago Alderman Paul Wigoda, he had testified that his alleged failure to pay federal income taxes had been under investigation by the federal government since at least 1970; that at one time he had been offered consideration in connection with his tax difficulties; and that his testimony was given under statutory immunity which had been granted to him on April 3, 1974.

In the Wigoda trial, Judge Marovitz had also stated that for the tax years 1968 through 1970, the Internal Revenue Service report containing detailed and substantial dollar amounts, claimed that Haskins had failed to report 54 per cent of his total income.

Defense attorney Tom Foran will hit this point again and again during the Bonk trial.

Foran wants Daley's and Haskins' tax returns from the government, along with any financial analyses of Haskins' incomes and expenditures made during the course of any federal tax or other investigation of him for the years involved.

"Insofar as the Government's financial analyses and the tax returns themselves disclose that Haskins (and Daley) have received monies and/or have been living in excess of their reported income for tax purposes, it is highly probative that monies Daley and Haskins were receiving from clients purportedly to pay off the defendant were, in fact, being retained by Daley and Haskins *in toto*," Foran charged.

Foran also raised the question of special consideration for Haskins in the Bonk trial, because of what happened in the earlier, Wigoda trial.

During the course of that earlier trial, material in the possession of the government relating to Haskins was presented to the trial judge for his *in camera* inspection. After his inspection, the trial judge (Marovitz) ordered that Internal Revenue Service reports compiled on Haskins be turned over to Wigoda's attorneys. In doing so, the trial judge commented on the information contained in the materials, stating that they showed the following facts regarding Haskins' income:

1. Total receipts not deposited of $110,517.49, including $76,000.00 in currency and $43,517.00 in checks.
2. For the period 1968-70, approximate-

ly 54% of Haskins' income was not reported.

"In his Wigoda trial testimony," Foran argued, "Haskins admitted that he had been talking with government agents since 1970 regarding his income tax problem, and that his failure to pay income taxes was still under investigation.

"According to Haskins, not only were his tax 'difficulties' discussed, but he was also offered 'consideration' for those 'difficulties' very early in the proceedings.

"The Wigoda transcript makes it clear, however, that Haskins had potentially serious income tax problems and that the Government had offered Haskins favorable treatment relating to those problems.

"As he was in the Wigoda case," Foran argued, "Haskins is a key witness against Defendant Bonk. The indictment in this case alleges that Charles S. Bonk, in his position as a Commissioner of the Cook County Board of Commissioners and as Chairman of its Zoning committee, used his position to extort money from, among others, Robert Haskins and John Daley. Defendant Bonk is in essence charged with using his official position to force payments from those seeking zoning changes in return for such changes.

"In the context of these facts, it is difficult to believe that a deal was not struck between the Government and Haskins," Foran said.

Daley, also immunized, also a zoning expert and attorney, may have been in a position exactly similar to Haskins, Foran argued. "He too was the so-called middle man who was, no doubt, identified by his clients as having received sums of money from them. Having received the money, he was charged with the responsibility of reporting it as income, which he probably did not do. Assuming he did not, he could face the fact that he had a problem and attempt to work out an agreement with the government. The government's primary trading point to encourage his testimony would, no doubt, be his tax liabilities."

Foran fought vigorously for Bonk — even before the trial started.

How can Charley Bonk have violated the Hobbs Act, Foran asked, for Counts 11 and 12, since there had been no effect on interstate commerce?

"Count 11, Origer's supposed $15,000 payment only alleges that Thomas J. Origer and Origer Builders generally engage in interstate commerce in the general pursuit of the building business," Foran said. "Count 11 does not anywhere allege that the extortion with respect to the particular 96-acre tract of land there concerned, had an effect on interstate commerce."

In fact, at a pretrial conference, the government had stated that the County Board's rezoning of the property for use as a multi-family planned unit development was later reversed in Court. Therefore, the property was never developed as a planned unit development, and the government conceded that no interstate commerce occurred with respect to that property.

"The government only contends that if the count 11 alleged extortion payment of $15,000 had *not* been made, this money would have been available for Origer's other real estate projects in which some extra state commerce was involved.

Likewise, Count 12 charged that Melvin Isenstein, a land developer, after obtaining the rezoning ordinance for a multi-family planned unit development there concerned, "intended" to purchase building materials which would move in interstate commerce. This count does not anywhere allege that the extortion with respect to the property and rezoning there described ever actually had an effect on interstate commerce.

In fact, at an earlier government conference, the government conceded that no interstate commerce had ever occurred with respect to the Count 12 rezoned property, even though nearly five years had elapsed since the passage of the relevant rezoning ordinance.

"The government only states that although Isenstein has not yet developed this property, he is now entering into contracts which may *eventually* involve interstate commerce," Foran said.

"Although the alleged extortion was successful, and the property was rezoned, no effect on commerce has occurred. In Count 11, it was because the rezoning was reversed in court; in Count 12, it's because the property had never been developed, even after 5 years."

Foran was fighting on another front as well.

"Additionally," he argued, "Bonk was charged with wrongfully and unlawfully using his governmental position and obtaining money from persons with their consent, money he has received "under color of official right!"

He argued with the U.S. Attorney that Charley Bonk could *not* have extorted money from the developers "under color of official right" because payments from them came *after* the County Board action which Bonk could have influenced. The passage, or non-passage, of re-zoning ordinance had already occurred.

"As a matter of law and plain fact," Foran argued, "there could be no unlawful Section 1951 'Inducement,' as there was nothing left for the defendant to influence, control or prevent at the time the unlawful money payments and alleged 'threats' were made."

The threats, of course, referred to the fact that Bonk allegedly had threatened to use his official position to prevent the property's rezoning unless money was paid to him.

Despite Foran's arguments, however, the counts in the indictment were not dismissed. Charley Bonk from 18th Street went to trial — facing two millionaire developers and two expert zoning lawyers, all of whom had immunity.

The trial moved rather quickly. Mike Igoe, secretary of the Cook County Board, testified about the procedure followed in zoning cases and to the fact that Charley Bonk was chairman of the Building and Zoning committee. But as the trial continued, evidence showed that Bonk always followed the recommendations of the Zoning Board of Appeals. In fact, out of 661 cases, Charley Bonk moved to defer only one — a case in which the applicant was the Federal Aviation Administration.

Up came the builders. Isenstein, immunized, testified on direct examination that he had to give money to Charley Bonk — that Haskins had told him that the money was to go to Charley.

Then Foran took over on cross-examination, which he later recapitulated in his concluding remarks to the jury.

"I said to him, Mr. Isenstein (and I will add my own thoughts; he knew Haskins, knew him inside out, had been with him all the time), what do you think, did you know then whether Haskins was giving the money to somebody or was he putting it in his own pocket?

"And he said, 'I don't know. Could have been either.'

". . . and I said to this guy, don't you wonder whether or not he might have put it in his own pocket, and he didn't really give it to anybody?

"And Isenstein said, 'Yes, yes, I wonder.'

"Isn't that reasonable doubt?" Foran asks the jury. "Isn't that doubt based on reason? Reason much better than what we have? Reason based on a long relationship with Haskins?

"Isenstein didn't know. Isenstein thinks he [Haskins] might well have put it in his pocket," Foran says to the jury.

Will the jury buy Isenstein's testimony? Will it buy that of Tom Origer? (Origer had a criminal tax case involving $200,000 pending, which was shifted to civil collection — an additional inducement for the immunity grant.) Origer said on the stand that he paid County Commissioner Floyd Fulle, on leave as chairman of the Republican County Central committee, "half as much as he paid to take care of the Democrats on the Board." Origer also said he gave Haskins about $85,000 in cash between 1966 and 1969 to arrange quick rezoning action by Board Democrats on zoning matters.

Then there was Daley.

Immunized, Daley revealed that he had first pleaded the Fifth Amendment when he went before a federal grand jury in June, 1974. But he said he agreed July 18, 1974, to testify after he was granted immunity from prosecution.

In all, Daley said he had made 17 payoffs to Bonk. But did he?

"Daley is in here trying to convince these fellows to give him immunity from prosecution for his crimes," Foran charged. "His crimes obviously include embezzlement among his clients.

"Daley's in it. You know he and Haskins are the two bigshot zoning lawyers. They are in it together. But can you imagine Daley coming in and trying to convince these decent guys to give him immunity, and have him say, 'I had 20 gas stations where I represented Standard Oil, City Service, Marathon Oil, Payless Stations, ARCO, all the great big gas stations, 20 of them, and I didn't make any payoffs. Non-zero, goose egg.' They say, 'Oh, come on, now! A gas station on a 1-acre residential lot that's worth maybe $7,500 and if you get it rezoned, it's going up to $100,000, you didn't make any payoffs? How can we believe this? We are not going to give you immunity on something like that. You are lying to us.'

"You weren't shook down," Foran told Daley. "They wouldn't give you a pass on something like that. Now why did he have to say he had some money to give, you know, out of his own pocket? Because otherwise he wasn't getting shaken down. Standard Oil and City Service and ARCO and the rest of them weren't giving him any cash, and he knew the government couldn't show that they did. He knew they couldn't come up with checks from an Isenstein or checks from a Kiney and Reichert or checks from a DiFranco to support an allegation that he was making payoffs on his gas station sites. And he knew his story had no credibility unless he told these fellows that he was shook down. So he had to say it came out of his own pocket. He *couldn't* show that he got it out of his own account. You know there was no way of showing that he had been cashing checks to get money to do it. So he had to find some money to say, 'I got shook down on all these gas station sites.'

"You know," Foran continued, "this is not a dumb man. You saw him, he's smart and he's smooth. He said, 'I've got to have some money where I can't prove, independently, that some cash came in. So he took 25 grand which he put in his pocket, that he got from Kiney and Reichert and he said, 'I gave 10 to Bonk,' so he'd have something to tell them. And then he said, 'I kept the other fifteen, and I made a deal with Bonk that we'd spread that over all the gas stations.' Now he had some way of saying to them that he had been shaken down on gas stations. Otherwise they wouldn't believe him. They couldn't give him immunity. They'd say, 'You had 20 gas station sites, and you didn't give the County Commissioners any money, and they let them all go through?' They wouldn't buy it.

"Even Mr. Hoffman, [one of the Assistant U.S. Attorneys assigned to the Bonk case], with his cynicism about the system, wouldn't buy this one. So Daley gave them one to buy, to bite, and Mr. Hoffman bit, just like a bass on a worm.

"Daley says he got $10,000 in cash from Chez. Chez told these young fellows that he got 30, that he gave $30,000 in cash to Daley. The same thing: He's got to have money to spread around where they can't prove it. He got into a pickle and he had to start balancing amounts. He had to start fooling with his amounts.

"But you have got to remember this man Daley knew an investigation was going on since 1971. Don't you remember Daley going out to see Kiney and Reichert and saying, 'Look, they're investigating County zoning. Now you guys sign this phoney letter I'm giving you, that is predated almost a year. I'll give it to you right in the exact words: 'Sign it, because if I get in trouble on this thing, you're getting in trouble too.' That's what he told Kiney and Reichert.

"So for three years before he was in immunity," Foran charged, "that smart alec was scheming and figuring out his bill of goods to sell these men, to sell to them, to get himself immunity."

Kiney described the phoney letter on the stand.

He and Reichert originally told the jury the fee arrangement had been $50,000. Then he changed it to twenty-five, and twenty-five in cash later on. Or, as Foran recalled for the jury in his closing remarks, both Kiney and Reichert testified "this phoney letter was phoney. It was a phoney letter."

Then Foran read from that part of the trial transcript in which the letter came up.

"Q. Would you give me the conversation he gave how he told this to you, Mr. Kiney? What did he say to you?

" 'He said, there was a special investigation going on at the zoning, Cook County, the Building and Zoning department and that something had to be done. Otherwise, he was going to be in trouble and if he gets in trouble, then we were going to be in trouble.'

"And I said, that is the way he put it?

"Mr. Kiney said yes.

"And that if I, Daley, prepare a letter that is predated back to when we first met, setting forth facts about our fee arrangement that are untrue - -"

"And Mr. Kiney interrupted me and said, 'That

199

is correct.'

"Then, 'I want you fellows to receipt for it.'

"Mr. Kiney said, 'That is correct.'

"Because if you don't, I, Daley, might get into trouble and if I get into trouble I will put you guys into it to. Was that the actual substance of the conversation?"

"And Mr. Kiney said, 'Yes it was.' "

Foran hammered on. It was a hardhitting, effective closing argument.

"Is it any wonder that each one of those clients, Kiney, Reichert, DiFranco, who knew Daley — oh, they knew him, they worked with him, person to person, alone in his office, preparing cases on matters that were important to them, and in this courtroom yesterday — each one of them told us that to this day, to this moment, they don't know whether Daley took their cash and passed it on to anybody, or just ripped them off and put it in his own pocket — to this day.

"Is that not a reasonable doubt?" Foran asked the jury. "What more can there be? A doubt based on reason. What better reason? Who knows better?

"There is absolutely no evidence, no evidence that Mr. Bonk ever, *ever* exercised his statutory duties and power unfairly, other than the testimony of those two corrupt bums . . .

"For you to convict Charley Bonk on their testimony, you will have to make a decision. You have got to be convinced that Mr. Bonk is guilty beyond a reasonable doubt to the level of belief that you use in making a decision in a really important matter in your life. You have got to be convinced.

"This case cries out reasonable doubt, reasonable doubt, reasonable doubt," Foran told the jury.

"Everybody in it who knew Haskins and Daley well say they might have put that money in their own pockets. They might have. I think they did. But from your standpoint, if they might have, Mr. Bonk is not guilty."

Charley Bonk from 18th Street waited — waited while the jury decided whether to believe Daley and Haskins, or to buy Foran's argument that they are shysters, thieves, "whore lawyers."

"Haskins and Daley play the game," Foran has charged, "and they play it to the hilt, and their patsy is not some judge [Foran had just referred to the shyster-lawyer practice of demanding money from a client to "fix" a traffic court judge and then pocketing the money]; their patsy is Charley Bonk. He's their patsy. He's the guy they wink and giggle about to justify getting cash which they don't have to report to the Internal Revenue Service.

"Look at Haskins. Isn't it a strange thing how his tax bill has gone down. When you add up everything — the $65,000 that Mr. Origer came up with, the $15,000 that Zizzo came up with, the $18,000 that Isenstein came up with in cash — you get $98,000. You will have it in evidence. In October, 1974, in that criminal tax investigation, the government was charging Haskins with not reporting $94,000 — some-odd dollars on his income tax. He's testified for the goverment. In April, 1975, it's down to 30. Now in this case he says as far as he knows he's up-to-date with the government. He claims he's paid all his bills," Foran said.

All these things were going through Charley Bonk's mind as he waited for the jury.

Then the jury returned.

In open court, the jury foreman said, "We, the

jury, find the defendant, Charles Stanley Bonk, NOT GUILTY as charged in the indictment."

Thompson was furious.

"In the four years I have been U.S. Attorney," he told the *Chicago Daily News*," this is the first case involving official corruption that I have ever lost.

"We put on every stick of evidence we had," Thompson continued. "I thought the evidence was overwhelming."

Bonk — in tears — goes free. Free to continue as County Commissioner, to serve once again as chairman of the Cook County Board's Committee on Zoning. In an act of faith and solidarity, Board President George Dunne, saying, "A man is innocent until proven guilty," had named Bonk as zoning chairman four days before the end of the trial. He had even expanded Bonk's authority by giving him two new chairmanships . . . of the public service and the building subcommittees.

It was, however, to be a short-lived period of happiness and vindication.

Seven weeks later, on August 1, 1975, the government petitioned for an immunity grant for Charley Bonk.

Thompson by this time had resigned. He had bigger things in mind than continuing as the United States Attorney. He had made a name for himself. There were scrapbooks full of glowing press clippings. For Thompson had been the darling of the media. He understood very well how to use the power of the office in dealing with the press—the afternoon deadlines; the leaked stories from "authoritative sources;" the cozy back-scratching relationships with certain favored reporters; and a special talent for using the vast but superficial coverage by radio and television to poison the public mind against his prosecutorial targets.

(The unusually cozy nature of Thompson's relationship with reporters who should have been more objective about his prosecutorial tactics is only now beginning to surface. *Chicago Tribune* Columnist Michael Kilian wrote this, for example, in a May 15, 1978, article in *Inquiry Magazine*: "From the beginning, Thompson courted the press as assiduously as a lovesick youth working the singles' bars. He still does today, although not quite so effectively as when half the reporters in Chicago could claim him as a drinking companion.")

So Thompson began pulling his Republican backing together and convincing the boys with the cash that he was the best bet in the Springfield, Illinois, 1976, gubernatorial sweepstakes.

Meanwhile, Thompson's assistant and intimate crony, Sam Skinner, had taken over as United States Attorney for Northern Illinois. There was extensive argument on the immunity grant for Charley Bonk. But on September 22, 1975, Judge Parsons granted the government's petition, and Bonk was compelled to testify.

An innocent Charley Bonk went back before the very same grand jury — the special March 1974 grand jury — which had indicted him, and was required to testify under the immunity grant or face contempt charges and the prospect of jail.

Of the 90 questions the prosecution asked, he answered 81. But on the other nine questions, he told the grand jury: "The question necessarily involves alleged transactions for which I have previously been indicted by this same Grand Jury, tried before a jury, and found by them to be not guilty.

"It is my position that you, as a Grand Jury, and the United States Attorney are presuming me to be guilty, contrary to my rights as a citizen, and are biased against me. Under these circumstances, I respectfully refuse to answer the question on the grounds that any answer I might give would tend to violate my rights under the Fifth Amendment, which protects me against double jeopardy, assures me the protection of due process of law, and my rights against self-incrimination." So said Charley Bonk.

Charley answered all questions not involving matters for which he had already been tried and acquitted. But the government was not satisfied. They asked Charley Bonk whether or not he gave money or anything of value to other County Commissioners in connection with the same zoning transactions for which he had been tried and acquitted! He had previously been charged with the receipt of money in connection with these same transactions. He had been found innocent of that charge.

One of the government's arguments in Bonk's trial was the allegation that he not only had received money for himself, but on behalf of all the Democratic Commissioners then on the County Board. (At that time, there were 10 Democrats and five Republicans on the Board).

By forcing Bonk into an immunity grant — which did not, of course, cover perjury — the government found itself in an unusual position! This may have been the first time in all the 200 years of the Republic that an American citizen, *acquitted* by a jury in a criminal proceeding in which he did not testify (and accordingly had not waived his Fifth Amendment privilege), had been compelled by the Government to answer under oath questions concerning the matters on which he was tried and acquitted.

Bonk was tried on 12 counts of extortion and five counts of tax evasion, which included all the sums charged in the extortion counts and some six additional transactions not counted in extortion counts. Haskins and Daley testified that they had paid the money in each case to Bonk. But implicit in the jury's verdict of not guilty on ALL counts (extortion *and* tax evasion) was the determination that Charley Bonk not only had *not* extorted, but had not even received monies from these government-immunized witnesses.

Why was Bonk worried about appearing again before the grand jury? He was acquitted — perhaps the only significant case Thompson had lost since starting his political corruption crusade. How could there be a problem with his testifying?

Bonk's position was that he could not be compelled to testify as to certain specific matters, and that the Fifth Amendment granted him this privilege. If he *could* claim his Fifth Amendment privilege and remain silent, there would be no possibility of an indictment for perjury against him.

But by this time, other members of the County Board had appeared before this same grand jury, Board members whom the government felt Bonk had, in fact, paid money to. It is reasonable to believe they testified that Bonk had *not* given them money. If this was indeed the case, any testimony

Bonk might give that would be inconsistent with his acquittal could be the basis of a perjury charge IRRESPECTIVE OF WHETHER IT WAS IN

FACT TRUE OR FALSE.

Bonk's lawyer Foran said this: "While the expectation of a perjury indictment is strongest if appellant [Bonk] testifies *consistent* with his acquittal, it should be noted that such indictment would also be possible if he testified *inconsistent* with his acquittal. In such event, there would be no assurance that the government would not choose to believe that he was *then* lying as a matter of expediency to avoid perjury prosecution and proceed with such indictment and prosecution."

Foran's involved reasoning on the possibility of Bonk being once again indicted and prosecuted — this time for perjury — *no matter what he might tell the grand jury* — becomes simpler to understand when we look at the prosecutorial psychology of Thompson and his assistants. One of the central elements of that psychology, an element that surfaced time after time in the criminal cases they prosecuted, is this: having once determined to convict someone of a crime, Thompson and his assistants then *defined* the man's every action as criminal. If, for example, they believed or said they believed that a man was lying about the true nature of his criminal activity, then every other thing the man might say or not say about his conduct would become — by definition — a lie.

This is what Foran meant when he claimed Bonk would lose either way by testifying on the same matters for which he had already been tried and acquitted — that Bonk could, and very likely would, be accused of perjury no matter what he said. The reason was that Thompson would simply "define" it as perjury.

The very same grand jury which indicted Charley Bonk . . . the very same prosecutor who subsequently, diligently, and forcefully, had presented the extortion and tax charges against him . . . could Charley Bonk even possibly get a fair shake from these people? Since it was obvious that the grand jury believed that Daley and Haskins were telling the truth, what would happen to Charley Bonk if he had testified consistent with his acquittal?

He had already been placed in jeopardy as to the subject matter the government wanted to question him about . . . there had been a final legal judgment of the facts involved . . . and the government previously had spent great amounts of time to "get" Charley Bonk, including extraordinary immunity grants to several badly tainted witnesses.

This is also the same grand jury that had indicted a string of political figures at Thompson's insistence; and that had gone home every night and read the newspapers and knew perfectly well that Bonk, whom they had previously indicted, was acquitted. Will they believe him? Or can they decide that he is perjuring himself — thereby leaving him wide open to another indictment and debilitating trial, very possibly followed by imprisonment for perjury.

It is reasonable to conclude, with Bonk's attorney Tom Foran, that Bonk was *not* facing an unbiased and impartial grand jury.

The government obviously pressured him. Finally, Charley Bonk did testify and answered the nine questions related to his earlier indictment and trial. How he answered those questions at the secret grand jury proceedings, since Charley Bonk died shortly thereafter, will never be known.

Charley's health was not good. The stress had

taken its toll. He was overweight. He had high blood pressure, and was always taking medication for it. Suddenly, on April 20, 1976, he died of a heart attack. He was only 55.

County Commissioner Mary McDonald, a Republican, remembers Charley Bonk warmly. "When I first came on the Board, she recalls, Charley could not have been nicer. He'd help me out and do all these real, nice things. He would say to me, 'Are you all right? Is there anything you want? Can I help you do research?'

"He stopped in my office every day. He was one of the friendliest men I ever met. Charley helped me more than any other single individual when I came into office," recalls Mrs. McDonald of Lincolnwood.

Perhaps the best way to express how others felt about Charley Bonk is to say that he had hundreds of people at his funeral . . . people who knew and loved Charley and appreciated having him around.

"Every day in my prayers," says Commissioner McDonald, "I mention the people who have been stars in my life, people who have been good to me and my relatives. Well, Charley was that kind of person. He made that much of an impression on me.

"I mention his name every day in my prayers. When Charley died, something special left the County Board."

(Attorney Thomas Foran's closing argument in the Bonk trial is reprinted as Appendix III in the rear section of this book.)

V

THE
PAUL WIGODA
CASE

Clear up to the morning of the day I was indicted, they were telling me there was still time to talk about Daley and Keane and others.

—Paul T. Wigoda

Circumstantial evidence!

It sent Chicago Alderman Paul T. Wigoda, one of 13 members of the City's Building and Zoning Committee — and a powerful member of Richard Daley's Democratic organization — to jail for wilfully and substantially understating his 1969 income. Wigoda, said the goverment, had not reported a $50,000 bribe in connection with rezoning of the Edgewater Golf Club property on Chicago's Far North Side.

Wigoda had allegedly received the $50,000 from Roy Gottlieb and Kenneth Tucker, owners of the Edgewater property.

Moreover, trial testimony showed that:

—Wigoda never asked for money, let alone demanded money, from *anyone;*

—Gottlieb, the man who with his partner Tucker generated the $50,000 bribe, never promised any money to Paul Wigoda, never personally gave the $50,000 to Wigoda, and never even directed that the money be given to Wigoda;

—Zoning lawyer Robert Haskins, who received a sealed envelope that Gottlieb said contained the $50,000, never opened the envelope.

Yet Wigoda served six months because this trial jury did indeed believe that Haskins had made the $50,000 "drop" and that Wigoda had taken possession of that sum of money. And Thompson chalked up a new triumph, along with plenty of page one headlines and other clippings about another "corrupt office holder" he'd put away.

Thompson's list of such high-profile public men is growing. *Kerner. Barrett.* Two top Democrats, each politically triumphant in an earlier era — both now in the maturity of their lives. If they had not fallen to Thompson's ambition, both of these veteran public men might have been expected to finish their careers with honor and dignity. Yet Kerner, sick and broken-hearted, sent home from Lexington for lung cancer surgery, dies a convicted felon, even though his friends push unsuccessfully for a posthumous pardon. And Eddie Barrett narrowly escapes being taken by ambulance to Federal prison, only to die not long after his trial, as a convicted felon, confined by court order to his Chicago home.

Bill Rentschler, the *Wunderkind* of the North Shore. *Charley Bonk* from Chicago's 18th Street, at this point under investigation, one of the only office holders Thompson would ever indict who would be acquitted — but whom Thompson would then subject to "double jeopardy" with another tortured interpretation of the immunity doctrine.

Now it is Wigoda's turn to defend himself against Thompson. Paul Wigoda, a 20-year stalwart supporter of Mayor Richard Daley, is in 1974 — when he's indicted — considered one of the leading Democrats in the Chicago City Council. The 56-year-old politician from the 49th Ward in Rogers Park has come up through the ranks of his organization. He's been a precinct captain, a lawyer, a corporation counsel, and since 1959 his ward's alderman.

The backdrop of Big Jim Thompson's political aspirations must never be overlooked in trying to reach a just assessment of the man's 3½-year record as U.S. Attorney. This is not by any means meant to obscure the facts of the Wigoda case, which will be summarized shortly, or the relevant facts concerning the alleged crimes of any other public figure Thompson's office moved against. Nor do these recurring references to Thompson's ultimate interest in elective politics suggest that Thompson was then or is now all bad.

U.S. Attorney Thompson had the merit of publicly castigating Vice President Spiro Agnew — *after* Agnew had pleaded *no contest* to federal charges that he'd been collecting bribes from Maryland contractors while holding the second highest American office. Thompson called Agnew what the Vice President's own abject plea admitted him to be: a crook. Nor was Thompson off base in his general understanding of the rather widespread pattern of official corruption in Northern Illinois.

But it is one thing to understand a general truth. It is quite another to apply that truth with one tortured legalistic interpretation after another — in order to amass an impressive string of courtroom victories.

And the latter practice — coupled with a characteristic tone in the Thompson that was at once manipulative and mean — did in fact constitute Big Jim's standard operating procedure. This characteristic tone and procedure fell far short of the spirit described by the late U.S. Supreme Court Justice Robert Jackson, who, when he was U.S. Attorney General, said a federal prosecutor should take

> *a detached and impartial view of all groups in the community. Law enforcement is not automatic. It isn't blind. One of the greatest difficulties of the position of prosecutor is that he must pick his cases, because no prosecutor can investigate all of the cases in which he receives complaints.*

What if Thompson's prosecutorial selection

process *was* anchored in his own political ambitions? How might that have reflected — during the 3½ years he was U.S. Attorney — on the actual men and the alleged crimes he chose to move against?

It would of course suggest, first of all, that many of Thompson's choices were made for mainly political considerations. Is that bad? No it isn't, *provided* that dismantling the Daley machine and rooting out official corruption in Chicago and Cook County amount in all cases to exactly the same thing. And it is a fact that in the minds of most Chicago and suburban political independents — and a vast number of downstate Illinois Republicans as well — the Democratic machine of the late Mayor Daley and official corruption do amount to the exact same thing.

What this meant for Thompson *the aspiring politician* was that he could have the best of both worlds: the judicial world, as a straight crime fighter; and the political world, as a *political* crime fighter. And, as long as he added just a few Republicans to his "hit" list, he'd be perceived in the press and elsewhere as an even-handed political crime fighter.

This is a beautiful theory. But what would happen to it in the event Thompson *wasn't* sure from the outset of an investigation that the *individual* Democrat or Republican he picked for prosecution was absolutely guilty? Then the U.S. Attorney would have to choose between putting another big dent in the Daley machine — or getting a needed Republican scalp — and serving the cause of justice in a more serious and truly even-handed way.

In practice, what would happen is that Thompson would be forced to lean one way or the other — once he'd picked the "corrupt office holder" and begun to move against that office holder with his federal investigators and legal assistants and mail inspectors. Why? *Because not every last Democratic office holder in Chicago was then or is now corrupt and venal. Because not every one of Thompson's Republican opponents was then or is now corrupt and venal. Because the people who think the Chicago Democratic machine is the most disgraceful political organization that ever existed are wrong. Because those who consider all politicians to be more or less crooked are wrong. And because Thompson himself, while fanning these and similar narrow prejudices, knew them to be wrong.*

Thompson would naturally defend himself by claiming he only prosecuted politicians whom he believed from the outset of an investigation to be absolutely guilty.

But that's not true.

And the Wigoda case is a perfect example of *why* it's not true.

Thompson prosecuted Paul Wigoda for allegedly taking a $50,000 zoning bribe and then not paying federal income tax on the extorted money. But there's no way on earth that Thompson even now can be certain that Wigoda received the brown envelope with all the cash.

Thompson may have been right that Wigoda took the money from Haskins.

The point is that Thompson never had *compelling* grounds to believe Haskins on that matter, because Haskins at different points in the grand jury investigation and the criminal trial changed his story significantly and also because his well-rewarded testimony was — by standards of truth and justice — *inherently unreliable.*

But the more important point is that Thompson didn't *have* to believe even Haskins' most solid version, the version where he testified he actually put the envelope in Paul Wigoda's hand. All Thompson had to do was *not* believe Wigoda's stout denial that the alderman had ever accepted or in any way took possession of the bribe.

The point is that only two people ever really knew whether Paul Wigoda took the $50,000 Haskins said he delivered to Wigoda: Haskins himself, and Wigoda himself.

The point is not that circumstantial evidence is no good or that there's anything wrong with using it to convict a man — providing it is *solid* circumstantial evidence. There isn't a smoking gun or an eye-witness in every murder conviction, and the conviction can still be just. But the government never solidly established that Gottlieb, the generator of the $50,000 bribe, ever had a discussion with his zoning-"fixer" Haskins about *whom* the money was supposed to go to. Nor did the government ever establish that Haskins and Wigoda had any conversation whatsoever when the money supposedly was passed. There was government speculation and inference about these "conversations" — but never even any hard *circumstantial* evidence that they occurred.

The point is that Thompson went after Wigoda — indicted and convicted him — without being absolutely certain from the outset of the investigation what exactly Haskins would end up telling the Wigoda trial jury. A grand juror who has seen an immunized zoning "fixer" like Robert Haskins — or anyone else who's been engaged in shady activities and then immunized — being nudged along by a government attorney at a grand jury proceeding knows how little the immunized person really wants to say. Because everything the government attorney nudges or coaxes or forces out of his reluctant witness makes that witness feel just so much dirtier in the sight of everyone in the room.

And the point is that Thompson's assistant Sam Skinner had to do just that kind of wheedling to get Thompson's reluctant, immunized witness to say enough to satisfy the conditions of the immunity deal that Haskins had gotten from Big Jim — an immunity deal that included tax relief for Haskins.

> *The point is that Big Jim had to lean one way or the other from the very outset of the Wigoda case. He had to lean towards making another big dent in the Daley machine — and to hell with judicial niceties. Or else he had to lean in the direction of giving Paul Wigoda the benefit of the doubt — a reasonable doubt that even a powerful Democratic alderman deserves when he is being accused of a crime by a self-confessed zoning "fixer."*

The point is that Big Jim leaned in the same direction with respect to Wigoda that he'd been leaning for the previous $2\frac{1}{2}$ years — toward the courtroom kill, away from the serious pursuit of justice.

Thompson's courtroom "kill" strategy made its most important appearance against Wigoda in the government's closing argument. Up to this point, remember, the government had never established that the briber and conduit and alleged extortionist had ever said a word to each other about *Wigoda* getting the $50,000 in bribe money. But somehow that gap had to be filled for the jurors to believe Haskins' immunized testimony and *not* believe Wigoda's own sworn trial testimony that he had never accepted or taken possession of the bribe.

Thompson had assigned two of the young stars on his staff to handle Wigoda's prosecution. One of those government attorneys was Joel F. Flaum, who entered the case near the end of the trial. The other was Dan K. Webb, 29, the man whom *Chicago Sun-Times* reporter Art Petacque on October 11, 1974, idolized in print by calling attention to Webb's

> *perfect conviction record in 23 cases, many involving political and police corruption. [By the time Webb left the U.S. Attorney's office in mid-1976, this record of convictions had become 44 out of 45 — as another Sun-Times reporter, Dennis Fisher, would gushingly write. What Fisher failed to mention in that same July 31 story was the fact that Webb's cases involved flagrantly excessive use of immunized witnesses even by the Thompson office standard — more than 100 by conservative estimate; and the directly related deduction that this promiscuous use of a highly questionable legal tool could not help but relieve Webb of at least some of the prosecutor's rightful burden of proving guilt beyond a reasonable doubt.]*

Nor did Petacque in the same 1974 story fail to

lionize Webb's boss Thompson or fail to live up to the standards of what the *Wall Street Journal* called Thompson's "adoring local press," Petacque wrote:

> *By gaining the convictions of two power-ful Chicago alderman on successive days, U.S. Atty. James R. Thompson has solid-ified his ranking as the nation's hottest federal prosecutor. Thompson's office now has retired more than 75 persons from public life as the result of convic-tions in government cases involving po-litical corruption.*

Getting back to Wigoda, who in Petacque's faithful recordkeeping for Thompson constituted Big Jim's 75th "score," let's think about a few rel-evant questions pertaining to the closing argument that Dan K. Webb delivered to the Wigoda trial jury.

> *How, specifically, did Webb prop up the shaky credibility of Haskins' testimony? How did he supply the verbal links that finally convinced the Wigoda jury that a $50,000 bribe could have been delivered to Paul Wigoda without a proved word ever passing between the admitted con-duit and the admitted generator of the bribe? What mode of argument did Webb use in that closing argument to make such flimsy circumstantial evi-dence stick?*

These are the most important questions that must be answered in order to understand how Paul Wigoda was convicted and thus became Thompson's 75th "score."

But there are other questions that must also be answered for a full illumination of Thompson's strategy in the whole case:

—What pre-trial government practices strongly indicate that Thompson was interested in far more than the alderman's own scalp?

—Why did the Thompson office choose to pass over in silence the bobbing-and-weaving zoning practices of Jack Sperling, the Chicago alderman in whose 50th Ward the Edgewater Golf Club property was located? Did the fact that Jack Sperling was a Republican have anything to do with that choice? Did it suggest that Thompson viewed Paul Wigoda, a leading representative of the Daley machine, as having greater potential value for a political crime-busting district attorney when he was working the *Chicago* side of the street?

—How many bribers and "fixers" and conduits did Thompson and his staff this time have to immunize against incriminating themselves?

—Did the Wigoda trial judge, Abraham Marovitz, help or hurt the rights of the accused? (Marovitz had expressed public friendliness to Wigoda during the trial, and according to Wigoda had addressed him privately as "pal" at the end of the trial.)

—What specifically did Judge Marovitz say about Thompson's wholesale use of immunity in this case, when he sentenced Paul Wigoda to prison?

—What else do those sentencing remarks by Marovitz seem to suggest about what he thought the trial may really have proved?

Let's go back to that closing government argument, and then consider all the above questions.

Webb must have known that it just does not make sense for so substantial an amount of bribe money as $50,000 to be generated, transmitted, and accepted with hand gestures and facial expressions alone. Somebody had to *say* something. Either the briber had to say, "Spread it around" . . . or, "Get so much to ...." and "so much to ...." Or else the bag man had to give the briber some idea, however general, of what he was going to do with so much money. Even a millionaire real estate developer cares about who gets cash of that magnitude — and especially if the millionaire real estate developer is a self-confessed briber.

So what did Dan Webb do to fill in the missing verbal link for the whole alleged bribery transaction? How did he frame his statements about that missing link in his closing argument?

The first thing he did was prepare the groundwork for that closing argument earlier in the trial. The self-admitted zoning "fixer" Robert Haskins was testifying — and his statements included nothing about any conversations with Wigoda about money or payoffs. Haskins had been asked, however, whether he talked with Wigoda about the Edgewater property during the first part of 1969, before one of the Chicago City Council's votes on the Edgewater zoning.

When Haskins said there had been such a conversation, prosecutor Webb prefaced his next question with:

> *I am not going to ask you to relate that conversation.*

Webb's statement seemed innocuous at the time.

If the early 1969 conversation Haskins described he'd had with Wigoda could have incriminated Wigoda, the Haskins testimony would probably have been drawn out at that very point in the trial. That's the way it then seemed — at any rate — to Paul Wigoda and his two defense attorneys, Warren Wolfson and Harry J. Busch.

Next on the stand was Roy Gottlieb, millionaire real estate developer and self-confessed briber. The government had already informed Judge Marovitz that it intended to introduce certain conversations between Gottlieb and Haskins — not as proof of the truth of what they said, but simply to establish that Gottlieb and Haskins were indeed discussing what they'd have to do to get the most favorable possible zoning of the Edgewater Golf Club property.

In fact, U.S. Attorney Thompson himself had stipulated — in a memorandum of law over his signature — that the Haskins-Gottlieb conversations did not incriminate Paul Wigoda. The relevant part of Thompson's memo about these conversations read:

> *During the trial testimony of Roy Gottlieb, the government intends to introduce conversations between Roy Gottlieb and Robert Haskins. In substance, Gottlieb will testify that Robert Haskins told him eventually certain public officials would have to be paid money in order for the Edgewater planned development to get through the Chicago City Council. Gottlieb will testify that after the rezoning passed the Chicago City Council, Haskins told Gottlieb to obtain $50,000 in cash so Haskins could spread*

it out.

It should be noted that these conversations do not incriminate the defendant Paul T. Wigoda.

These conversations will not be offered into evidence for the truth of what Haskins says to Gottlieb, but will only be offered into evidence to prove that certain words were spoken to Gottlieb by Haskins, and that as a result of these words being spoken to Gottlieb, Gottlieb and other government witnesses then proceeded to raise $50,000 in cash.

The government has tendered to the Court a limiting instruction to be read to the jury pointing out the limited purpose for which these conversations are to be considered by the jury.

So here again Thompson proved that he did not have any outside evidence — even outside circumstantial evidence — that corroborated what Haskins had told him about having "bribed" Wigoda. He simply "decided" to believe Haskins.

After Gottlieb had taken the stand, Judge Marovitz himself decided the substance of the Gottlieb-Haskins conversations was unduly prejudicial to Wigoda — *since the conversations in no way incriminated Wigoda* — and that the government could not therefore draw out that substance in Gottlieb's testimony. Marovitz commented

Why should Wigoda be guilty of the sins of others?

Attorney Webb, apparently obeying the Judge's ruling, then used as a preface to his next question to Gottlieb: "I am not going to ask you to relate the conversation —"

This was Webb's second, seemingly innocuous reference to the excluded substance of the Gottlieb-Haskins conversation — the conversation that did not in any way refer to Wigoda.

As the final arguments began, the government was faced with a difficult problem. No one — not Haskins, Gottlieb, or anyone else — had testified to a conversation with Wigoda about a payoff. The jury might think it illogical that $50,000 was passed without anyone talking about it.

Dan Webb solved the problem in his closing argument. He did so by inviting the jury to speculate on the contents of the *inadmissible* conversations. Thus, he was able to do indirectly what he could not do directly — and he did it in a way more devastating than the actual conversations would have been.

He began:

> *Think about it: **The bag man Haskins has a conversation with Wigoda**, the bag man goes to the developers, the developers then get the money and bring the money back to the bag man and the bag man delivers it to the defendant Wigoda.*

The seed planted during Haskins' direct examination germinated. It reached full bloom when Attorney Webb issued his broad invitation to speculate on the contents of all conversations not admitted into evidence. Webb, again:

> *Now, it doesn't really matter what took place in those conversations between the parties **that were not admitted into***

evidence. However, you, the eleven jurors, may use your common sense and you may call upon your own human experience and common sense and I don't think you have any difficulty in inferring what was said in these conversations.

Mr. Wolfson: I object, your Honor, please, because that is improper.

The Court: What?

Mr. Wolfson: He is asking the jury to infer something from nothing.

The Court: I think the lawyers are entitled to make such logical inferences as the evidence warrants. It is up to the jury to judge those inferences which are not warranted and they may certainly disregard them.

The message from Dan Webb to the jury — with an imprimatur from Judge Marovitz — was clear.

The government possessed important and damaging evidence it had not been allowed to introduce. The conversations dealt with payoffs. Since the government was charging that Wigoda received a payoff, the conversations must have dealt with the payment of money to Wigoda.

Those are the inferences invited by the government. In fact, the government *knew* the Gottlieb-Haskins conversations did not mention Wigoda. And the government itself had not chosen to offer the Haskins-Wigoda conversation *for their truth.*

In his offer of proof, Thompson himself conceded that the Gottlieb-Haskins conversations could *not* be admitted for their truth. It was improper for Dan Webb to tell the jurors they might infer the contents of the conversations for use in their deliberations.

What Dan Webb should have done and what he actually did, however, were different. His perfect 23-straight conviction record didn't come out of nowhere. Nor did Thompson's 75th score, Paul Wigoda.

For Webb expressly told the jury there were "conversations between the parties that were not admissible into evidence." He made the statement while arguing that Haskins was the middle man who received money from Gottlieb and delivered it to Wigoda.

> *Webb's meaning was obvious. He, Webb, knew the contents of the conversations. He was not able to get them before the jury. But if the jury had heard them, they, too, would know what he knows — the conversations dealt with payoffs to Wigoda.*

To defendant Paul Wigoda's serious detriment, then, his jury could very possibly have regarded Dan Webb as an unsworn but quasi-infallible witness attesting to the devastating impact of the conversations that had not been introduced.

Those Wigoda jurors, after all, didn't have much other good reason to believe the twisting stories and words of the self-confessed "fixer" Robert Haskins. It may well be that Dan Webb gave them the best "reason" of all.

And the jurors ended up believing what Haskins told them about bribing Paul Wigoda.

It's impossible in our system of criminal justice, as trial attorney .F. Lee Bailey correctly points out, to fault or second-guess a jury that has believed a lying witness. Or a jury that has been misled into speculating falsely and without any factual basis. On the basis of either of those two things happening in a jury's deliberations, there are just no legal grounds for appeal by the person convicted. That not-so-little flaw in our system seems to be the necessary price we pay for the "right" to a jury trial by our peers.

> *But it is possible to fault a U.S. Attorney — especially one like Big Jim who claims to know where the "bodies are buried" in Chicago politics — when he too easily believes, or says he believes, almost anything a rich briber or a zoning "fixer" tells him to the detriment of a public officer. Even if Thompson as a federal prosecutor had more real experience than he brought to the job — or even as much as he then claimed to have — he would still have needed to find some corroborative evidence to justly back up the testimony of a Robert Haskins. Thompson or any other federal prosecutor should feel conscience-bound to do this for two reasons: it well serves the interest of justice, and it protects the prosecutor himself from becoming someone's fool.*

By immunizing Haskins in the Wigoda case — and later in the Charley Bonk case — Thompson probably didn't become a gullible fool. But he didn't serve justice either. Big Jim is quoted as saying — in the March 21, 1975, of the Waukegan *News-Sun* — that it would have been

> *impossible to prosecute some cases with-
> out it [immunity]. We only give immu-
> nity when it's the only way.*

Well, in the Wigoda case, it *was* the only way.
The Haskins stories about his payoffs to the alderman were not corroborated by any other evidence.
A reasonable and impartial observer might well
conclude from that that Thompson's best policy,
therefore, would be to quash the proceedings
against Paul Wigoda. But not Big Jim. He *knew*
Wigoda was guilty. Besides, he had to get his 75th
"score." And Robert Haskins showed how far
Thompson this time leaned away from justice.

Robert E. Haskins. Zoning attorney. The man
who filed the application for a zoning change on
the Edgewater property. The man who will also
testify as Thompson's immunized witness against
County Commissioner Charley Bonk, and there
tell how he went back to Bonk a total of eight
times as the "victim" of an extortion shakedown
of his clients.

Haskins' two clients in the Wigoda case are Roy
Gottlieb and Ken Tucker, principal officers and
shareholders in Kenroy, Inc. Gottlieb and Tucker
are the two men who'd been wheeling and dealing
in northside Chicago real estate developments for
years before the opportunity came along for them
to buy the 92-acre Edgewater Golf Club in Chicago's Rogers Park. And like Haskins, Gottlieb
and Tucker were immunized in the Wigoda trial.

So was Oscar Tucker, uncle of Ken Tucker,
brought by the government from the federal penitentiary at Marion, Illinois, to testify under an
immunity grant in the Wigoda trial. Oscar Tucker had been serving for receiving bribes and

evading income tax while serving with the Cook County Assessor's Office.

To understand the story these men tell — and deal Wigoda is charged with making — you need to know about the Edgewater Golf Club and the Rogers Park area.

With quiet, tree-lined streets, brick apartment buildings, and commercial traffic pretty much limited to two or three north-south streets, Rogers Park has been a solid, steady neighborhood for more years than it's been part of Chicago. Many parts of Rogers Park have been built in the last 20 or 30 years, but most of this farthest north lakeside sector of Chicago still exhibits the values of an old-fashioned neighborhood. In the late 1960's and early 1970's, Democrat Paul Wigoda is alderman of the 49th ward, just east of the Golf Club property. Republican Jack Sperling is alderman for the 50th ward, in which the Edgewater tract lies.

The large 92-acre property, bounded by Western, Damen, Albion, and Pratt Avenues, was a private golf club for many years — a club losing money that decided to sell. In 1965, Wigoda tried to get the Chicago Board of Education to buy the land for a community college site and park. By March of the following year, a special citizens committee sponsored by the Allied North Side Community Organizations (ANSCO) also was pushing the college-park concept.

The golf club property had been purchased in 1965 by Roy Gottlieb and Kenneth Tucker, principal officers and shareholders in Kenroy, Inc., a real estate developing firm. The men formed a limited partnership, called The Edgewater Company, for the purpose of acquiring and develop-

ing the site. In July, 1965, Chicago attorney
Leonard Ash, who had acted as a nominee for
Gottlieb and Tucker, executed a contract of purchase for the golf club property, in which he
agreed to buy the land for a total price of $7.6
million. Under the contract, an initial earnest
money payment of $200,000 was required, and
that was made. The rest of the purchase price
was originally due on November 1, 1966.

Chicago zoning is extremely complicated. There
are roughly 11 steps taken by all applications for
residential planned developments. The Edgewater
property went through all of them.

*Chicago has a comprehensive zoning
code. It's made up of zoning R-1 through
R-7. R-1 and R-2 are single-family, and
you can only put single family houses on
the property. R-3 is for 2-flats. R-4,
R-5, R-6, and R-7 are for multiple-unit
dwellings.*

*Now Chicago has what's called a den-
sity zoning code — not height. Suppose,
for instance, a home on a property 50 x
150 — 7,500 sq. feet — happens to be
zoned R-4. The owner can build apart-
ments on this property, if he wants to,
but each apartment must be a minimum
of 600 square feet. So the owner divides
600 into the number of square feet, and
that's how many units he can put up.
That's density. Chicago was the first city
in the country to have that kind of zoning
code.*

*Different zoning classifications mean
different rules. For an R-5 — that's a
low-rise —you only need 400 square feet*

per apartment.

Some properties are businesses. They tell you the business you can put in there — usually a business which is not obnoxious or uncharacteristic of the neighborhood, like service stores or beauty shops. Then you have commercial zoning. And then you have manufacturing.

Over the years, the Chicago City Council found there were certain zonings that fitted no pattern, so it devised a system called PUD, planned unit development. That gives the Department of Development and Planning and the Chicago Plan Commission and the Committee on Building and Zoning a chance to control the density, yet allow certain variations that the builder can't get under a rigid code. Obviously, it's to the builder's advantage to go into a planned development, because he can put up more units. It lets the City control his setbacks, his side yard lot lines, and how much open space. In return for that, the City allows him to go up a little higher, and he makes more money.

There are basically only two ways that zoning is introduced in the City Council. One way is by an alderman who can introduce the zoning any place he wants. Out of aldermanic courtesy, he only does it in his own ward.

The other way — the most common way — is for the property owner to introduce the zoning through the City Clerk. The reason most aldermen don't introduce any zoning is that they don't know what opposition they are going to have in the community. They like to see the lay of the land. They count noses. How many for it? How many people against it? They've got more votes this way than that way.

Once the property owner introduces the zoning request in the clerk's office, the clerk brings it to the City Council and reads it. Then it automatically goes to the committee on Building and Zoning, which then sends it back to the City Council for final approval if the Committee first approves. There are even more steps if the zoning requested is a planned development — sending the application to various planning agencies for study and recommendations — but the Chicago City Council is always the final authority in Chicago zoning.

At the time of its sale, the Edgewater Golf Club property was zoned R-4 — a Chicago designation which meant that 5,221 multiple family residences of not less than 900 square feet each could have been built on the property, and that there were no provisions which would limit the height of any of the structures. While there were requirements for parking and open spaces, these were minimal under the City Code.

Gottlieb and Tucker, in 1965, retained zoning expert Robert E. Haskins, a Chicago lawyer, to apply for a zoning change from the R-4 zoning to a residential planned development, paying him a retainer of $1,500 and not setting a specific fee. In the 35 years that Haskins had practiced law, he had handled several hundred zoning cases in the City of Chicago. Knowledgeable, experienced, and competent in dealing with the lengthy procedures Chicago and its various departments followed in zoning matters, Haskins was the attorney that a number of developers used when they wanted to get a zoning change through the system.

So in May, 1967, Haskins filed an application asking for a change in zoning. Under the proposal, a $100 million shopping center would have been built on a piece of the land which fronted on Western Avenue, already a commercial street; between 4,000 and 4,200 highrise apartment units would go up; and a number of townhouses would also have been built.

The application for the zoning change that Haskins filed in 1967 was referred to the Chicago Plan Commission — a group of 17 members whose task was to review the application, hold public hearings on it, and make a recommendation to the Committee on Building and Zoning. Paul Wigoda was one of the four Chicago alderman who were Commission members.

On June 20, 1967, a public hearing was held by the Plan Commission. Both Wigoda and Alderman Sperling, in whose ward the property was located, attended. Opposition ran high against the planned development among residents, who felt that the property should be bought for a park. Because the Commission had not received a recommendation, either from the Department of Development and Planning, or from the Zoning Administrator, the Commission did not take action on the application. "I was not pleased with the plan," said Wigoda, who supported the motion to defer consideration. "I didn't think it was a well-thought-out plan."

Next month (June, 1967), the proposal also came before the Committee on Buildings and Zoning in a public hearing. Those who wanted the zoning changed testified about the planned development; Sperling and various civic groups stated their opposition. Wigoda seconded a motion to defer consideration of the proposed change because there had been no recommendation from the Department of Development, from the Zoning Administrator, or from the Plan Commission. He also felt the plan was not well thought-out, and that he would still prefer to try to have a public agency purchase the site for a public park.

By October, 1967, however, a building permit had been issued to begin construction of several 6-story apartment buildings on the property — and promptly pulled back.

> *A friend of mine called me from the Chicago Building Department, Wigoda says, and told me that Joe Fitzgerald, Building Commissioner, had issued permits. I called Kay Spear, the Mayor's secretary, and said I had to talk to the Mayor. It was Columbus Day. He was already at the parade, and she finally got hold of him in his car. I told Mayor Daley I had to see him not later than 9 or 10 o'clock the next morning. I met with him, and he pulled the permit and ordered the building stopped. I made sure he understood the feelings of the community. I still wanted to save the land for the public, and I felt it would be tragic to allow helter-skelter building without any plan. It would have been destructive to the neighborhood.*

Later that month, an article appeared in the

Lerner newspapers, a neighborhood chain, indicating that the Mayor had told ANSCO, the citizen's group, that if they didn't like the existing zoning of the property, they should request their alderman to apply for a downgrading. Another article in the same issue quoted Alderman Sperling as saying that he was considering filing an application to down-grade the zoning.

> *The **only** thing I ever really wanted to permit the developers to build was a planned development, says Wigoda. With a planned development, they could build more, but we would have had more control. When I found out Jack Sperling was going to introduce the downgrading ordinance, and that Alderman Robert O'Rourke and John Hoellen were going to co-sponsor it, I went to the Mayor. Jack and I weren't enemies, but we just didn't like each other. The Edgewater property bordered on both our wards, so to speak. And I didn't like the idea of Sperling making political hay out of the matter, since the zoning had such large implications that it affected the whole north side of Chicago.*

About that same time, Haskins and Gottlieb came to see Wigoda, partly to give him news of the development corporation's financial problems. One of the golf club property's purchase provisions was that the time left in which the balance of the purchase price could be extended to November 1, 1968, if anyone other than a party to the contract started proceedings to downgrade the zoned status of the property. Haskins, in a 1970 sworn deposition, also said he'd been seeing Sperling during this period.

Gottlieb told Wigoda that such an application would not only help the purchasers, but would go along with the apparent wishes of the people who lived in the community. Wigoda told Gottlieb he wasn't interested in the financial problems of the purchasers, but that he had already decided to introduce a downgrading ordinance at the next City Council session — to reflect the wishes of the community and to delay the question in order to give him a further chance to find a public agency to purchase the property for public use.

On November 1, 1967, the City Council met. Wigoda did in fact introduce the downgrading ordinance. So did Aldermen Sperling, Hoellen, and O'Rourke, although neither of the ordinances was ever acted upon.

By early 1969, the developers filed a new application for a residential planned unit development. This PUD had a number of changes from their planned development of 1967, most importantly including a fewer number of units.

Despite loud and continuing objections from various community organizations and neighborhood residents, Commissioner Lewis Hill of the Department of Development and Planning recommended approval of the 1969 planned development to the Chicago Plan Commission.

As Hill testified in Wigoda's trial, he recommended approval because he believed that "the planned development — as described in the 1969 ordinance — was a much more desirable development for that area than to have that area built solidly by 4-flat developments." Hill cited many reasons — open space, off-street parking, the facing of townhouses rather than 4-flats on Pratt Avenue — for his decision.

Next step for the Edgewater property: it went to the City Council Committee on Buildings and Zoning, which considered the developer's application on January 23, 1969. Both Hill and John Maloney, the Zoning Administrator, submitted their favorable recommendation to the Committee. Hill also wrote to the Committee giving his independent favorable recommendation.

On March 14, 1969, the zoning application came up for action by the entire Chicago City Council. Jack Sperling, Republican alderman for the 50th ward — in whose ward the Edgewater property was located — moved to defer action on the report from the Committee on Buildings and Zoning. Wigoda spoke in favor of the recommendation of the Committee on Buildings and Zoning, and supported the proposed change.

When the City Council voted on the zoning proposal, that vote was taken in roll call fashion. The "call of the wards" began with the 1st ward and ended with the 50th ward. In order for the ordinance to pass, it needed a majority of those who were voting. By the time the vote reached Paul Wigoda, alderman for the 49th ward, 32 votes in favor of the ordinance had already been cast, and the ordinance had been passed. He voted in favor of the ordinance, though aldermen for the 40th, the 47th, the 48th, and 50th wards voted against the ordinance. Final vote was 33 in favor to 10 against.

A new factor had come into the Edgewater zoning situation roughly five or six weeks earlier —

the possibility of the State of Illinois buying the land.

Phillip S. Krone, a political opponent of Wigoda's, and public relations consultant with the Illinois Department of Conservation, called on Paul Wigoda — about late January or early February, 1969. (This was the same Phillip Krone who in 1973 was to be appointed — by Cook County GOP Chairman Edmund J. Kucharski — to "represent" the 20th legislative district in Chicago, replacing one of the district's representatives who had died. But Krone had a problem: he had not lived in the district the legally required two years — had even moved to this West Side Chicago area immediately after the death in order to enable Kucharski to appoint him. Anyway Krone attempted to backdate his apartment-lease application, earning him the well-deserved and severe criticism of the General Assembly's Election Commission. Krone resigned from this position one week after his appointment, knowing his colleagues were moving successfully to have him expelled from the legislature.)

Krone said he'd come to see Wigoda to ask him for help in getting the Edgewater property bought for public use. Illinois State Rep. Copeland, a Republican State Representative for the area which included the Edgewater property, was planning to introduce a bipartisan bill in the Illinois legislature which would call for purchase of the property by the State, Krone said. He told Wigoda that he was concerned because the City Council was going to be acting on the planned development for the property — that if the zoning proposal passed the City Council, it might make it more difficult for Copeland's bill to get past the state legislature. Even if Copeland's bill passes, said Krone, it will be more difficult to purchase the whole 92 acres of the Edgewater property, because the value of the land would be increased by the zoning change.

Wigoda's answer was simple: since the State had not taken any action up to that time — and since he could not conceive that downstate representatives would let a bill pass that so obviously aided Chicago — he felt the matter had been delayed long enough. It was not fair, he said, to keep the developers in the lurch.

Krone said he too felt the developers had rights, but he did not think they should get the additional windfall that they'd receive if the ordinance on zoning passed the City Council. Use your influence, Krone asked Wigoda, to table the planned development till June 30.

The point of the bill Krone was pushing was to enable the State of Illinois to buy and convert the still-undeveloped property and convert it into a State park. The bill specifically appropriated $950,000 to be used as a downpayment for the purchase.

State Rep. Copeland went ahead and introduced the bill on April 22, 1969, more than a month after the Chicago City Council had changed the property's zoning status — and value.

The General Assembly and State Senate also went ahead and passed the bill in the hectic, zany closing hours of the legislative session — that traditional time in Springfield when the state clock "stops" just before midnight and thus permits the legislators to take care of pending business before the session officially closes. And the following October 9, Governor Richard Ogilvie signed the appropriation and committed the State to buy 55 acres of the property. (This became 59.3 acres in 1970, the year the State actually bought the property. About two years later, the State consigned its entire interest in the land to the Chicago Public Buildings Commission, which in 1978 is in the process of selling the 59.3 acres to the Chicago Park District.)

One of the last major acts in the long struggle to do something with the 92 acres came on June 18, 1970, when the Chicago Public Buildings Commission agreed to buy the remaining 32.7 acres in the name of the City of Chicago.

The importance of the zoning changes in the property becomes clear when looking at what Gottlieb and Tucker were able to charge Illinois and Chicago for the entire property. For the acreage they'd sold the State, the developers received $8 million. For the smaller parcel they'd sold the City, they got $10.3 million.

That's $18.3 million! They'd paid, remember, $7.6 million for the same property in 1965. Even subtracting the legal fees and bank-financing charges they probably had to pay, the whole series of events of the five years had netted them several *million* dollars.

> *The government's position in prosecuting Wigoda was that his actions as an important member of the Chicago City Council had provided the developers with exactly the help they'd needed on two crucial occasions. Which made possible their financial bonanza. Which in turn explained the alleged payment of $50,000 to Wigoda.*

Almost nothing that a local government does matches its zoning actions in sheer magnitude of technical detail. Since those actions so importantly bear on people's lives, they also assume gigantic proportions in terms of their potential for stirring public controversy. Zoning can obviously make or break a land developer.

But beyond all this, almost nothing in government lends itself so well to trickery as zoning. The mass of technical detail is so great that tricky politicians who know how the game is played can quite easily cover their tracks. Tricky zoning lawyers like Robert Haskins know all the moves that can gain them big fees and that don't necessarily have to be reported, if it is their intention not to report the income.

Thompson may well have been right in suspecting that somebody was playing tricks in order to inflate the value of the Edgewater Golf Club's 92 acres — from $7.6 million in 1965 to $18.3 million in 1970. Gottlieb and Haskins testified *they* had played a few tricks. Wigoda said he didn't play any tricks at all. The Chicago Republican whose ward contains the property — Alderman Jack Sperling — aparently seems to have been suspected by Thompson's office of playing tricks but was never indicted or prosecuted. Others also seem to have been suspected, and they weren't prosecuted either.

Let's quickly re-scan the several key actions where the tricks may have occurred. Keep in mind that the community organizations in Rogers Park didn't ever like the idea of Gottlieb and Tucker building *anything* on the 92 acres — these groups wanted open, public-use land. Keep in mind also that an alderman in Chicago has got to be a pretty good nose-counter in order to keep getting elected. And keep in mind, finally, that especially skillful aldermen with a little larceny in their hearts can *seem* to be supporting community sentiment in zoning matters while the real motives may include jacking up a developer for a payoff — or for a larger payoff.

May, 1967: Haskins files zoning-change application — *from R4* (5,221 multiple-flat residences ... either highrise or 4-flats) *to a Planned Unit Development* (about 4,000 highrise units plus a planned $100 million shopping center facing the main north-south arterial street bordering the property, Western avenue).

Oct., 1967: Faced with community opposition to their PUD idea, Gottlieb and Tucker get a permit from the Chicago Building department, enabling them to go ahead with plans to construct several 6-story buildings (in compliance with the original zoning).

Oct., 1967: Apparently in response to the screaming from North Side community organizations about developer's plans, *Alderman Sperling voices loud public opposition to the plans and threatens to try to get the property downzoned. Alderman Wigoda* — who, like any politician, hates to be upstaged by a colleague — *sees Mayor Daley and has the building permit pulled back from the developer.*

Nov., 1967: Gottlieb and Tucker can't come up with the more than $7 million they still owe and need a time extension. Gottlieb tells Wigoda that if someone other than a party to the original purchase gets the property downzoned — to single-family residences, for example — the developer will get a year's extension on his debt.

Wigoda responds that he intended anyway to downzone the property in light of the community feeling, *even though he himself favors a reasonable-density planned development.* All through this period, Haskins is seeing Sperling, according to the 1970 deposition of Haskins.

FACT: Both *Sperling and Wigoda introduce separate ordinances to downzone the property at the November, 1967, meeting of the City Council.* Both ordinances are referred to the Building and Zoning committee, on which Wigoda sits; *neither ordinance is ever acted on by the committee.*

GOVERNMENT INTERPRETATION OF FACT: That Wigoda acted — *and then did not act —* so that Gottlieb and Tucker could get an extension on their $7 million debt.

Jan., 1969: Haskins files new application with City for different kind of Planned Unit Development — with slighty fewer highrise units, some townhouses, 1½ acres of open space, more off-street parking, and the $100 million shopping center on Western Avenue.

Jan., 1969: Lewis Hill, Commissioner of Chicago Department of Development and Planning, submits favorable report on new PUD — calls it better than the 1967 PUD.

Jan., 1969: Developer's application for the PUD voted out of the 13-member City Council Committee on Building and Zoning. Wigoda is on this committee.

March, 1969: City Council passes ordinance changing property zoning from original R4 to the planned development status recently applied for by Haskins, recently recommended by Hill, recently approved by the Building and Zoning committee. The vote is 33 to 10, with Wigoda voting for it, Sperling and other minority aldermen voting against it.

FACT: Value of developer's 92 acres now skyrockets.

GOVERNMENT INTERPRETATION OF FACT: That Wigoda acted so that Gottlieb and Tucker could make a stupendous windfall profit.

April 8, 1969: The date Haskins says he delivers the brown envelope containing $50,000 to Wigoda at Wigoda's law office.

June 29-30, 1969: Illinois legislature passes bill that will enable state to buy 59.3 acres of the property, ultimately, for $8 million.

June 18, 1970: Chicago acquires remaining 32.7 acres from Gottlieb and Tucker for $10.3 million, with land to be used as a Chicago park.

Do Paul Wigoda's actions show a pattern of extorting the developer or even "earning" a big bribe? Look at them.

In 1965 he's publicly for turning the site, which the Golf Club owners want to sell, into a community college and a park.

In 1967, after two years of inaction by the developer, Wigoda supports the developer's preference for a Planned Unit Development — although he backs off from a storm of community sentiment against the developer's threat to start building high-density apartment buildings. So by satisfying the community and stopping the builder from going through with his threat, Wigoda is later said to be conspiring illegitimately with the builder.

In 1969, after another 2-year period of inaction by the builder, Wigoda again supports a PUD. *And a planned development such as Gottlieb and*

Tucker were suggesting, it should be said, makes pretty good sense in a land-short urban area. So Wigoda votes for the zoning change that may finally enable the builders to do something with what by this time is becoming an unkempt community eye-sore. Obviously, Wigoda knows the price of the land will increase enormously when it is zoned this way.

Does the Chicago alderman have to be a grafter to want 92 acres — that have been going to seed for four years — *used?*

Does he have to have larceny in his heart to want a builder to succeed — even a builder whose plan he occasionally opposed? Since Wigoda can't even get *Chicago* to buy the land in 1965, what would suggest to him that the *State* would want to buy a big chunk of it in 1969? How many *other* state parks are there in cities over 25,000 people anyplace in Illinois? And doesn't the fact that the State Department of Conservation resold its parcel of the 92 acres — only two years after its purchase of the land, and after doing less than nothing to develop a state park — suggest that the purchase was a thoughtless, flukey piece of show-boat politics in the first place? Something that tired Downstate legislators did to make Ed Copeland happy or get him off their backs or just get the session over with and the hell with the money?

Hindsight is so great for putting together the pieces of a supposed conspiracy. Maybe Wigoda was a grafter and had plenty of larceny in his heart and worked hard as an alderman for all those years just so he could knock Roy Gottlieb down for $50,000. But if you think that,

> *you have to be giving even a pretty*
> *bright and well-connected man like Wi-*
> *goda credit for an almost incredible*
> *amount of political muscle and a godlike*
> *ability to peer into the future and a very*
> *patient sort of larceny.*

Thompson may have given Wigoda credit for all that. But it's easy for someone who's never held elective office to exaggerate the real powers of even as well-thought-of an alderman as Paul Wigoda. And it's especially easy for someone like Big Jim — who had to prove, after all, that he knew where "all the bodies were buried" in Chicago and Cook County.

But one thing about Wigoda Thompson did not mistake. That was the fact that Paul Wigoda was a law associate of the most politically muscular Chicago alderman of them all, Thomas Keane. And Wigoda and Mayor Daley seemed to have a pretty good relationship, too. All of which made Wigoda a prime target and not only for the value of his own scalp.

> *"I think the government thought that*
> *I knew a hell of a lot more than I actu-*
> *ally knew," Wigoda recalls. "They wanted*
> *to talk about Daley. They wanted to*
> *talk about Keane. They wanted to talk*
> *about other people. But I had no inten-*
> *tion of talking to anyone. And I didn't.*
> *Clear up to the morning of the day I*
> *was indicted, they were telling me there*
> *was still time to talk about Daley and*
> *Keane and others."*

The government, however was doing plenty of talking.

Thompson's investigators went on a fishing expedition, looking for people who knew Paul Wigoda. More than 25 people who were subpoenaed never were called to testify before the grand jury.

"They had a cute system," Wigoda says. "They took you into a private room; and if you had nothing bad to say, they wouldn't take you before the grand jury."

Wigoda probably has a point. Grand jury testimony is secret, so nobody is even supposed to say they've testified. But would anyone like to wager $10 that Wigoda's grand jurors were permitted to hear what a former 2-term chairman of the Rogers Park umbrella organization ANSCO had to say? ANSCO, remember, had fought tooth and nail from 1965 on to stop Gottlieb and Tucker from building anything at all on the former golf course — ANSCO wanted open land, period. And for two of those years, 1967 and 1968, and for three other years (1971-73), Dr. James Barry, an English professor at Loyola University, served as chairman of ANSCO.

Barry's organization did not share Wigoda's liking for the planned development approach, but Barry a few days after the 1974 Wigoda indictment was quoted by the *Lerner Newspapers* as saying:

> *My conviction, based on working closely with Paul Wigoda for more than 10 years, is that he has not engaged in improper conduct in connection with the 1969 rezoning of the former Edgewater Golf course.*

ANSCO had watched Wigoda's actions on the rezoning with close scrutiny and frequent disagreement, and yet its chairman was still able to say that. What if Dr. Barry had been able to say it to the Wigoda grand jurors *before* the indictment, instead of in a newspaper a few days *after* the indictment.

Trotting out only the unfavorable witnesses at his grand jury proceedings was a well-honed technique of Thompson's for the 3½ years he was prosecutor. And in the context of his own case, Wigoda gives the reason:

> If they had brought favorable witnesses before the grand jury investigating me, my lawyer could have asked them, "How many people did you subpoena before the grand jury? Did any of them have any adverse testimony against Wigoda?" No, Thompson's boys didn't do that. Well, it makes the government look bad. So they don't take witnesses before the grand jury unless they can talk them into having something bad to say. They even subpoenaed some lawyer I gave a $10 check to. I owed him the money, because he had filed an appearance in a case for me. Yet because I'd given him a check, they subpoenaed him.
>
> "Now the grand jury under Thompson was a sieve. They must have thought the grand jury came under the open meeting law. There weren't very many prominent people that were under investigation under Thompson that everything before the grand jury didn't hit the newspapers the next day."

Wigoda is right. Though the indictment against him is not brought until April 5, 1974, a 7-column front page headline on the March 12 *Chicago Daily News* charges: "REPORT ZONING PAYOFF, PROBE KEANE, WIGODA . . . U.S. JURY SIFTS EDGEWATER LAND DEALS."

In a copyrighted story by two *Daily News* reporters, readers were told that "a federal grand jury is investigating reports of payoffs made to the City Council's 1969 rezoning of the Edgewater Golf Club, which later became a park, the *Daily News* learned Tuesday. A Loop attorney, who had inside knowledge of the reported payoffs, has been providing the federal government with detailed information, investigators said. Investigators said they were told that recipients of the reported bribes were permitted to keep them because the club was a financial bonanza for the developer, even though it became park land."

Grand jury testimony is confidential and secret. That's the law. And yet on March 13, *Chicago Today* ran a story about the continuing federal investigation, saying Wigoda and another alderman were "under scrutiny by federal officials. Another story on that date says, "An official of the U.S. Attorney's Office refused to comment when asked if (Jack) Sperling or Wigoda is under investigation. But the official did confirm that a grand jury is investigating the rezoning of the property."

The *Chicago Sun-Times* carried a March 14 story that "more than 200 zoning cases handled by Robert E. Haskins, a politically connected Loop lawyer, are being examined by federal investigators, it was learned. The investigation is part of an over-all inquiry into political corruption that is being conducted by prosecutors under U.S. Atty. James R. Thompson with help from other federal investigatory agencies. Specifically, a federal grand jury is investigating whether payoffs were made to obtain City Council approval for rezoning of the multimillion-dollar Edgewater Golf Course on the North Side. The federal inquiry is being handled by Anton R. Valukas, deputy chief of the Special Investigations Division. Valukas was assigned to handle cases involving official corruption. They also declined to comment on the investigation. However, it was learned that several present or former Chicago aldermen have appeared or are scheduled to appear before the grand jury."

And the *Chicago Daily News* of March 14, 1974 says that "federal investigators are in the final stages of pinning down how many aldermen shared in a $50,000 fee paid at the time the City Council was considering the lucrative rezoning for the Edgewater Golf Course. Agents already have traced payment of the $50,000 to one alderman and reportedly have readied a tax case based on his failure to report all the money on his 1969 income tax return. Investigation has indicated that the unreported remainder was shared with at least one other alderman and maybe as many as two others plus a city planning official."

On April 5, 1975, with the fishing expedition over, the indictment finally came.

Haskins, the chief government witness against Wigoda, was in tax trouble — serious tax trouble.

The Internal Revenue Service had been checking his tax returns for 1968, 1969, and 1970. Though Wigoda's defense attorneys argued forcefully that the IRS files, and in particular a report by IRS Agent Starr, were essential material that should be turned over to them, Judge Marovitz announced tHat only Starr's report was relevant to the trial. Instead of turning the report over to Wigoda's attorneys, Marovitz said that the report contained information that

> *Haskins' total unreported and undeposited legal receipts were $83,767; that there was a total of $110,517.49 total receipts not deposited; that $76,000 of that in currency and $43,517.49 in checks; that there were unreported partnership income or losses unreported for the years 1969 and 1970 and that he admitted a non-deposit of these items; that he did not include on his returns his share of profits . . . **He failed to report 54 per cent of that total income for the years 1968 through 1970.***

Could Haskins have been pressured into testifying against Wigoda? Could he have negotiated that immunity grant against criminal prosecution, even though he failed to report 54 per cent of his income, in return for his testimony that he gave Wigoda an envelope?

Certainly there were those who thought so.

Veteran newsman John Madigan described it this way, in his Oct. 14, 1974 commentary on WBBM, Newsradio 78:

> *The Alderman Wigoda case has again raised some questions about granting immunity to witnesses who themselves are suspect.*
>
> *Some charge it is the same as buying*

perjury . . . or using prosecutorial clout.

The federal immunity statute has been tested before the U.S. Supreme Court and has been upheld. But just as in search-and-seizure . . . capital punishment . . . wire-tap . . . probation . . . criminal procedures run in cycles.

Veteran prosecutors don't preclude that the high court may take another look one of these days and . . . perhaps . . . relimit the scope and use of immunity.

Take the testimony of Attorney Bob Haskins who said he handed the envelope to Alderman Wigoda. He was under investigation for income tax evasion. He was granted immunity.

The prosecution was aware that Haskins wanted to save his own neck. It had to weigh the importance of getting Wigoda . . . an elected official . . . as against getting Haskins . . . an old hand at the wheeling-dealing life of zoning law.

The generating of $50,000 from land developers to Haskins was indisputable. The latter said it was for political payoffs. Haskins said he didn't look in the envelope. Just gave it to Wigoda. The alderman said he didn't. The defense claimed Haskins pocketed the money.

There was no corroborative evidence to back up Haskins. How then did the prosecutors elect to believe him and give him immunity?

The gestalt of the whole thing. The pattern. Haskins' meeting with Wigoda. The alderman's actions in behalf of the land developers.

All inferential. Circumstantial! As far as putting the $50,000 in Wigoda's hands. A heavy burden for the prosecution to drop on a jury.

Robert Kennedy pushed through the first immunity statute. John Mitchell got Congress to broaden it . . . to get gangsters. But it turned around and bit him . . . and Wigoda and Kerner too . . . and may continue to chew up public officials unless the Supreme Court takes another look.

Never, during the trial, did government attorney Webb explain *why* the $50,000 bribe which Wigoda never asked for and never was promised had been paid to him.

Gottlieb, one of the Edgewater developers, testified that he gave the $50,000 to Haskins. Several weeks after the date on which the Chicago City Council has passed the planned development ordinance, Gottlieb said, he and Haskins talked about the Edgewater property in a meeting at Haskins' office — and that subsequently, he and his partner, Kenneth Tucker, had several meetings related to the Haskins conversation at their Lincolnwood offices.

Gottlieb told the Wigoda trial jury that at a meeting in April, 1969, Kenneth Tucker had brought $50,000 in cash to his office, and that he and Tucker counted it there. Later, said Gottlieb, he took an envelope with the $50,000 in cash in it to Haskins' office.

"When you met with Mr. Haskins on this occasion," the prosecutor asks, "what if anything did you give to him?"

"The envelope with the $50,000 in it," Gottlieb says.

"Did Mr. Haskins count the money in your presence, to your recollection?"

"No."

"After you gave him the money, did you remain in the office, or did you leave?"

"I left," says Gottlieb.

Later, Gottlieb testified that he "absolutely" did *not* tell Haskins to give the $50,000 bribe to the defendant.

Was this the answer the U.S. Attorney expected?

Apparently not.

"I came home from the trial, picked up the newspaper, and the newspaper had a story that Roy Gottlieb had admitted that he gave me $50,000," Wigoda recalls. "Now Roy Gottlieb was a star witness for the government. And he testified that he did *not* tell Haskins to give me the money, that I never asked for anything, and that he never offered anything.

> *"Now stories have to be given to the press by a certain time so they make their deadlines," Wigoda says. "We used the same trick when I was on the city council. When we had anything hot on the agenda, we'd hold it till last so the press wouldn't get it. We aggravated them. They hated us. But we knew how to use deadlines.*
>
> *"Well, it looked to me like the government gave the story to the press before the testimony, because Gottlieb said he*

> *didn't give me the money. So I didn't*
> *even ask my lawyer — I called up the*
> *newspaper, and the story was pulled out*
> *of the paper because it was an outright*
> *lie."*

If Thompson's prosecutors never really knew what their immunized briber Gottlieb was going to say next, they must have been *mystified* by their immunized conduit Haskins.

The story he ended up telling the Wigoda trial was firm enough. He had received a manila envelope about the size of a brick from Gottlieb, Haskins testified, but was not told what was in the envelope or what to do with it. *So,* his testimony continued, *he phoned Wigoda* — their offices were in the same building but on different floors — and then went to the Alderman's office to deliver it. That was April 8, 1969, he testified.

Under oath, Haskins testified he then entered the outer office, met Wigoda at the doorway to Wigoda's private office, handed him the envelope, and said, "Gottlieb wanted me to give you this." Then, Haskins testified, he left.

But Haskins also had other versions of the same set of events. Only days after Haskins himself testified for the first time at the Wigoda grand jury — that was April 4, 1974, one day before the indictment was returned — Haskins met for lunch with John P. Coghlan. John Coghlan is a special state's attorney of Cook County, appointed by a judge of the U.S. district court to act in that capacity. Haskins and Coghlan and Haskins met at a South Side Chicago restaurant on April 16, 1974.

As Coghlan took notes on a pad of legal-size

paper, Haskins talked. And among other things, Haskins said that when he took the brick-size manila envelope from Gottlieb to Wigoda's office, he could not remember for sure whether the Alderman was there at the time. He told Coghlan — and Coghlan's notes show this — that he did not know to whom he gave the envelope. Possibly to one of the office girls. Possibly just put in by the glass window in the receptionist's room or on her desk.

People in positions like that of Robert Haskins tend to have a poor memory, probably on purpose, so they can always use it to slip and slide and duck when someone's trying to pin them down.

And Paul Wigoda's attorney Harry Busch was doing just that with Haskins on the stand. Before bringing up the meeting Haskins had had with Coghlan shortly after the Wigoda trial opened, Attorney Busch asked Haskins:

> *Did you ever tell anyone that you took the envelope to Wigoda's office but you weren't sure that he was there, you don't know who you gave it to, it is possible that you gave it to one of the girls, it is possible that you gave it to the receptionist, or put it by the glass at the receptionist desk, it is possible you could have dropped it on the receptionists's desk; did you ever say that to anyone?*

Haskins' answer, unqualified: "No sir, I never did."

Then Busch asked Haskins:

> *Did you tell Coghlan that you took the envelope to Wigoda's office and that he may have been in the office but you*

> *don't know for sure and you didn't know*
> *who you gave it to, it's possible you*
> *gave it to one of the girls, it's possible*
> *you put it by the glass in the reception*
> *room, it is possible you put it on the re-*
> *ceptionist's desk?*

Haskin's answer this time was: "I don't recall the conversation."

These memory lapses and equivocations and shifting stories by the government's immunized witnesses did not seem to bother the Wigoda trial jury. With the help of government prosecutor Webb's well-timed and smoothly insinuated allusions to unsubstantiated Gottlieb-Haskins conversations, the jury believed this government evidence. It chose not to believe Wigoda's stout denials, under oath, that he ever asked for or indeed ever received the $50,000 bribe.

As mentioned earlier, this is not meant to demonstrate that Haskins lied and Wigoda told the truth on the witness stand. It is meant to demonstrate that Haskins and the other shaky government witness Gottlieb were just that: shaky. Coached and nudged along — when they weren't threatened with prosecution themselves. Interviewed over long periods of time — and in Haskins' case, for at least four years — by prosecutors in private offices. Prosecutors who then leaked stories to the press and finally hauled Haskins before the grand jury — weeks after government-leaked stories about a $50,000 bribe began appearing in Thompson's adoring Chicago press.

An outside observer would think that all the immunized stories could have been firmed up and all the memories refreshed under those ordeals.

But Gottlieb and Haskins kept slipping away.

Had they gone to Thompson's men originally with *firm* recollections of their financial dealings with Wigoda? Doubtful. For then there would have been no earthly reason for the stories to get *shakier* as time went on. And the stories did.

The stories started out shaky. But Big Jim believed them all the same.

The reason that the Gottlieb and Haskins stories were shaky from the beginning is that these are slippery people. They are the people Jim Thompson chose to believe and then put every ounce of federal muscle against to force them to help him convict Wigoda. They are the people he also rewarded with immunity against incriminating themselves, and in Haskins' case with apparent and substantial tax relief.

They are the same shaky, dishonest, not especially believable people who convicted Alderman Paul Wigoda.

But these Thompson-immunized witnesses — the two bribers, Ken Tucker and Roy Gottlieb; and their front man Robert Haskins — also convicted themselves in the Wigoda case, as the trial judge seemed to understand when he sentenced Wigoda to prison. For Judge Abraham Marovitz said this on December 2, 1974:

> *As I presided over the case of United States v. Wigoda, it became increasingly clear to me that the drama involved many guilty — but only one defendant. Almost every single person involved in the zoning payoff was granted immunity, with the sole exception of Paul Wigoda.*

Judge Marovitz failed to mention two things in

that short passage. One, that even though the jurors believed Alderman Wigoda guilty of being "involved in the zoning payoff," Paul Wigoda may not *in truth* have been "involved in the zoning payoff." Two, there were several public figures in Chicago — figures whom both the Thompson office and Judge Marovitz decided not to make known in the course of the investigation and the Wigoda trial itself. These people were *not* granted immunity but they may *in truth* have been "involved" in the zoning payoff. Haskins said he was taking envelopes many places, to many people, in his 1970 sworn deposition. He said the same thing to newspaper reporters.

> *And don't forget, either, that at Wigoda's trial Judge Marovitz it was who first decided **not** to admit evidence of the substance of the Gottlieb-Haskins conversations . . . but who also in the government's closing argument let the government prosecutor invite the jurors to speculate falsely and without any factual basis on the substance of those same conversations.*

None of this dismays peppery Paul Wigoda, now back in Chicago after serving six months of his year-long sentence in the Lexington, Kentucky, federal penitentiary. Wigoda is a proud man who thinks he was railroaded and hopes to get back his law license soon. On June 30, 1978, a hearing panel of the Illinois Attorney Registration and Disciplinary Commission recommended that he be reinstated to the Illinois bar. Five past presidents of the Rogers Park Community Council and leaders of ANSCO were among those who submitted affidavits attesting to Wigoda's integrity: Dr. James Barry and Dr. Homer Johnson of Loyola University; Fred A. Wolf; Harry S. Nachman; and Joel Van Ryzin.

And Wigoda still *likes* government as much as ever. "I had great joy," he says, "throughout all the years in the City Council! I still got excited the night before the meetings! Because it was the challenge. I was the speaker on the floor, defending the administration.

How does a man who loves government feel about what the government did to him?

"It was the night of the long knives and a reign of terror we had," Wigoda says. "There were some guys who obviously were guilty. And I think anybody that takes a bribe should lose his office, and should get everything he's got coming to him. But there were a lot of borderline cases, and a lot of them were used . . .

"I think the U.S. Attorney should go after everybody who's guilty of dereliction of duty, who's guilty of bribery, who's guilty of extortion. I believe in those things — but I believe it should be done within the framework of the law.

"We had a period where that didn't happen. And the newspapers and the U.S. Prosecutor had a field day at the expense of lots of people — some of whom were guilty, and some of whom were not."

And Big Jim would continue to have a field day, as Wigoda puts it, for the remainder of his term as federal prosecutor. He still had a lot of "scores" to make after he'd convicted Paul Wigoda.

A prosecuting attorney under our system has tremendous power, and with that power there is the potential for abuse. Particularly when a prosecutor is politically ambitious and thinks of his office as the road to the governorship or other high elected position, the temptation to seek personal publicity out of the functions of the office can be very real. Abuse of the office begins to creep in when a prosecutor makes decisions based on his own personal stake in the publicity that might result . . .

—WHITNEY NORTH
SEYMOUR, JR., attorney in
private practice, and former
U.S. Attorney, Southern
District of New York

●

CROMWELL: (Straightening his papers, briskly) Sir Thomas is going to be a slippery fish, Richard; we need a net with a finer mesh.

RICH: Yes, Secretary?

CROMWELL We'll weave one for him, shall we, you and I?

RICH: (Uncertainly) I'm only anxious to do what is correct, Secretary.

CROMWELL: (Smiling at him) Yes, Richard, I know. (Straight-faced) You're absolutely right. It must be done by law. It's just a matter of finding the right law, or making one. Bring my papers, will you?

—*A Man for All Seasons*,
a play by Robert Bolt

VI

THE
RONALD COLES
CASE

A lawyer . . . shall not . . . from the time of indictment . . . make or participate in making an extra-judicial statement that a prudent lawyer would expect to be disseminated by means of public communication and that relates to:

(6) Any opinion as to the guilt or innocence of the accused, the evidence, or the merits of the case.

—Canon 20, the American Bar
Association's Canons of
Professional Ethics

Ron Coles is pretty sure his troubles began with Linda's wedding.

It's a simple story of Coles' secretary getting married, and a boss who wanted her to have a nice reception.

But by the time is was all over, Ronald R. Coles was no longer Chairman of the Board of Commissioners of Lake County or Township Supervisor of Lake Villa or Lake County Liquor Control Commissioner.

Instead, he was a convicted felon, on probation for three years, and paying off $25,000 in legal fees and expenses.

The Thompson office only succeeded in getting Coles convicted on two of the seven counts for which he'd been indicted on April 24, 1975. That number of alleged crimes, seven, may seem short by the standard of Big Jim's characteristic shotgun approach to forcing indictments through his sheep-like grand juries. Coles' indictment list is not as short as it seems, however.

Two of the seven counts pertained to Coles' alleged abuse of his power — on separate occasions — as liquor control commissioner for Lake County against the "legitimate" business interests of the sleazy owners of a nude-dancer bar. Two other counts pertained to Coles' alleged federal tax cheating, in two separate years. So the seven counts of the indictment really represented inflating five alleged crimes into a larger number, with the fairly apparent purpose of stampeding the layman grand jurors into the feeling that when a man is accused of so many things he must be guilty of *something*.

But the experienced U.S. District Judge Prentice H. Marshall, who presided at Coles' subsequent bench trial for the seven alleged crimes, was not stampeded by Thompson's where-there's-smoke-there's-fire tactic. The tall and tousled Judge Marshall — rated recently, by the Chicago Council of Lawyers, as the finest federal district judge in Chicago — dismissed all four of the nudie-bar-harassment and tax counts. And in finding Coles *not* guilty on five of the seven counts, Judge Marshall also scathingly criticized Thompson's office for immunizing not only the two nudie bar operators, Martin L. DeFoor and William Hagood; but also for immunizing the chief deputy sheriff of Lake County, Jerome Schuetz, a man who testified under full immunity protection in the Coles trial that he, Schuetz, had extorted tavern owners and other Lake county businessmen as a routine day-to-day activity. Thompson's then-assistant Sam Skinner had tried desperately to protect one of the nudie-bar owners, DeFoor, from all post-trial criminal and civil actions by the federal government, the State of Illinois, and the Lake County Liquor Commission.

Judge Marshall said of these three tainted witnesses, DeFoor, Hagood, and Schuetz: "Testimony from *the likes of these men* does not overcome the presumption of innocence as far as Mr. Coles is concerned."

The Judge did not of course mention in his public statements that U.S. District Attorney Thompson and his first assistant Skinner had gotten these men immunized in the first place, had shielded DeFoor especially from paying taxes on the huge amounts of money he admitted skimming from the receipts at his nudie bar, had even tried to shield him from any post-trial liquor license examination by the State of Illinois for his criminal activity of skimming money for purposes of bribery. But by condemning the credibility of sleazy self-admitted criminals like DeFoor and Schuetz, Judge Marshall *by the same token* called into the question the integrity of Thompson and Skinner, the two chief law-enforcement officers for the federal government in northern Illinois, the same two who got DeFoor and Schuetz their extraordinary immunity in the first place.

To understand more about what happened to Ron Coles — and why — you need to understand Lake County.

The northeasternmost county of Illinois, wedged up against Wisconsin on the north, Lake Michigan on the east, its southern border little more than 20 miles from Chicago's Loop, Lake County bears little resemblance to Cook County's dominant suburban sprawl of housing developments.

Rich Illinois farmland to the west contributes heavily to Lake County's $2.5 billion assessed valuation, which has been going up about 17 per cent each year. Only 50 square miles of the county are developed residential land, but they include some of America's most affluent suburbs, communities like Highland Park, Lake Forest, Lake Bluff, Deerfield, and Libertyville, where $100,000-plus homes are the rule rather than the exception and where a substantial segment of Chicagoland's commercial leadership congregates.

Only 6.6 square miles are developed commercially, with some of that concentrated in milltowns like North Chicago and Waukegan, the county seat where Ron Coles had his office, much of the rest in shopping and office complexes.

The county's nearly 600,000 residents are spread out through 18 townships, with many living in unincorporated areas outside 48 cities and villages, which range in size from Waukegan's 65,000-plus to tiny Hainesville's 142 population.

Unlike Cook County, where a government seems at times to be sophisticated and professional enough to be a way of life, Lake County still retains the slightly old-fashioned charm of informality. Call up its Regional Planning Office, for instance, to ask how many square miles the county contains, and you'll get the answer, "Four hundred sixty, give or take, depending on how high Lake Michigan is."

Lake County, in short, with two-thirds of its land officially characterized as non-urban, is still a county where things move more slowly, where informal friendships and a handshake can still be as good at times as a written contract. Yet it's a county divided, as one observer puts it, into "eastern Republicans" and "western Republicans."

Eastern Republicans, most within easy commuting distance of Chicago, tend to prefer Highland Park, with its Ravinia symphonies and ballet concerts, or Lake Forest, with its sprawling estates and 1976 median income of $33,800. Western Republicans are more rustic, informal, and clannish, dependent for their incomes on farming, lake resorts, and small business. Inevitably, there is a kind of guarded relationship between the two factions. The Easterners tend to classify the Westerners as a little too "countrified," while the westerners see the lakefront Republicans as rich and at least somewhat "uppity."

Ron Coles was a western Republican who had ascended to the chairmanship of the Lake County Board of Commissioners, a powerful post. And there are those who wonder how many of his problems stemmed from the fact that he got in the way of an eastern Republican. Or that he made a headline-grabbing target for an ambitious U.S. Attorney who suddenly, when his gubernatorial aspirations flowered, took an interest in suburban corruption, especially in the collar counties around Cook where Republicans are strongest.

Linda's wedding may well have been the start of it, just as Ron Coles believes.

"She was a very efficient and wonderful girl," he remembers. "I had strong personal feelings for her, because her family were long-time friends. I knew she was having trouble finding a nice place for her wedding reception. One day, she told me she'd decided on the Gurnee Holiday Inn.

"Back around 1965, shortly after I came on the County Board, I'd voted to help the Holiday Inn get its zoning, despite opposition from nearby farmers. I figured it would bring in more revenue, and would be a good thing. Then when I became the liquor commissioner, I got to know John Brooke, the owner, because he had to come in for a license. We'd never had any problems.

"When Linda said she was going to have her wedding there, I figured I'd see what I could do to make it a little bit easier on her, by asking John Brooke to see what he could do to keep the food-and-drink costs to a bare minimum. Linda was paying for the wedding herself. She had no father, and her mother worked. I stopped on my way home one night, and asked for Mr. Brooke. He wasn't there. I said, fine. I stopped in a couple of days later, and he still wasn't there. So I left my card and said, 'Have him call me. It's important that I talk to Mr. Brooke.'

"He never called me." Coles shakes his head slowly. "He never did nothing.

"And I called out there, but I couldn't get him to respond. Finally, I talked to some other manager. I said, 'Look — this guy knows where to call us when he has problems, but now that I want to talk to him, he's too big a man to call us.'

Coles shrugs, reminiscing. He finally was able to talk to one of Brooke's assistants. "I said there was no problem. All I wanted was to make sure that Linda gets a fair deal for her wedding. If there's any way I can help in doing anything, or can contribute so she has a nice wedding, I'll be glad to do it."

"So this guy says to me, 'Don't worry about it. I understand. I know the girl hasn't got much money. We'll do our best for her.'

"I said fine, and we left it at that.

"Linda had a nice wedding, with a formal wedding dinner. It wasn't a big crowd, not a drinking crowd by any means.

Some time after the wedding, she came into the office, just as crabby as a son-of-a-gun. She was stomping around a bit. I said to her, 'What the hell's wrong with you? What affects you affects me. What's wrong?'

"She told me she'd gotten the bill for the wedding. 'I think it's terrible!' she said.

"I looked at the bill," Coles says, "and I thought it looked exorbitant. In fact, I got damn upset. I called out there, and said, 'This is bullshit.' I tried calling Brooke again and again, and finally got hold of Sherm St. Pierre, who was Brooke's landlord for the Holiday Inn.

" 'What's the problem?' he said.

" 'I think you screwed up Linda,' I told him." Coles face tightens, remembering his anger. It is as if he is reliving the conversation.

" 'Have you seen her bar bill! There's no way the group could drink all that! You guys said you would take good care of her, but I think you hurt her instead of helping her! I'm not too happy about it.'

"Right away, he asked me, 'What do you want?'

" 'I don't want anything,' I said. 'All I want is a fair bill for Linda. You guys sure as hell didn't bend over backwards to help her.' And really, in the past, she'd done a lot of things for them. So I told him, 'I think you really owe the girl something.'

"I know he felt I was leaning on him," Coles said. "Which I was. No doubt about it. I was upset.

"Again, I went over to the Holiday Inn weeks after the wedding. And I was angry. I noticed that the jukebox didn't even have a license. Now that's against the county ordinance. So I told the bartender, 'Tell your boss to get a license on that machine. It's only $25. I'm sure he can afford it.' " Brooke could indeed afford the fee. He owns a string of Holiday Inns.

"We started a drive on these jukeboxes," Coles continues, "and I probably should have been smarter than to pick Brooke to start on. But Brooke still didn't respond! I signed a complaint against him at the suggestion of an Assistant

State's Attorney. He was served with the necessary papers; but before the case went to court,
he sent Sherm St. Pierre to me. Sherm wanted
to know what I was doing, what the hell I wanted,
and what the problem was. He wanted me to
forget the complaint.

"I said, 'I'm telling you — I don't want anything
for me. But you sit down with Linda and try to
shave the bill. If you added up all this alcohol, I
think no one in the world could have drunk it all!'

"So they finally came in with a check for $700,
and tried to give it to me." Coles shakes his head,
remembering. "And I said, 'No way. That's the
girl out there. Her office is right out in front.
You go see her. If she feels that's ample, it's fine.'
Because I really thought they had ripped her off.

"Anyway, they gave her the check. I guess she
bought some furniture with it. And that was
that."

And the Holiday Inn was fined $50 when the
jukebox complaint went to court.

But Coles, running for the County Board, began
to hear rumbles. "Finally, the story broke in the
Waukegan *News-Sun* that I was going to be indicted for extorting the Holiday Inn," he says.
"Sure it upset me, having the story leaked so very
conveniently just before the election. It was a
tough race. Here I was, running for the county
board, and it looked as if I was going to be subpoenaed and maybe indicted.

"A couple of FBI guys came out to the house
just before the election," Coles says, "and questioned me about the Holiday Inn matter. They
wanted to talk to me about it.

"The two FBI guys told me that I was the subject of their investigation. They said I didn't have to talk to them.

" 'Hell,' I said. 'I got nothing to hide. I'll tell you exactly how it happened.' We sat down, and they asked me a lot of questions. I told them the whole story. Then they slapped me with a subpoena to appear before the grand jury.

"I went to the phone and called an attorney. I I guess I shouldn't have talked to the FBI guys; but that was around November, 1974, and I didn't *really* get indicted till the following spring."

Coles got indicted, all right.,

The Special March, 1974 Federal Grand Jury was hard at work.

Normally, a federal grand jury is made up of 23 citizens who serve for a one-month period, unless they are hearing cases that need a few extra working days to finish up. This particular grand jury, however, had already been sitting for more than a year, coming down to the Federal Building at Dearborn and Jackson two and three times a week during that whole time. This jury was identified as the Special March, 1974 Grand Jury — to distinguish it from the Regular March, 1974 Grand Jury, sitting at the same time and in the same building, but serving for only a month. On April 24, 1975, the group of citizens returned the indictment against Coles.

That April 24 date is important for understanding one of Thompson's most flagrantly unethical practices as a federal prosecutor. For it well illustrates his method of using the mass media to try to poison public opinion against his prosecutorial targets and anything those targeted people might

270

subsequently present in their defense in court. For Big Jim, standing tall in front of the television cameras and in front of the Chicago reporters, many of whom were his drinking buddies, made a statement on April 24 that in its net effect condemned Coles, called him guilty beyond question.

Thompson had no way of knowing at the time that U.S. Judge Prentice Marshall would subsequently try the case as a bench trial. None of Thompson's big cases had previously been tried as bench trials; all had been tried by juries composed of generally unsophisticated and easily confused laymen. So Thompson could safely assume that as he stood before his press cronies and the television cameras that he would get his message to at least a few future jurors in the Coles case, along with millions of other decent-minded Illinoisans who hate corruption in public officials.

What Thompson said on April 24, 1975, the same day his grand jury had returned the 7-count indictment against Coles, included this:

> *Coles had a great deal of power. The situation was that if you wanted a liquor license up there [Lake County], you had to pay off. Coles had a real club over the head of any potential liquor licensee.*

Thompson's wholly unsupported blanket condemnation — that every last liquor license in Lake County was the result of a bribe paid to Coles or one of his predecessors — is an affront to the common sense of any intelligent person, and an especially gratuitous insult to the law-abiding tavern owners in Lake County. That blanket condemnation was so fallacious that it of course could not be included in the actual indictment counts against Coles, as indeed it was not.

But the statement is even worse than unprovable nonsense. It is unethical. It is unethical by the standard of the unwritten code of decent U.S. district attorneys, who merely report the facts of an indictment to the media and to the public, with restraint and objectivity. And it is unethical by the standard of the *written* canon of ethics subscribed to by all lawyers practicing in Illinois. That canon of ethics states:

> *A lawyer ... shall not ... from the time of indictment ... make or participate in making an extra-judicial statement that a prudent lawyer would expect to be disseminated by means of public communication and that relates to:*
>
> • • •
>
> *(6) Any opinion as to the guilt or innocence of the accused, the evidence, or the merits of the case.*

But in arrogant contempt for such ethical restraints, Thompson said, and the press reported him as saying, that not only was Coles guilty; but that he, Thompson, had knowledge of many more offenses than were set forth in the indictment. This was an obviously prejudicial statement, putting charges on Coles that he was never allowed to meet and refute.

Thompson's public statement made the 5 o'clock news on Chicago's Channels 5, 7, and 9 — and was repeated on WBBM radio — on the day of Coles' indictment. The U.S. Attorney's statement was quoted in the Chicago *Sun-Times* on

April 25, the day after the indictment, and in various other papers circulated in the greater Chicago area. And his words were subsequently circulated widely in Lake county, as well as in the remainder of the Northern District of Illinois.

Thus we see in clear focus Thompson's technique of poisoning the wells of public opinion. He poisoned the public mind against Ron Coles by anticipating public suspicion and mistrust of corrupt public officials and then by almost casually "defining" Ron Coles as that sort of official.

The grand jury said that the Lake County Board had the power to enact ordinances regulating the retail sale of alcoholic liquor in the unincorporated areas of Lake County; that the ordinance provided that no one should be selling liquor at retail without first having a liquor license from the Lake County Liquor Control Commissioner; that licenses ran for a one-year period, but could be renewed; that Ronald R. Coles was both Chairman of the Lake County Board and, as such, designated the Lake County Liquor Control Commissioner; and that Coles had the power to issue or to refuse to issue available liquor licenses, as well as the power to suspend licenses, for not more than 30 days, or to revoke them for cause.

Then the indictment got down to business.

Count One described the application of Cathy Ann Petrucci for a liquor license for Marino's Lounge — an application, said the grand jury, "caused" by Marino Petrucci, her husband. Cathy got the license. Marino "intended to and did purchase alcoholic beverages and other articles made by manufacturers and producers in various states, other than the state of Illinois, and that said alcoholic beverages and other articles were to move and did move in interstate commerce from said manufacturers and producers outside the State of Illinois to Lake County, Illinois, to be used in Marino's Lounge."

Ron Coles, in other words, was charged with affecting commerce (as the term is defined in Title 18, United States Code, Section 1951), and affecting the movement of alcoholic beverages and other articles in commerce.

The government also claimed that on or about August 7, 1972, Ronald R. Coles "knowingly, wilfully, and unlawfully" committed extortion; that Coles wrongfully used his position as Lake County Liquor Control Commissioner to unlawfully obtain $400 in cash from Marino Petrucci — money which was not due Coles, his office, or Lake County — and that Marino Petrucci's consent was induced under color of official right.

Count Two of the indictment charged Ron Coles with wrongfully using his position as Lake County Liquor Control Commissioner to obtain approximately $2,500 in cash not due him, his office, or Lake County from Martin L. DeFoor, president of Cheetah Enterprises, Inc., under color of official right, between June and early August, 1972.

Count Three said that between June, 1973, and July, 1974, Ron Coles had extorted approximately $15,000 in cash from DeFoor, under color of official right.

Count Four said Coles had extorted approximately $1,500 in cash from William E. Dugan, president of Country Music Inn, Inc., between January 3 and Feb. 16, 1973, under color of official right.

Count Five dealt with the renewal of a liquor license previously issued to Budy, Inc., for the Saraha Inn. Coles was charged with wrongfully using his position as Liquor Control Commissioner to extort $300 from Joseph Budy, under color of official right. Budy, the indictment said, filed his renewal application on or about June 29, 1973, and the license was renewed about July 30, 1973. The government claimed Coles' extortion of Budy took place about July 30.

Count Six claimed that Ron Coles had filed a 1972 federal income tax return for himself and his wife that he did not believe "to be true and correct as to every material matter" — that they had reported total income of $35,862.59 that year, but had actually received substantial other income in addition. Count seven was a similar income tax charge, for 1973.

Seven counts, five extortions. But nothing about Linda's wedding. Why, then, does Coles believe his troubles started with her reception?

"I can't prove anything," he says. "I only know how I feel. But John Brooke, from the Holiday Inn where Linda had her reception, has a big, wonderful estate, I've been told, and opens it up to politicians. He had a big bash for Jim Thompson when Thompson decided to run for governor. He and Sam Skinner, who became U.S. Attorney after Thompson stepped down, both live in Lake Forest, and I've heard they go to social events together. Skinner was the prosecutor during my trial. Now the only guy I ever really leaned on in my capacity as Liquor Control Commissioner was John Brooke. Since my trial, Mr. Brooke ends up

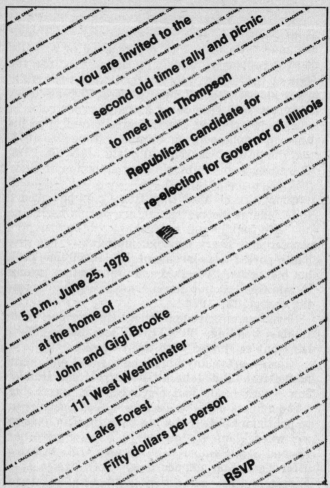

You are invited to the
second old time rally and picnic
to meet Jim Thompson
Republican candidate for
re-election for Governor of Illinois

5 p.m., June 25, 1978
at the home of
John and Gigi Brooke
111 West Westminster
Lake Forest
Fifty dollars per person
RSVP

This is the same John Brooke who evidently helped Big Jim find the downstate Republican scalp he needed: Coles.

with the bid on the new lodge at the state park in

Zion. I don't know if there is anything to it" — Coles pauses — "but it seems strange." [Brooke ultimately received from the State of Illinois the right to convert the lodge at the State Park in Zion to a Holiday Inn which he operates. Governor Thompson was an honored guest at the grand opening ceremonies.]

Coles smiles dryly, recalling the only two indictment counts he was found guilty on — the two relatively minor counts involving Budy's Sahara Inn and Dugan's Country Music Inn.

"I get convicted of extorting $800, and then Jim Thompson turns around and goes to the Kentucky Derby for free and gets all kinds of donations from guys who have contracts from the state.

"It's very clear that Thompson got all kinds of flak because he was mainly picking on Democrats. It was well known up here that his office was going to go after Republicans to take the heat off himself because he was going to run for governor.

"I said to a friend of mine, 'Why me?' "And my friend told me. 'Hey, you're a tiger. He don't want any little pussycats. He wants a guy who is high in public office. He wants the notoriety. If you were just one of the Coles running the grocery store, he wouldn't even bother with you . . .'"

The phrase *under color of official right,* appearing in all five of the Coles extortion counts, is very important for understanding extortion in its most subtle form. Legal experts still disagree about the intent of the Congressional language that put the phrase into federal law, in the 1943 Hobbs Act. The way the courts have been consistently interpreting the language for the past 35 years, in any case, amounts to this: a public official somehow uses his office to "induce" someone to pay the official for performing (or not performing) a legitimate governmental service — and to pay an amount over and above whatever stated legitimate fee attaches to that service.

The official must perform some act that causes the person he's dealing with to *believe* that this extra payment is necessary for the accomplishment of the desired governmental "act." The psychology of the interaction between the official and the person seeking the governmental action is obviously important. But just as obviously, it's a very tricky matter to subsequently judge that psychology and to determine that the public official was in fact inducing such an illegitimate payment. Part of the trickiness stems from the fact that an applicant for governmental service might sometimes have a little — or a lot — of larceny in his heart; and may therefore misinterpret what he "hears" an official say, misinterpret it to mean that the official wants a payoff in order to do his legitimate duty.

Moreover, extorting money under color of official right represents only one of several ways the law specifies that a public official might extort valuable property from an applicant for government service. Another method of official extortion, as defined by Title 18, U.S.C. Section 1951, is the wrongful use of actual or threatened force.

While finding Ron Coles not guilty of the bulk of the charges on which he was indicted, Judge Prentice Marshall also made an interpretation of the color-of-official-right phrase that went against Coles in the Budy and Dugan matters. Judge Marshall decided that Coles did not threaten to misuse his power as Lake County Liquor Control Commissioner and that he did not even ask Budy and Dugan for money, which Coles nonetheless took and subsequently used for political purposes in a reelection campaign. But Judge Marshall said that Coles did not *have* to ask for the $800 in campaign contributions in order to be guilty of extorting under color of official right.

All that needs to be established, according to Marshall, is that the payment be "induced" by the alleged extortioner — induced by some deliberate act that causes or precipitates the payment. The Judge found no compelling reason to believe that all the conditions for this type of extortion were present in three of the government's charges that Coles extorted tavern owners. But he had reason to believe that such conditions were present when Coles took the two small campaign contributions from Budy and Dugan.

The impartial observer need not conclude that Coles was unfairly treated in the two findings against him, although it is hard to see malice in actions that netted his campaign a grand total of $800 and in a defendant who may himself have been confused by a very tricky law and who did in any case apologize publicly for his action and pay back the $800 to his "bribers."

But the impartial observer should also have cause to ponder Coles' basis for wondering what makes his illegitimate actions any different from the various campaign contributions Governor James Thompson has received from state contractors. Ron Coles does not accuse the Governor of "causing or precipitating" those campaign and other contributions (the Kentucky Derby "freebie," for example) "under color of official right;"

but Coles can be excused, certainly, for wondering just who might really have been doing the "inducing" in those matters. Surely the principle is the same.

Games the government plays — that's how Coles himself remembers his pre-trial period. "They call you all the way down to Chicago, and you sit there for hours. Then they tell you, well we can't get to you today — go home. They haul you back down again, and they take it all in bits and pieces. By then, you're so tired of coming down there and telling your story that you'd agree to anything," says Coles.

"I have very little use for my government, any more.

"I've learned that they are not for us. They did not want to listen to anything good. I had people call me and tell me — people the government wanted to talk to — that said the government absolutely shut them off if they started saying anything good about me. The government didn't want to hear that. They said to one guy, 'Look — do you know anything bad about Mr. Coles? We're not here to hear the good things. We want to know anything bad about him.'

"Then you're called before the grand jury.

"Do you know what you feel like up there, before the grand jury? Anybody would indict me, the way they act. My God! The jury only hears what they want them to hear!

"Now I'm a fearful person," Coles says. "I never found anything in life before that I had to fear, to the point of being nervous, but I'll tell you, after a couple weeks and months of this, you just get to feeling terrible!

"My wife and I lived in fear. It got so that I wouldn't want anybody to come near me, because on some occasions when guys did call me up, they were subpoenaed, or the feds came out to talk to them.

"We were being watched and followed. One day, I led the guys I thought were following me into a deadend driveway. They stood there, looking at me . . . they didn't know what the hell to do with themselves. A woman said to them. 'What are you doing in my driveway?' I had led them into a driveway — I knew I could screw them up, because I knew I was being followed.

"We were certain our phone was tapped. George Collins, my lawyer, called me one day and said, 'I have proof that they have been given permission to use electronic surveillance on you. Be careful. Don't talk to anybody about anything! Don't say anything about anybody!'

"I told him, 'George, I haven't talked to anybody or said anything since this whole damn business started!'

"You lead an awfully lonely existence. You almost get to the point where you crawl into a shell, and it's very hard to come out."

In finding Coles not guilty of Count One, the alleged extortion of $400 from Marino Petrucci, Judge Marshall said the facts of the allegation "paint for me the picture of a man [Petrucci] who became totally frustrated in his efforts [to secure a liquor license] and that frustration was not occasioned in any way in my opinion by any misconduct or wrongful conduct on the part of Mr. Coles or his staff; and that as a result of that frustration, an animosity developed on the part of Mr.

Petrucci to such a degree that I cannot say that I am persuaded by his testimony beyond a reasonable doubt as to Mr. Coles' guilt under Count One of the indictment."

Judge Marshall also found Coles not guilty of Counts Two and Three, the two alleged extortions of the owners of a nudie bar called the Cheetah II. These were the allegations, remember, that Thompson and Skinner wanted so badly to establish that they even tried to immunize one of the bar owners from post-trial liquor license investigations by the State of Illinois. The background of the two counts is interesting.

Martin L. DeFoor and his partner, William Hagood, owned a club called Cheetah I in Kenosha, Wisconsin, a club that opened in August, 1970. By January, 1971, they began to feature nude dancing. They went into a local court and were granted an injunction prohibiting the city of Kenosha from enforcing an ordinance that Kenosha had against nude dancing. By Spring 1972, they had lost their injunction and could no longer feature nude dancing. The pair decided to relocate the Cheetah, and began looking for a location in Lake County, Illinois. DeFoor called Jerome F. Schuetz, Chief Deputy Sheriff for Lake County, whom he had known for 15 years, who told him he'd have to get a Lake County liquor license. At Schuetz's suggestion, DeFoor went to Coles' home.

"I pulled into the driveway about four o'clock," DeFoor testified, "and Mr. Coles came out to meet me and invited me to come in. I told Mr. Coles I would like to open a club in Lake County, and wondered what his feelings were, and how I would go about obtaining a liquor license.

"He said that he had heard that I had a nude club in Kenosha, and asked me what kind of club I planned to have in Lake County," DeFoor said.

"I told him that I had done some research with my attorney in Lake County, and I found they had no ordinance against it. But we found that in Kenosha, Wisconsin, even under a federal injunction, we got a hell of a lot of harassment from the police department and from the city council. I wondered if I could expect that, or would he merely go by the law, as such.

"I pointed out to him that in Wisconsin, we had operated under an injunction," DeFoor continued, "and if necessary, we would attempt to do the same thing in Lake County.

"At that point," DeFoors recalled, "Coles became rather angry. I believe his comment was that I could stick the injunction up my ass if I had that type of attitude in coming to Lake County.

"Coles said that even though he realized there was no law against it at the moment, he nevertheless would make a decision on whether I would have a license or whether I wouldn't. He was in charge of the issuance of liquor licenses at that time, and he just didn't like my attitude on coming in, telling him what I was going to do, or something to that effect.

"Mr Coles questioned me a little further on my type of operation. I think he wanted to know if I planned to have any prostitution or drink solicitation or dope or operate after hours or do anything that might be illegal," DeFoor said.

"And when I assured him that I didn't plan any of these things, he said, 'Well, then, I see nothing wrong with it. Go ahead and try to find your location, and as soon as you do that, well, then, get back to me.'

DeFoor met with Schuetz a day or two later to discuss the liquor license for his club. "Schuetz told me," he said, "the license would cost me $3,500. He said Mr. Coles wanted the money. I got a bit angry over it because I knew the face value of the license was only a thousand dollars, and I felt it was a very unreasonable figure to have a pay to get the license. Schuetz told me that he had nothing to do with it, that he wasn't getting a penny out of it, and basically that I could take it or leave it. A couple days later, Schuetz told me, 'Well, hell, why don't you just give me $2,500 and I am sure that he will take it."

DeFoor testified that the next day he withdrew $2,500 from his safe deposit box at a Kenosha bank, phoned Schuetz, and arranged to meet him that night to give him the money. So Schuetz got DeFoor's $2,500 and, as Judge Marshall would later say, very likely put it in his own pocket and then lied to DeFoor that he had transmitted the bribe to Ron Coles.

"The next step in getting the license was going to the Sheriff's Department in Lake County, filling out the forms, being fingerprinted, and applying for a liquor license," DeFoor testified. "A week later, Schuetz called me to tell me that my prints and everything had checked out. He said the next step in getting a liquor license was to appear before the County Board, and that I should see Ron Coles before I went up there.

"Coles and I met in his kitchen," testified De-Foor, who said that Coles had told him and his partner to come before the Board for a formal hearing.

"He said, 'There are certain questions that I will have to ask you at the meeting,' DeFoor testified. 'One of them will be whether you intend to have nude dancing in Lake County or not.' He said, 'Well, you can't say you are going to have nude dancing. I don't think that would go over very big.' So I said I won't. [Coles disputes this testimony.]

"A couple of days later, my partner and I drove down from Kenosha for the license hearing. I believe there were three other Board members, an attorney, and a secretary. Coles gave me a book on the laws regarding a liquor license holder," DeFoor said, "and pointed out to me that he would not tolerate being open after hours, serving minors, prostitution, dope, or anything else that might be illegal.

"At the conclusion of the meeting, I wrote out a check for a thousand dollars for my liquor license and submitted it along with my application. I was told that the license would be forthcoming within a few days. Approximately a week later, I received the license."

The Cheetah II opened for business on August 25, 1972. It was located in Half Day, Illinois.

Despite DeFoor's promise, by October, 1972, the Cheetah featured totally nude entertainment. And that led to problems.

By December 5, 1972, a decision in a case involved nude dancing (California vs. Larue) came down. Jack Hoogasian, the State's Attorney of Lake County, told the press he now had the tools to work with to eliminate nude dancing. By February 13, 1973, an antinude dancing ordinance strongly promoted by Ron Coles was passed by the Lake County Board, and by February 28, about two weeks later, the lawsuit the Cheetah II had filed was heard, and the club had injunctive relief — relief against the Cheetah's being deprived of the right to sell liquor at retail during the time an appeal was pending, and the right to be able to feature nude entertainment without being stopped.

Eventually, the Appellate Court decided against the Cheetah II. After they lost in that court, they petitioned for rehearing, and then petitioned the Supreme Court for leave to appeal. During that entire procedure they stayed open.

By June, 1973, however, according to DeFoor's testimony, he had not received his application for the renewal of his liquor license. "I called Jerry Schuetz on the phone, and asked him if he had any idea why," DeFoor said. "A couple days later, he called me and told me to talk with Ron Coles about the matter. I met with Coles in the kitchen of his home, and asked him why the renewal application had not been mailed to me. I believe his reply was something to the effect that the Cheetah II was causing him a great deal of concern, that he had had a lot of complaints on it, a lot of heat, a lot of aggravation, a lot of adverse publicity.

"I don't know whether I started this conversation, or whether he did, but at any rate, I expressed the fact that I needed my license, it was my only source of income, it was my livelihood, and it meant a great deal to me to be able to remain open. And further in our conversation, I believe he asked me how much was it worth to

me to remain open, *or perhaps I asked him* — I don't recall the conversation exactly.

"But I know that at that meeting, we determined that I would give him a thousand dollars a month if he would issue my license for renewal, and he told me he would mail my application to me for me to send my check in, and the license would be forthcoming. We agreed that as soon as I was in receipt of the license, why, at that time, then I would begin to pay him a thousand dollars a month in advance, around the first of each month," DeFoor said. He also said he'd paid Coles a total of $15,000 to get the Cheetah II's liquor license renewed.

Where did the money come from?

Earlier, DeFoor had testified that when he took $2,500 from his safety deposit box, the source of the money was from the Cheetah I door receipts that he skimmed.

"We felt like we had to get some money together quickly in order to try to get into some other type of business, when our nude dancing ended, and we were in a 50-per cent tax bracket. We felt like it would be to our advantage not to report it so that we could have the entire money, rather than pay half of it to the Government," DeFoor said. "The skimmed money — well, we split it — but it went into our safety deposit box for us in the future for trying to get into another business.

"We had a daily cash report which was accurate, both with the door receipts and the bar receipts. But in order to be able to accurately check our cash registers on bar sales, we didn't bother with any of that money. On the other hand, the money that came through the door was strictly a cash transaction. On our daily cash report, I would use the true figure. At the end of the week, we would determine what moneys we had over and above our expenses, and we would skim from it. At that point, then, I would transfer the false figures to a ledger sheet which I turned in to my book-keeper, and then destroy the daily cash reports," DeFoor testified. He said the ledger sheets he turned over to the bookkeeper 'did not reflect the skimmed money. Skimming operations on the Cheetah II, according to DeFoor, began from prac-tically the very day we opened," and ended "ap-proximately two years later, when — I think, at the time that I was supoened to come down here to see the government," I kept a daily cash report merely to show to my partner the actual amount that we took in, and then the part that we were skimming off the top."

"Did you ever pay any income tax on the moneys you skimmed?" asked government attorney Ann C. Tighe.

"No, I didn't," DeFoor replied.

Like Schuetz, DeFoor was an immunized wit-ness, but immunized with an important difference. He and Bill Hagood, his partner in Cheetah opera-tions, not only had a grant of immunity for any criminal proceedings, but also a grant which pro-vided that their testimony could not be used against them in any liquor license proceedings after the trial.

Compare that extraordinary protection against the crimes DeFoor himself admitted, under oath, at the Coles trial. He testified that he had skim-med — both from the Cheetah I and Cheetah II operations — "all totaled, possibly in a two-and-a-half-year period, *perhaps $100,000.*" DeFoor also admitted using "half the skimmed money to pay certain officials and the other half . . . for our own personal use, which basically was for expenses."

DeFoor's immunity grant, issued at the request of Thompson's First Assistant, Sam Skinner, surfaced importantly in the closing arguments of the Coles Trial. U.S. Assistant Attorney Michael O'Brien discussed that grant with Judge Marshall.

"By coming in as he did," O'Brien said, "DeFoor did nothing but enhance his own civil tax liability. If you were to read the disclosure of inducements, you would see that we told the IRS to hold off because of a misunderstanding on DeFoor and his attorney's part of what we had told them about that, but by testifying in the courtroom, what he says will be used against him for civil tax proceedings.

"He and his attorney," O'Brien continued, "have a reasonable understanding of the law, which is that DeFoor will pay income tax on the dollars he paid to Mr. Coles. That is reasonable. The IRS will go after him for that money. I have every reason to think they will collect that. DeFoor is going to pay taxes on those dollars."

Judge Marshall countered promptly.

"He is not going to be prosecuted, though, for income tax evasion. He is not going to be prosecuted for the use of interstate facilities in the commission of a crime, namely, bribery. He is not going to be prosecuted for violating the Mann Act. He is not going to be prosecuted for anything."

"Right," O'Brien answered.

"And he is probably guilty of all of them," Judge Marshall said.

"Right," **O'Brien said,** *"but on the basis of his*

testimony, could he be convicted?"

"Not the Mann Act," Judge Marshall answered. "Interstate transportation and furtherance of a crime, he could. Income tax evasion, he could."

"Not the Mann Act," said O'Brien. "Then I agree with you."

What an extraordinary piece of cynicism those statements by Attorney O'Brien represent! A federal judge has just told him that his sleazy immunized witness against Coles is probably guilty of massive income tax cheating, of using interstate facilities for bribery also on a massive scale, and of peddling female flesh as if it were a dirty rag. And what does this government attorney say in response? "Right."

And what is his countering "argument" to the Judge, who has just brought to his attention important matters involving truth and goodness and justice? That even though he knows the Judge is correct about DeFoor's crimes, it doesn't make any difference — because DeFoor is immunized against incriminating himself, and because De-Foor *therefore* can't be convicted of any of these violations.

So here we can see O'Brien and his superiors, Thompson and Skinner, once again demonstrating their cynical disregard of what the role of the federal prosecutor is supposed to be. In their zeal to destroy high-profile public figures — at least some of whom deserved to be indicted and possibly convicted — Thompson's people demonstrated time and again that they would not be restrained by any sense of ethics or fair play or the impartial wish to see justice done. Perhaps they had never read the words of former Solicitor General of the United States Simon E. Sobeloff, who said the main job of the federal prosecutor is that of an advocate . . .

> *but an advocate for a client whose business is not merely to prevail in the instant case. My client's chief business is not to achieve victory but to establish justice.*

Justice does not win in the courts when illicit means are used even to gain legitimate ends. It is one thing to use the immunity doctrine with restraint in order to convict a corrupt public official; but it is quite another to "wink and giggle," as former U.S. Attorney Tom Foran puts it in another context, at the self-admitted felonies of your tainted immunized witness — and to dare a federal judge, in effect, to try to get that tainted witness convicted after you have immunized him. That is not wanting justice to be done. It is not even caring whether or not justice is done. Attorney Michael O'Brien showed in those remarks about DeFoor's massive admitted crimes a woeful lack of ethical sense, the same lack displayed in prosecution after prosecution by the Thompson-Skinner office.

Earlier in the trial, another key government-immunized witness, Jerome Schuetz testified that he had extorted other people—Paul Mueller from Birchwood Builders; Ronald Larson, a trucking contractor in North Chicago; and Gene Marsh, a lie detector operator in Waukegan. Plus others, whose names he couldn't recall at the moment. Schuetz also testified that in the Mueller, Larson, and Marsh extortions Ron Coles had nothing to do with them, did not know Schuetz was extorting money, and was not involved in any way.

Schuetz admitted under oath that he had collected more than $20,000 from his self-confessed extortion activities.

He also testified that none of these payments had been reported on his income tax returns, but he'd disclosed the payments to the government during the course of the Coles investigation; and that the immunity grant he had been given included any criminal income tax liability for these payments, as well as those he testified to with respect to Ron Coles.

When defendant Ron Coles took the stand, he testified about his dealings with DeFoor. "In 1974," Coles said, "I was faced with a primary, and a general election in November. Eventually I got through to DeFoor. I told him I would like to talk to him. He wanted to know about what. And I told him: he had made an offer to help me, and I wanted to talk to him about it. We met in the early morning or early afternoon at the coffee shop right across the street from the Township Office," Coles continued, "and I asked him. 'Does the offer still stand to help me in my campaign?'"

The offer still stood, apparently, because Coles testified under oath that a couple of weeks later DeFoor gave him a $2,000 campaign contribution.

"And other than that $2,000, did you ever receive any money from Mark DeFoor?" Coles' attorney George Collins asked him.

"No, sir," Coles answered under oath.

"Other than responding and making the phone call you stated, did you ever ask DeFoor for anything?"

"Just that," Coles said.

Testimony continued in relation to the Cheetah II operation. Jack Hoogasian, State's Attorney of

Lake County, described the county ordinance against nude dancing, and the legal difficulties it caused for the Cheetah II. Hoogasian also told of a phone call he'd received from Samuel Skinner, the United States Attorney at the time of Coles' trial, but First Assistant to James Thompson at the time of the phone call. Skinner is a resident of Lake Forest in Lake County.

"We discussed the immunity factor" Hoogasian testified, "and I said, 'Well, for too long, Cheetah II had been operating contrary to law, and for too long we have been looking for respective legal avenues to close Cheetah II and put them out of business.'

"And since we had the allegation of bribery through his statements to the U.S. Government, I told Sam I would request a hearing. Sam then indicated that he wanted me to have knowledge of the fact that DeFoor had federal immunity — and that a Mr. James Shellow, a lawyer for DeFoor, had been trying to contact me. He asked me to consider these facts for whatever value I deemed necessary."

Cole's attorney, George Collins, later asked Hoogasian: "Have you ever had a call from Mr. Skinner about any other liquor license holder in Lake County, other than the Cheetah II?"

"No, sir," said Hoogasian. This response by the chief prosecutor of Lake County came after the Court overruled a government objection and determined that Skinner's unusual attempt to influence Hoogasian in behalf of DeFoor was indeed admissable.

Of all the testimony concerning Ron Coles allegedly extorting money from the owners of the Cheetah II, Judge Marshall said this at the end of the trial:

There are some corroborative circumstances, but in the main, the government's case, it seems to me, stands or falls on the testimony of Martin DeFoor and Jerome Schuetz. Both of these men were granted extraordinary use immunity by the government in order to induce them or to compel them to testify against Mr. Coles.

I shan't repeat here Mr. DeFoor's general background and evident purpose in life. In addition to running his tavern, Cheetah II, he also runs a so-called talent agency through which, according to his own testimony, literally hundreds of nude dancers have passed during the period in question.

Accepting his testimony in regard to his alleged transactions with Mr. Schuetz, it's apparent that he committed crimes and used interstate facilities in connection therewith. By his own admission, he grossly evaded income taxes in connection with his Kenosha Cheetah I operation, and his Lake County Cheetah II operation. For all of these things, he was granted immunity.

Schuetz, on the other hand, a confessed extortionist, is Chief Deputy Sheriff of one of the largest counties in the state, a metropolitan county in many respects of the word. He admitted that extortion was a day-to-day thing with him. He extorted tavern owners. He extorted in respect to zoning transactions.

He even extorted from the Moose Club in respect to their bingo games.

Mr. Coles took the stand. He was a credible witness. He denied receiving the payments from DeFoor. DeFoor's testimony, so far as I am concerned, is essentially uncorroborated, and I cannot credit him against Coles beyond a reasonable doubt.

Insofar as the $2,500 is concerned, Mr. Schuetz comes into play. He is not only the person that I have heretofore described, but the record shows that he is a duplicitous extortionist . . . I come away with the same feelings with repect to Mr. Schuetz as I did Mr. DeFoor.

You put money in Mr. Schuetz's hands, and you better have him under constant surveillance if you want to know what's going to happen or what did happen with the money. And when he says, as he did, that he was the courier of $2,500 from DeFoor to Coles, I cannot say that I am not persuaded — or that I am persuaded beyond a reasonable doubt that that is what occurred to the money. I think it is just as likely that Schuetz pocketed it.

During his lengthy summary of the weakness of the government case against Coles in the Cheetah II matters — a weakness based on the slimy activities DeFoor and Schuetz admitted to, and the consequent flimsy credibility of their testimony against Coles — Judge Marshall also touched on the way the Thompson office selected its prosecutorial targets. The Judge found no reason to quarrel with the selection of Ron Coles, although he found many reasons to praise in his concluding remarks the civic work Coles had done; and he found no reason to dispute the government's choice to grant extraordinary immunity and extraordinary rewards to the likes of DeFoor and Schuetz, although he flayed those two men in his final remarks.

But if Judge Marshall had enough to do in just sorting out the rights and wrongs of the government's actions against Ron Coles, it is now necessary to examine the values of a prosecutor's office that would give a total "pass" on criminal charges to a possible violator of the Mann Act and a large-scale tax cheat, on the one hand; and on the other to a self-confessed extortionist in the highest ranks of Lake County police work.

For even if Ron Coles used poor judgment in accepting campaign contributions from two tavern operators, how does that offense compare against the sexual pandering and exploitation that made Martin DeFoor personally wealthy? How does it compare to the activities of a deputy sheriff who admits he is a corrupt, contemptible police officer? And what do those comparisons say about Jim Thompson's sense of ethical values in his choice of prosecutorial targets?

They say his ethical sense is highly questionable at best, and perhaps even missing.

Listen to what the late United States Supreme Court Justice Robert H. Jackson, who presided at the Nurenburg trials of the Nazi war criminals after World War II, once said about what he considered the greatest potential abuse of the federal prosecutor's office:

If the prosecutor is obliged to choose his

> *cases, it follows that he can choose his*
> *defendants. Therein is the most danger-*
> *ous power of the prosecutor: that he will*
> *pick people that he thinks he should get,*
> *rather than pick cases that need to be*
> *prosecuted.*

Ron Coles isn't the only person who thinks Thompson needed a downstate suburban Republican target at the precise point in Thompson's political career when Coles' possible offenses surfaced. And it only stands to reason that Coles, a top official of a key Republican county, was a juicy prize for a prosecutor whose political ambitions had changed from Mayor of Chicago to Governor of Illinois.

Others who use the king's English just as well as Justice Jackson, but whose style is less scholarly and more gutsy, know that Jackson was right in believing that a federal prosecutor in the United States can hang just about anybody on earth. Here, for example, is what the street-wise and eloquent Tom Foran says about the power of an office he himself once held and with credit:

> *Nobody alive's a striped-ass saint, and if*
> *a federal prosecutor decides you're a bad*
> *guy and wants to get you, he's gonna get*
> *you. No question about it.*

And the way that federal prosecutor goes about getting anybody he wants to get, returning to the scholarly words of the late Justice Jackson,

> *is not a question of discovering the com-*
> *mission of a crime and then looking for*
> *the man who has committed it; it is a*
> *question of picking the man and then*

> *searching the law books, or putting in-*
> *vestigators to work, to pin some offense*
> *on him. It is in this realm — in which*
> *the prosecutor picks some person whom*
> *he dislikes or desires to embarrass, or*
> *selects some group of unpopular persons*
> *and then looks for an offense, that the*
> *greatest danger of abuse of prosecuting*
> *power lies.*

Ron Coles, then, is guilty — not of everything the government charged, but of extorting a total of $800 from William E. Dugan and Joseph Budy. The conviction comes March 26, 1976; sentencing by Judge Prentice H. Marshall comes nearly three months later. Judge Marshall puts Coles on three years' probation, after praising him as "a man who has struggled very hard to serve his people well.

"I do not mean to minimize the two transactions upon which Mr. Coles has been convicted," Marshall says, noting that Coles "has made a couple of very serious mistakes." But he points out that only four charges of extortion have been presented by the government — and that two of them had been dismissed at the end of the trial.

"There may be some who say that I have just seen the tip of the iceberg," Judge Marshall says; "but I do not think that is the case."

The judge mentions the fact that Coles had been a full-time public official, who had not engaged in any private business while in office. "It is rather uncommon today for a man of public office to stand in front of a judge and say that he had no private business," Marshall notes. "In my experience, a number of public officials have in some subtle way gone into this business and that business just happens to prosper while he is in office."

Coles, meanwhile, had given the $800 back to Dugan and Budy. At sentencing, he tells the judge, "I can't blame anyone but myself. But the word extortion . . . I never extorted anyone in my life. I just wish a different word could be used.

"I have been paid well as a public servant, but I gave the public every dollar's worth of my salary. I do apologize."

No longer is Ron Coles a member of the Lake County Board, or the township supervisor of Lake Villa. Those offices are declared vacant, when Coles is sentenced.

Ron Coles is still bitter about the conviction — not only about the trial and its outcome, but also about Jim Thompson.

"Take Thompson himself," Coles said, in an interview. "He took about $2 million in campaign contributions, a lot of it from people who expect favors. That's where the mystery of my conviction comes in. What's the real difference?

"People tell me, 'Be happy, Ron, you're on probation and out of the penitentiary.' But that's not the way I feel," Coles said.

George Collins, Coles' attorney, is also unhappy. "This is very depressing to me," he says. "What it means is that if a political officer takes a dime or any gift from a person or persons doing business with that office, he has committed a crime, regardless of whether it was solicited," Collins tells the Waukegan *News Sun*.

Meanwhile, things are going far better for Martin L. DeFoor, immunized owner of Cheetah II. He by this time is running Cheetah III in Florida, while his attorney in Illinois is trying to fend off post-trial actions to close Cheetah II by the Lake County Liquor Control Commission and the Illinois Liquor Control Commission.

Cheetah's attorney argues that "in accordance with the mandate of the United States District Court and in reliance on discussions with representatives of the U.S. Attorney's office about the scope of the immunity order, Martin L. DeFoor gave the testimony compelled by the immunity order. The use of this testimony in a liquor license proceeding in violation of the specific terms of the immunity order constitutes a denial of DeFoor's right to due process of law. The immunity which has been granted is co-extensive with the privilege against self- incrimination."

Whose authority is greater — federal or state?

The Illinois Liquor Commission argues that Congress has limited the scope of immunity to simply prohibit federal and state prosecutors from later on using immunized testimony against the witness in a criminal case.

"In addition to going beyond statutory authority,"the state Commission continues, "the (immunity) order in question violates the 10th Amendment of the United States Constitution" — an amendment which reserves powers for the states that have not specifically given to the federal government. The Commission continued:

> The general power to prohibit or regulate the sale of intoxicating liquors rests in the police power of the state. In purporting to grant the witness immunity with respect to liquor license proceedings, the Federal government has usurped power reserved to the state of Illinois.

Thus, not only does the federal court lack statutory authority to enter such an order, but the order is, on its face, unconstitutional and a violation of the 10th Amendment.

After a lengthy legal fight, Cheetah II finally lost its liquor license although the owners maintained to the end that the immunity granted protected their license from revocation.

Nor was this any skin off Thompson's back. While the sleazy witness he'd immunized was now off and running in Florida, Big Jim himself was off and running for the Illinois governorship. He'd picked Ron Coles as one of his last political targets before moving on to his higher political ambitions. And even though Thompson's tactics had been scathingly criticized by the same federal court judge who convicted Coles of two minor counts of extortion, Big Jim had at last got himself a downstate Republican scalp.

Thompson had done to Coles what former U.S. Attorney Tom Foran says *any* federal prosecutor can do to *anybody alive,* saints being very rare. And it seems just as clear, all things considered, that Thompson got Coles in the exact manner described by the late Justice Jackson in the context of the abusive potential of a federal prosecutor's power — by picking his man, then searching the law books, then putting his investigators to work, then immunizing crooked businessmen and police officers, and finally pinning some offense on Coles.

EPILOGUE

Most who read this book understandably will be troubled by it. It does not leave one with good or reassuring feelings. It raises unsettling questions of gravest import in a free society. It raises serious doubts about one of the fundamental institutions of our society, and shows how easily it can be perverted by men of overwhelming personal ambition and flexible scruples.

This is not a book about some ancient civilization, buried under layers of historical dust. It is as recent as Watergate. It is now, and it is the future. It is a convincing indictment of a U. S. Attorney become Governor of a major state, a powerful figure in American politics by virtue of that high office.

It is remote (but not impossible) that James R. Thompson will be summoned before the bar of justice and compelled, as were his victims, to prove his innocence.

For this book suggests that *no less than reasonable doubt* exists in each of the cases discussed here.

There can be little doubt that the prosecutors, Thompson and Skinner and their anointed associates, were far more interested in their personal stakes than in the rights of defendants and the ends of justice.

It may well be that laws were violated and criminal acts committed by Thompson and his prosecutorial force, but those are matters which can be resolved only by a grand jury hearing evidence presented by an unbiased special prosecutor, and ultimately a trial jury.

At the minimum, this book demonstrates conclusively that James R. Thompson as U.S. Attorney — and certain of his closest associates — violated their solemn oaths.

For the federal prosecutor's obligation, stated with such force and nobility by the former Solicitor General of the United States, Judge Simon E. Sobeloff, is clear:

> *The prosecutor is not a neutral, he is an advocate, but an advocate for a client whose business is not to achieve victory but to establish justice.*

APPENDIX

This Appendix contains observations and statements by eminent jurists and legal scholars and experienced courtroom attorneys which serve to place in perspective the text of **THE THOMPSON INDICTMENT,** *as well as the actions and tactics of the federal prosecutors during the Thompson tenure as U.S. Attorney in the Northern District of Illinois.*

Appendix I

ELIMINATE THE GRAND JURY

BY

JUDGE WILLIAM J. CAMPBELL

OF THE

UNITED STATES DISTRICT COURT

NORTHERN DISTRICT OF ILLINOIS

BEFORE

THE CHICAGO CHAPTER OF THE FEDERAL BAR ASSOCIATION

THE PALMER HOUSE

CHICAGO

MAY 17, 1978

(*Reprinted with the permission of U.S. District Judge Campbell*)

As a former U.S. Attorney of this district, may I clarify at the outset that I do not propose any restrictions upon the power or authority of the prosecutor. Quite the contrary, I would increase both. My proposition is simple although not simplistic. It is this:

> *The grand jury should be abolished and its powers vested in the prosecutor. Prosecution should be commenced upon as information filed by the prosecuting official and followed by a probable cause hearing before a judicial officer, such as a magistrate, who would determine whether there is sufficient evidence to permit the prosecution to continue.*

Abolition of the grand jury is not a revolutionary idea. In England, from whom we borrowed this noble institutios of the past, the grand jury was abolished in 1933. Many of our own states, including Illinois, have to a greater or lesser degree followed suit.

Although the early history of the grand jury is clouded, the ancestor of our present-day inquest made its first appearance in England when King Henry II summoned laymen to the Assize of Clarendon to ferret out crimes in their locale and inform the Crown.

Although it did not specifically refer to any grand inquest, the famed Magna Carta — wrested from King John at Runnymede by his barons on June 15, 1215 — is frequently credited with having started the process which we know as the grand jury. The procedure, however, remained completely and absolutely within the control of the Crown — and was generally public in the nature of its hearings.

The concept of the grand jury as a body free from royal influence did not appear until 1681 during the famed Earl of Shaftesbury's case. In that case, the jury insisted on secrecy and later refused to indict despite extreme pressure from the Attorney General. With this advent of secrecy in its proceedings, this council of laymen soon developed into a guardian of individual rights, standing between the prosecutor and the accused and protecting the citizen from unfounded accusation of crime.

It was this type of grand jury that was transported to our continent by the early colonists; and it was preserved, after independence, through the Fifth Amendment to the Constitution of the United States. It thus became entrenched in our judicial heritage despite many early criticisms that it was not necessary to protect individuals from governmental oppression in a country with a representative form of government. The Supreme Court, for obvious constitutional reasons, has consistently resisted any efforts to limit the broad powers of this body in the federal field.

The grand jury is an arm of the court. Its responsibilities are essentially threefold: (1) the investigation of crimes or "public offenses" committed within the boundaries of its jurisdiction; (2) the identification of persons suspected of having committed the offenses, and the related determination of whether there is probable cause to charge a person with an offense; and (3) the publication of its findings to the court by way of an indictment, presentment, or report.

Although grand jury proceedings are technically independent, the prosecutor actually conducts the proceedings. The scope of the grand jury's inquiry, although unlimited in theory, is therefore subject to the skillful control and direction of the prosecutor. So also is its result limited by its inability in the federal system to return an indictment without the prosecutor's written approval.

In my 40 years of judicial experience, which includes 12 years as Chief Judge and a term as United States Attorney, there has not been a single criminal investigation begun by a grand jury.

THE THOMPSON INDICTMENT

If the independence of the grand jury constitutes the rationale for the grand jury clause of the Fifth Amendment to the Constitution — as the Supreme Court has so frequently suggested — then I respectfully submit that, as we did with our unfortunate "noble experiment" concerning prohibition, we should eliminate by constitutional amendment the requirement of grand jury indictment. In response to the exigencies of modern society,

> the grand jury has long ceased to function as an agency independent from prosecutorial influence. It is today but an alter ego of the prosecutor. It has abandoned its claim to be a bulwark of democracy. Indeed, it is that very pretension that has led some to suggest that the grand jury has become instead the bulwark of prosecutorial immunity, encouraging abuses by permitting the prosecutor to do his work with complete anonymity.

The grand jury has become in effect an administrative agency, executing in secrecy and with unlimited discretionary power, the policies — also determined in secret — of law-enforcement officers. And those same law-enforcement officers continue to maintain the fiction that the grand jury is a free autonomous body impartially ferreting out objective truth. This proposition is simply no longer believable.

The shocking number and type of grand jury abuses that recently caused the American Bar Association to consider 27 different reform measures and adopt 25, have also caused other new voices to speak out in protest. A recent Wall Street Journal article, for example, chronicles the numerous criticisms made of the grand jury system. Many of these abuses are now being articulated by the corporate lawyers of America, such as the counsel for General Motors and International Paper Company. No longer are the critics of our archaic grand jury system confined to the poor or the politically oppressed; the abuses of the grand jury now reach across all color and class divisions.

Many of the far-reaching grand jury abuses are discussed in a newly published book, *The Grand Jury: An Institution On Trial*, written by United States District Court Judge Marvin Frankel and former Assistant U.S. Attorney Gary Naftalis.

As I stated at the outset, I favor a system which would bring theory into line with reality by placing the responsibility for initiating criminal prosecutions where it in fact already exists — with the prosecuting attorney. Prosecutions should be commenced upon the filing of an information signed by the prosecutor, and be followed by a probable cause hearing before a judicial officer who would determine whether there is sufficient evidence to allow the prosecution to continue to trial. A most salutary result of such a process would be the removal of the anonymity presently enshrouds the exercise of prosecutorial discretion through the vehicle of the grand jury.

My suggestion would encompass the transfer to the prosecutor of all powers which currently belong to the grand jury. Thus for example, the subpoena power would be lodged with the prosecuting officer. Indeed, most federal regulatory agencies already possess subpoena power. Witnesses could be examined under oath as well as in secret, their testimony being recorded by an official court reporter. Testimony would thus be preserved for use at trial, if necessary. Authority to extend immunity from prosecution in exchange for testimony would also be given the prosecuting attorney. Federal prosecutors already enjoy to a degree such authority under the Omnibus Crime Act.

Upon reaching a determination that a prosecution should be initiated, the prosecutor would then file a criminal information with the court in much the same fashion as indictments are now presented. A hearing to determine whether there is probable cause to proceed with the prosecution would then be scheduled. The hearing would be conducted before a judicial officer, the magistrate. I suggest that the hearing be adversary in nature, with the accused given the right to appear with counsel, cross-examine the prosecution's witnesses and present evidence in his own behalf.

The benefits which would accrue from the system which I have described seem to me to be unlimited. The determination of whether a citizen would be required to answer criminal charges brought against him would be made by a member of the judiciary.

> *The sham of the "autonomous" grand jury would be discarded in favor of a judgment made by one trained and skilled in the law, and more importantly not subject to the direction and control of the prosecuting agency.*

True independence would be restored, thereby revitalizing the concept that a citizen should be protected against unfounded accusation of crime, whatever its source.

Investigative powers so necessary to the ordinary maintenance of a peaceful society would not be curtailed. They would simply be lodged with the prosecuting authority, where their *de facto* exercise has already come to reside. Constitutional guarantees would not be diluted in the slightest. Judges would remain available to entertain motions seeking to prevent any over-reaching by prosecutors. A civil analogue to such a procedure is the protective order now issued in the context of discovery disputes. Also, a transcript of the prosecutor's investigative proceedings would always be available for review by the judge.

The advantages which some contend flow from the secret nature of grand jury proceedings would also be preserved under the system I propose. Although this secrecy has been the subject of well-intended criticism in recent years, no one can question that in some cases it has its benefits, during the investigatory phase of a prosecution. It is said to encourage disclosure by witnesses who have information concerning the commission of a crime, to prevent outside influences from contaminating the investigation, to prevent the accused from fleeing prior to being charged, to limit subordnation of perjury, and to protect the innocent from the harm that might be visited upon them by disclosure of an investigation not leading to a formal charge.

Another important contribution which would result from the system I advocate would be a substantial increase in the efficiency and economy of our system of criminal justice. It cannot be doubted that the daily operation of multiple grand juries in the communities across this land constitutes a very expensive project. Nor can we underestimate the unnecessary waste in the energies of our law enforcement and prosecuting personnel generated by the totally repetitious task of making presentations before the grand jury. The elimination of this needless squandering of resources would be a great boon to the administration of justice.

Before the ever-growing demands placed upon our system of justice completely overwhelm us, it is time to face reality. A constitutional amendment is necessary to effect the change I propose on the federal level. The enormity of that task must not deter us. The time to begin is now. Legislation to this end is pending in the present Congress.

I fully realize the difficulty presented in any attempt to amend or repeal any provision of the Bill of Rights. I feel however, that the public outcry against the Grand Jury is so great and the media so receptive at this time in our history that it is now possible of achievement. Indeed, if our profession does not take the lead in this effort and in the general reform and streamlining of the administration of criminal justice by bold positive action, the people may soon take this important function of government from us. It's later than you think!

Appendix II

THE FEDERAL PROSECUTOR

BY

MR. JUSTICE ROBERT H. JACKSON

OF THE

UNITED STATES SUPREME COURT

(1941-1954)

(The late Mr. Justice Jackson delivered the following remarks when he was U.S. Attorney General, before a meeting of federal prosecutors from the several districts of the United States.)

The federal prosecutor has more control over life, liberty, and reputation than any other person in America. His discretion is tremendous. He can have citizens investigated and, if he is that kind of a person, he can have this done to the tune of public statements and veiled or unveiled intimations.

Or the prosecutor may choose a more subtle course and simply have a citizen's friends interviewed. The prosecutor can order arrests, present cases to the grand jury in secret session, and on the basis of his one-sided presentation of the facts, can cause the citizen to be indicted and held for trial. He may dismiss the case before trial, in which case the defense never has a chance to be heard. Or he may go on with a public trial. If he obtains a conviction, the prosecutor can still make recommendations as to sentence, as to whether the prisoner should get probation or a suspended sentence, and after he is put away, as to whether he is a fit subject for parole.

While the prosecutor at his best is one of the most beneficient forces in our society, when he acts from malice or other base motives, he is one of the worst.

These powers have been granted to our law-enforcement agencies because it seems necessary that such a power to prosecute be lodged somewhere. This authority has been granted by people who really wanted the right thing done — wanted crime eliminated — but also wanted the best in our American traditions preserved.

Because of this immense power to strike at citizens, not with mere individual strength, but with all the force of government itself, the post of Federal District Attorney from the very beginning has been safeguarded by presidential appointment, requiring confirmation of the Senate of the United States. You are thus required to win an expression of confidence in your character by both the legislative and the executive branches of the government before assuming the responsibilities of a federal prosecutor.

Your responsibility in your several districts for law enforcement and for its methods cannot be wholly surrendered to Washington, and ought not to be assumed by a centralized Department of Justice. It is an unusual and rare instance in which the local District Attorney should be superseded in the handling of litigation, except where he requests help of Washington. It is also clear that with his knowledge of local sentiment and opinion, his contact with and intimate knowledge of the views of the court, and his acquaintance with the feelings of the group from which jurors are drawn, it is an unusual case in which his judgment should be overruled.

Experience, however, has demonstrated that some measure of centralized control is necessary. In the absence of that control, different district attorneys were striving for different interpretations or applications of an Act, or were pursuing different conceptions of policy. Also, to put it mildly, there were differences in the degree of diligence and zeal in different districts. To promote uniformity of policy and action, to establish some standards of performance, and to make available specialized help, some degree of centralized administration was found necessary.

Our problem, of course, is to balance these opposing considerations. I desire to avoid any lessening of the prestige and influence of the district attorneys in their districts. At the same time we must proceed in all districts with that uniformity of policy which is necessary to the prestige of federal law.

Nothing better can come out of this meeting of law enforcement officers than a rededication to the spirit of fair play and decency that should animate the federal prosecutor. Your positions are of such independence and importance that while you are being diligent, strict, and vigorous in law enforcement you can also afford to be just. Although the government technically loses its case, it has really won if justice has been done. The lawyer in public office is justified in seeking to leave behind him a good record. But he must remember that his most alert and severe, but just, judges will be the members of his own profession, and that lawyers rest their good opinion of each other not merely on results accomplished but on the quality of the performance. Reputation has been called "the shadow cast by one's daily life."

Any prosecutor who risks his day-to-day professional name for fair dealing to build up statistics of success has a perverted sense of practical values, as well as defects of character.

Whether one seeks promotion to a judgeship, as many prosecutors rightly do, or whether he returns to private practice, he can have no better asset than to have his profession recognize that his attitude toward those who feel his power has been dispassionate, reasonable, and just.

The federal prosecutor has now been prohibited from engaging in political activities. I am convinced that a good-faith acceptance of the spirit and letter of that doctrine will relieve many district attorneys from the embarrassment of what have heretofore been regarded as legitimate expectations of political service. There can also be no doubt that to be closely identified with the intrigue, the money raising, and the machinery of a particular party or faction may present a prosecuting officer with embarrassing alignments and associations. I think the Hatch Act should be utilized by federal prosecutors as a protection against demands on their time and their prestige to participate in the operation of the machinery of practical politics.

There is a most important reason why the prosecutor should have, as nearly as possible, a detached and impartial view of all groups in his community. Law enforcement is not automatic. It isn't blind. One of the greatest difficulties of the position of prosecutor is that he must pick his cases, because no prosecutor can even investigate all of the cases in which he receives complaints. If the Department of Justice were to make even a pretense of reaching every probable violation of federal law, ten times its present staff would be inadequate. We know that no local police force can strictly enforce the traffic laws, or it would arrest half the driving population of any given morning. What every prosecutor is practically required to do is to select the cases for prosecution and to select those in which the offense is the most flagrant, the public harm the greatest, and the proof the most certain.

If the prosecutor is obliged to choose his cases, it follows that he can choose his defendants. Therein is the most dangerous power of the prosecutor: that he will pick people that he thinks he should get, rather than pick cases that need to be prosecuted. With the law books filled with a great assortment of crimes, a prosecutor stands a fair chance of finding at least a technical violation of some act on the part of almost anyone. In such a case, it is not a question of discovering the commission of a crime and then looking for the man who has committed it, it is a question of picking the man and then searching the law books, or putting investigators to work, to pin some offense on him.

It is in this realm — in which the prosecutor picks some person whom he dislikes or desires to embarrass, or selects some group of unpopular persons and then looks for an offense, that the greatest danger of abuse of prosecuting power lies. It is here that law enforcement becomes personal, and the real crime becomes that of being unpopular with the predominant or governing group, being attached to the wrong political views, or being personally obnoxious to or in the way of the prosecutor himself.

In times of fear or hysteria political, racial, religious, social, and economic groups, often from the best of motives, cry for the scalps of individuals or groups because they do not like their views. Particularly do we need to be dispassionate and courageous in those cases which deal with so-called "subversive activities." They are dangerous to civil liberty because the prosecutor has no definite standards to determine what constitutes a "subversive activity," such as we have for murder or larceny. Activities which seem benevolent and helpful to wage earners, persons on relief, or those who are disadvantaged in the struggle for existence may be regarded as "subversive" by those whose property interests might be burdened or affected thereby. Those who are in office are apt to regard as "subversive" the activities of any of those who would bring about a change of administration. Some of our soundest constitutional doctrines were once punished as subversive. We must not forget that it was not so long ago that both the term "Republican" and the term "Democrat" were epithets with sinister meaning to denote persons of radical tendencies that were "subversive" of the order then dominant.

In the enforcement of laws which protect our national integrity and existence, we should prosecute any and every act of violation, but only overt acts, not the expression of opinion, or activities such as the holding of meetings, petitioning of Congress, or dissemination of news or opinions Only by extreme care can be protect the spirit as well as the letter of our civil liberties, and to do so is a responsibility of the federal prosecutor.

Another delicate task is to distinguish between the federal and the local in law-enforcement activities. We must bear in mind that we are concerned only with the prosecution of acts which the Congress has made federal offenses. Those acts we should prosecute regardless of local feeling, regardless of whether it exposes lax local enforcement, regardless of whether it makes or breaks local politicians.

But outside of federal law each locality has the right under our system of government to fix its own standards of law enforcement and of morals. And the moral climate of the United States is as varied as its physical climate. For example, some states legalize and permit gambling, some states prohibit it legislatively and protect it administratively, and some try to prohibit it entirely. The same variation of attitudes towards other law-enforcement problems exists. The federal government could not enforce one kind of law in one place and another kind elsewhere. It could hardly adopt strict standards for loose states or loose standards for strict states without doing violence to local sentiment. Is spite of the temptation to divert our power to local conditions where they have become offensive to our sense of decency, the only long-term policy that will save federal justice from being discredited by entanglements with local politics is that it confine itself to strict and impartial enforcement of federal law, letting the chips fall in the community where they may. Just as there should be no permitting of local considerations to stop federal enforcement so there should be no striving to enlarge our power over local affairs and no use of federal prosecutions to exert an indirect influence that would be unlawful if exerted directly.

> *The qualities of a good prosecutor are as elusive and as impossible to define as those which mark a gentleman. And those who need to be told would not understand it anyway. A sensitiveness to fair play and sportsmanship is perhaps the best protection against the abuse of power, and the citizen's safety lies in the prosecutor who tempers zeal with human kindness, who seeks truth and not victims, who serves the law and not factional purposes, and who approaches his task with humility.*

Appendix III

A COURTROOM EXPOSITION
OF TWO THOMPSON-IMMUNIZED WITNESSES

BY

THOMAS A. FORAN

FORMER U.S. ATTORNEY, NORTHERN DISTRICT OF ILLINOIS
(The following transcript material comes from Mr. Foran's
closing argument on behalf of Cook County Commissioner
Charles S. Bonk, accused of having accepted bribes from
two self-confessed zoning "fixers" — John Daley and
Robert Haskins. The Thompson office rewarded these two
men with more than criminal immunity. In Daley's case,
Thompson tried as well to protect this witness from facing
State of Illinois proceedings to disbar him from the legal
profession. In Haskins' case, there was an apparent low-
ering of federal tax obligations in return for the testimony.
Mr. Foran here dissects for the Bonk jury the quality of
the testimony from these two star government witnesses.)

CLOSING ARGUMENT FOR THE DEFENDANT

By Mr. Foran

Your Honor, Counsel, Ladies and Gentlemen of the Jury:
I think the most surprising thing in this case to me was
when we were told that this was an indictment of a system.

It's not the indictment of a system at all. It is
the indictment of Charley Bonk, sitting over there.

In order to generate some kind of support for a government case that is built on sand and mud and slop, the
government tries to use political rhetoric to decide a criminal lawsuit. Mr. Hoffmann said in his opening statement,
"We are going to structure a house." And I said in response
that the government's house has a problem. It's built on
one foundation, a foundation that consists of two poles:
Daley and Haskins.

Daley and Haskins alone, totally uncorroborated — uncorroborated. Not one, single, solitary thing that corrob-
orates their testimony that Mr. Bonk was involved in this
case. We heard from Mike Igoe. Was that to corroborate
that there are zoning cases in Cook County? We are the
ones that stipulated to all the cases that there were in
1967, '68, '69 and '70. Was Igoe's testimony meant to corroborate that interstate commerce is involved? We stipulated to all that.

We heard that Kiney, Reichert, DiFranco, Origer, Chez, and Isenstein all gave money to Haskins and Daley. Good Lord, we all *know* they gave money to them. They all sat up here and told you the phenomenal amounts of cash that they gave to Daley and to Haskins. Rather than corroborate Daley and Haskins, they told you beyond question what Daley and Haskins truly are.

Does it corroborate Haskins and Daley that Charley Bonk was chairman of the Building and Zoning Committee? No. He has, by his legal duty, all of the obligations to put things on the Agenda. And by the way, if he thinks something is wrong, he also has the obligation to defer or vote against. The only problem is that there is absolutely no evidence at all that Charley Bonk ever held anything off the agenda; that he ever did defer anything; that he ever voted against the Zoning Board of Appeal's approval.

So those things are supposed to put it on Charley Bonk, because he had power and he never used it bad. He never did anything wrong with it. Is that against him? Does that corroborate Haskins and Daley? The government's case corroborated just two facts. One, that Haskins and Daley are shysters. And the other, that Haskins and Daley are rotten thieves. Haskins and Daley are their witnesses.

We are going to talk about indictment of political systems. As I go along in this argument I want you to wonder if perhaps that kind of cynicism isn't what generates the improper use of a phenomenal power, a power that only came into existence in October of 1970. *Immunity.* Immunity which wipes out one of the most important constitutional powers in the history of the United States, right out of the Bill of Rights. The right against self-incrimination.

And you see how a couple of diabolically evil guys like Haskins and Daley can take that cynicism about a political system in something like immunity and use it to make a patsy of Charley Bonk or a judge or anybody in public life. Now, just remember — I'll go into it in detail, but I want to hit it in order, because I want to meet what Mr. Hoffmann said in somewhat the same context that he did.

We know that Daley and Haskins are shysters.
We know they're thieves. We know that. They
told us that themselves, out of their own mouths.

We know that Haskins has a criminal tax case pending against him. We know that Daley on his own testimony took $15,000 in cash away from Kiney and Reichert. We know he got $25,000 in cash from them to give to somebody. He took $15,000 of it and put it in his own pocket and used it, on his own testimony, for his own purposes.

He used it to help his clients: Marathon Oil, Standard Oil, City Service, and the rest of them. And to save himself some money.

Mr. Hoffmann says, "Why that proves that Daley's telling the truth." Stop and think again of that statement and then remember the testimony. Daley is in here trying to convince these fellows [government lawyers] to give him immunity from prosecution for his crimes. His crimes obviously include embezzlement among his clients, and obviously include all sorts of interactions with Haskins. Daley's in it. You know he and Haskins are the two biggest zoning lawyers. They are in it together.

> Can you imagine Daley coming in and trying to convince these decent guys to give him immunity, and have him say, "I had 20 gas stations where I represented Standard Oil, City Service, Marathon Oil, Payless stations, ARCO, all the great big gas stations, 20 of them, and I didn't make any payoffs. Non-zero, goose egg." They say, "Oh, come on, now! A gas station on a 1-acre residential lot that's worth maybe $7,500 and if you get it rezoned, it goes up to $100,000, you didn't make any payoffs? How can we believe this? We are not going to give you immunity on something like that. You're lying to us."

You weren't shook down, Daley; they wouldn't give you a pass on something like that. Now why did he have to *say* he had some money to give, out of his own pocket? Because otherwise he *wasn't* getting shaken down. Standard Oil and City Service and ARCO and the rest of them weren't giving him any cash; and he knew the government couldn't show that they did. He knew the government couldn't come up with checks from an Isenstein or checks from a Kiney and a Reichert or checks from a DiFranco to support an allegation that he was making payoffs on his gas station sites. And he knew his story had no credibility unless he told these fellows that he was shook down. So he had to say it came out of his own pocket. He *couldn't* show that he got it out of his own account. You know there was no way of showing that he had been cashing checks to get money to do it. So he had to find some money to say, "I got shook down on all the gas station sites."

You know, this is not a dumb man. You saw him, he's smart and he's smooth. He said, "I've got to have some money where I can't prove, independently, that some cash came in." So he took 25 grand which he put in his pocket, that he got from Kiney and Reichert and he said, "I gave ten to Bonk," so he'd have something to tell them. And then he said, "I kept the other 15 and I made a deal with Bonk that we'd spread that over all the gas stations." Now he had some way of saying to them that he'd been shaken down on gas stations. Otherwise they wouldn't believe him, they wouldn't give him immunity.

They'd say, "You had 20 gas station sites, and you didn't give the County Commissioners any money, and they let them *all* go through?" They wouldn't buy it. Mr. Hoffmann, with his cynicism about the system, wouldn't buy that one. *So Daley gave them one to buy, to bite; and Mr. Hoffmann bit, just like a bass on a worm.*

Daley says he got $10,000 in cash from Chez. Chez told these young fellows that he gave $30,000 in cash to Daley. This same thing: He's got to have money to spread around where they can't prove it. He got into a pickle and he had to starting balancing amounts. He had to start fooling around with his amounts.

But you have got to remember this man Daley knew an investigation was going on since 1971. Don't you remember Daley going out to see Kiney and Reichert and saying, "Look, they're investigating County zoning. Now you guys sign this phoney letter I'm giving you, that is predated almost a year. I'll give it to you right in the exact words; "Sign it, because if I get in trouble on this thing you're getting in trouble too." That's what he told Kiney and Reichert.

So for three years before he was in immunity, that smart aleck was scheming and figuring out his bill of goods to sell these men, to sell to them in order to get himself immunity. They really have a gullibility about this immunity, just a gullibility.

> *A public official in this regulated society of ours is an absolute patsy, just a pushover. Look at the position of a guy like Haskins. He's in a position where his client knows that he's got to go to the government to get something through; and the client has been inundated with reports of political corruption, simply inundated. So people like Haskins wink and giggle and say, "You know what it's got to be. Now I really only charge you a $10,000 fee; unfortunately I've got to charge you 20, and 10 of it's got to be in cash. You know I've got to take care of somebody."*

In the profession we have got a name for it, it's a vulgar name, we call them *whore lawyers*. That is what we call them. Usually you'd think of them in terms of the guy over in Traffic Court for drunken driving, where they are winking, saying "I'm going to fix the Judge. You know, slip me a little under the table. I have got to fix the Judge." And it all goes in their pocket, and they cream a judge. Haskins and Daley play that game, and they play it to the hilt, and their patsy is not some judge, but Charley Bonk. He's their patsy. He's the guy they wink and giggle about to justify getting cash which they don't have to report to the Internal Revenue Service.

Look at Haskins. Isn't it a strange thing how his tax bill has gone down. When you add up everything — the $65,000 that Mr. Origer came up with, the $15,000 that Zizzo came up with, the $18,000 that Isenstein came up with in cash — you get $98,000. You will have it in evidence. In October of 1974, in that criminal tax investigation, the government was charging Haskins with not reporting $94,000 — some-odd dollars on his income tax. He's testified for the government. In April, 1975, it's down to 30. Now in this case he says as far as he knows he's up-to-date with the government. He claims he's paid all his bills.

What was true in the beginning of this case is true right now. The government's case rests lock, stock and barrel on the testimony of Haskins and Daley, totally and absolutely uncorroborated.

> *If Haskins and Daley are lying, if they are liars and more than that — even if you have some reasonable belief that they are lying — you have got to find Mr. Bonk not guilty. You have got to. That is your duty, that is your obligation.*

Haskins testified about eight cases, three clients: Origer, Isenstein, and Zizzo. The government would have you believe that two of them corroborated Haskins. Origer who, time after time, said things happened; things that Haskins in his own testimony denied happened, or couldn't remember happening.

At one time it was said that a lack of memory is the refuge of the intelligent lawyer — of the intelligent *liar*. Sometimes they are the same, unfortunately for all of us here.

Remember how Haskin's government testimony would go? "Where did you see Mr. Bonk." "In his office or mine." "What did he say to you, and what did you say to him?" "He said, 'I need $500.' And I said, gee Charley, I don't want to give it to you. I am being pained by this, and I am fearing economic harm." "And what happened then?" "I agreed to give him the $500." "What did you do then?" "I went back to the office." "And several days later, what

318

happened?" "I went back and saw him and gave him $500."

And he and Daley said it over and over and over again.

> *Say Coca Cola enough and everybody buys Coca Cola; but we don't pay any attention to an individual mention of the name Coca Cola. You would have thought, that is ridiculous to prosecute a man on. But these men said it over and over again; so it is supposed to be a case. The only thing that changes it was that if Haskins or Daley thought the government could show where some cash came from, then the price of their testimony went up. If it was a case that the government couldn't show cash coming from a client, then Daley and Haskins said they didn't get any cash from a client.*

Like Daley said about the gasoline stations, "I had to come up with the money myself." He couldn't show any money coming from his account of any substance, so he had to create an account. He had to admit he stole *some* of Reichert's and Kiney's money rather than admit he stole it all, which is what he did.

Let's go back to Isenstein. By the way, he was immunized, too.

Somebody should say something about this. Isenstein, a millionaire, or Origer, millions of dollars worth of property, immunized. Rich, fancy Jack Daley: immunized. Smart, clever hot shot lawyer, former Master in Chancery Haskins: immunized.

> *All to get Charley Bonk. Is this the way we are supposed to be? Are people like a Haskins and a Daley supposed to be more believable because they were able to con these people into not prosecuting them for all their crimes? That is supposed to add to their credibility? Good heavens, what has happened to us.*

If I am willing to be a rat fink because you are not going to prosecute me, that is supposed to make me more believable. I don't know. If that is what it is, it has changed a long way from when I was probably the biggest target of the tattletale all through grammar school. I didn't think much of him then. I didn't believe him then either.

But, Isenstein. Isenstein on direct telling all about how he'd been told he had to give the money to Charley Bonk. Haskins telling him he had to give the money to Charley Bonk.

By the way, on cross examination, arriving on the scene he got sent to Fulle by Haskins, to try and move Fulle; but then on cross examination I could see the man felt distasteful. He felt dirty.

> I said to him, "Mr. Isenstein" (and I will add my own thoughts; he knew Haskins, knew him inside out, had been with him all the time) — "What do you think, did you know then whether he was giving the money to somebody or was he putting it in his own pocket?" And he said, "I don't know. Could have been either."
> I said, "To this day" (and here he was in here testifying under immunity for the government; in a case to corroborate Haskins) and I said to this guy, "don't you wonder whether or not he might have put it in his own pocket and he didn't really give it to anybody?"
> And, Isenstein said, "Yes, yes, I wonder."

Isn't that reasonable doubt? Isn't that doubt based on reason? Reason much better than what we have? Reason based on a long relationship with Haskins?

Isenstein didn't know. Isenstein thinks Haskins might well have put the money in his own pocket.

And Daley. Lord help us. Handsome, talented, born with a golden spoon in his mouth, clever, and so capable. You saw him. Smooth as glass.

He wouldn't talk at all. His buddy Haskins was talking at the time, but he wouldn't talk at all, not a word, *until they got him immunity.* Then after he was home free, he left his clients abandoned and alone.

Remember? He hadn't talked to them for four years. The last thing he said, if the government comes to talk to you, don't talk; because if I get in trouble on this, I will put you into it.

Boy, he did that all right, didn't he? All of them who testified, DiFranco, Kiney, Reichert, his clients. Those men, by the way, were given no immunity. They are sitting up there testifying under oath to crimes, false statements to Mr. Thompson, the IRS agent.

Remember Daley on direct testimony? How smooth he was, giving the impression he had helped Kiney and Reichert with his coverup letter. He made it sound as if he wanted to be sure that they didn't make any mistake on their Internal Revenue reports.

He repeated his admonition to Reichert on direct testimony, stating that Mr. Reichert some time later asked him about what to do. "And I said, be truthful. Tell them the truth. Tell them the exact truth." *As if he was a nice, decent man.*

He told us he told the guy to get a lawyer, and he gave the clear impression that he did all this long before he had himself focused the government on these guys by telling the government about it, after he figured he himself was home free.

When he told it on direct testimony, he really sounded like a swell guy. Remember poor Reichert tried to get hold of Daley after he got the subpoena, going out to Olympia Fields, finding Daley's car and sitting there on the car waiting for him because he couldn't get him on the phone? And, here, he had just told a lie to a federal agent. And that is when Daley says, "Well, I told them all about it and they wouldn't let me call you. So now, tell the truth."

A little different story, isn't it?

You know, sometimes in the thrust of courtroom combat a lawyer loses his cool, as I did, and Judge Will properly slapped me down. If you think about why I was angry, though, you will not hold it against Mr. Bonk. I should have known after all these years in courtrooms that I have been around that after a little bit of patience the truth will out, because thank God, it does.

What was the truth? I am going to give it to you just exactly the way it was. And remember, because it tells Daley right down the line.

The time of the meeting with Kiney and Reichert was not June 21. It was March of '71 just before tax time.

The purpose of the meeting was not to help Kiney and Reichert or to establish, as Daley told the Judge, the true fee arrangement. Remember, he said the true fee arrangement was $25,000 by check and $25,000 cash.

Mr. Kiney and Mr. Reichert told you originally the fee arrangement was one flat fee of $50,000. Then Daley changed it to 25 right then and 25 in cash later on. They said that this phoney letter was phoney, Kiney and Reichert said. It was a phoney letter.

Let me give it to you.

"Q. Would you give me the conversation he gave, how he told this to you, Mr. Kiney? What did he say to you?

"He said, there was a special investigation going on at the zoning, Cook County, the Building and Zoning Department, and that something had to be done. Otherwise he was going to be in trouble and if he gets in trouble, then we're going to be in trouble."

And I said, "That is the way he put it?"

Mr. Kiney said yes.

"Q. And that if I, Daley, prepare a letter that is pre-dated back to when we first met setting forth facts about our fee arrangement that are untrue" —

And Mr. Kiney interrupted me and said, "That is correct."

Then, "I want you fellows to receipt for it."

Mr. Kiney said, "That is correct."

"Q. Because if you don't, I, Daley, might get in trouble and if I get in trouble I will put you guys into it it to. Was that the actual substance of the conversation?"

And Mr. Kiney said, "Yes, it was."

What a difference between the smooth, arrogant Daley sparring with me, and beating me after I lost my cool, and the true, rotten, corrupt person that he is.

> *And is it any wonder that each one of those clients, Kiney, Reichert, DiFranco, who knew Daley — oh, they knew him, they worked with him, person to person, alone in his office, preparing cases on matters that were important to them, and in this courtroom yesterday, each one of them told us that to this day, to this moment, they don't know whether Daley took their cash and passed it on to anybody, or just ripped them off and put it in his own pocket — to this day.*

Is that not a reasonable doubt? What more can there be? Men who have much more reason to be able to judge these men. Isenstein with Haskins; DiFranco, Kiney, Reichert with Daley. Does any one of them to this day know what Haskins and Daley did with their money? No. They testified they might have been ripped off.

There is no better evidence that any defendant could ever find for himself.

You saw the men who dealt with Haskins and Daley, the men the government says corroborate Haskins and Daley, telling you, "I wouldn't believe them when they said they gave it to somebody else. I think they might have stolen it from me and put it in their own pockets."

A doubt based on reason. What better reason? Who knows better? Who knows best?

> *There is absolutely no evidence, no evidence that Mr. Bonk ever, ever exercised his statutory duties and power unfairly, other than the testimony of those two corrupt bums.*

The evidence is absolutely to the contrary. There is no evidence or even anybody speculating in this case about when the application was filed and when it was referred to the Zoning Board of Appeals, of that being a problem of delay. Nobody mentioned it. Or, you know, when it is

filed, it goes to the County Board. They then refer it to
the Zoning Board of Appeals. Nobody ever talked about
any delay at that time. That is Mr. Bonk's responsibility.
It is filed. It goes to his committee. It is referred to the
Zoning Board of Appeals.

Mr. Igoe said, it goes so fast it is almost automatic.
It is almost automatic.

There is absolutely no evidence there is anything wrong
in the Zoning Board of Appeals, which by the way, might
help Mr. Hoffmann get over his cynicism. This is a
Board of Appeals that is appointed by Mr. Bonk's Board;
the County Board appoints the Zoning Board of Appeals.
Everybody said they do a great job. They are top rated
people. They give good hearings, everything else.

If we are going to say that because Mr. Bonk *might*
have done something bad, he *did* do something bad, which
seems to be the government's case; then we should say
that he might have done something good, and we should
give him credit for what he might have done.

99½ percent of all those things recommended by the
Zoning Board of Appeals, recommended approval, were
passed by the County Board.

The evidence shows that Mr. Bonk always followed
the recommendations of the Zoning Board of Appeals.
Motions to defer are almost all Fulle; Chaplin is there
pretty regularly; Piotrowski is in there, who is the one
by the way who deferred the DiFranco matter. It wasn't
Charley Bonk. This woman named Lillian Piotrowski, now
dead. It wasn't Charley Bonk. Even though that is the
classic example, according to Mr. Hoffmann, of how Mr.
Bonk delays things, the record shows it was Lillian Piotrowski who delayed it, not Charley Bonk.

Charley Bonk moved to defer one out of 661. The applicant was the Federal Aviation Administration. That
is the only motion to defer that Charley Bonk made in
600 cases. There were a lot of the other commissioners,
by the way, who hardly ever deferred anything either.

> *Daley is their witness. Oh, Mr. Valukas will
> get up and say, "Well, we don't choose our wit-
> nesses. We take them where we find them.*
>
> *You don't have to take them.*
>
> *He'll say, "We have to give immunity to those
> who are willing to talk."*
>
> *They don't have to. Nobody puts a gun to their
> head. There is a thing called prosecutor's discre-
> tion.*

How could Charley Bonk have got $146,000 and not
have Don Thompson, a pretty good agent, find something,

find a safe deposit box, find a deposit slip, find that Charley bought a big car, or that he had a beautiful house, or that he was a big shot, or that he chased girls, or gambled, or did something else that cost a lot of money?

A good agent like Don Thompson couldn't find anything. You know, even if you put it under your bed, $146,000 would put a pretty good lump in the mattress.

Nothing! They found cash deposits on Haskins, $25,000 worth. They had a criminal tax case going on him, matching his unreported income to his reported income. Can you imagine the guy who makes $248,000 in one fee reporting $16,000 of taxable income in '68? Who makes $60,000 from Isenstein in one fee, and then says he forgot it? I mean, he testified he didn't get it.

Again, what does he think? Does he think these young men are like him and that they wouldn't disclose the facts? They did it themselves. They had Mr. Isenstein tell you he did pay him. He must have been as astounded by that comment as anybody could be.

The evidence shows this ability to use somebody as a patsy so well. Daley, I think, does it better. He is the best.

On direct examination he insisted that he was a victim of Charley Bonk. That is where I lost my cool. That smoothie. *Some victim.*

> *You know, recently the public and the media have been expressing horror about one of the most heinous of all crimes — rape — and how the prosecution treats a rape victim.*
>
> *When the woman who gets raped goes into the police or the prosecution, they question her virtue. They make her prove she is virtuous before they will prosecute; and that is terribly disturbing to her.*
>
> *Unfortunately, to some degree it is true. The law does permit a guy to go into whether or not the woman is virtuous when she charges some man with assault. You know that is tough on a victim.*
>
> *But this victim Daley tells you he is an honest-to-God victim — and 17 times he goes back to the same assailant?*
>
> *Haskins, another self-styled victim, testifies he goes back eight times to the same guy in the same office over a period of years. Some victim.*

The prosecutor would be fairly within his rights to question the virtue of that witness, I would think. The believability, the credibility of such a witness, just isn't there.

And do you know why Daley told it that way? And, this is the cleverest of all. His immunity order, 39. Look at it, Government's Exhibit 39, the only one that has a little extra action in it. You can't use anything that he says here against him in any disciplinary proceedings before the Bar Association.

If he came in here and if the story that he had made up was straight, flat-out bribery — that he was going in and saying, here is the dough, do what I want you to do — he would be in a position that lawyers might question him. Lawyers might say, get away, beat it, get out of our profession.

So, he tried to make himself a victim. That smoothie. That guy who had the gall to think and justify himself, not only to me, but to the Judge, that he was justified in taking the money from Kiney and Reichert to take care of his other clients, and he was doing it because he feared economic harm.

A former state's attorney. Of course, he never had gone to the law. Oh, he wouldn't do that. But, here is a guy who loves money so much, whose testimony is that he was really hurting economically, so he had to do this.

Charley Bonk, big bully Charley Bonk picked on poor little Jackie Daley, who was only as far away as the nearest phone from calling up his cousin, the Mayor of Chicago.

"Cousin Dick, Charley Bonk is shaking me down. Hang him up by his ears. Put him in Lake Michigan and throw him out of the Democratic Party."

And, Jack Daley said, well, I didn't do that. The Judge said you had five years to call a policeman. He was that far, a telephone call away from saving himself some money.

What a fake. What a phoney. What a shyster.

Do you think that smoothy wouldn't have called either the police or his cousin Dick to save himself a few bucks? For him to say he *wouldn't* do it is absolutely ridiculous. For him to say he *couldn't* do it is sensible from his standpoint, however, because all he could say is: "I am shaking my clients down. I am shaking my clients down. I am stealing from my clients and I am corrupting the reputation of your party, cousin Dick, in the course of doing it." So, he wouldn't call because that is what he was doing.

And, Haskins. For every dollar he says he gave Charley Bonk, his own tax liability goes down. You know, that is why these guys want cash. They don't have to pay taxes on it. They don't put it in their books. It is that simple.

That is the way they catch them. Don Thompson catches them. They cheat on their income tax. Then they start maneuvering. They have got to get out. Who will I pick? Well, boy, there is a perfect pick. Look at him. Charley Bonk in a position where he could hurt them. He never did, even though he could have. Not an articulate guy, not an aggressive guy. Let's not pick on George Dunne or Dick Ogilvie. They can take care of themselves. Let's pick on Charley Bonk.

Great guys.

These two scum are unbelievable to me because of what they do to all of us in the legal profession. Ours should be the best profession; we should be the voice for people who are afraid. But scum like Daley and Haskins corrupt us in your eyes. I know they are lawyers, and that is why I hate them, because I know they are liars. They shame me so.

Just ask yourselves this. Would you, if you needed a lawyer in a matter where his integrity was important to you — in a matter of most importance in your life — would you, next Monday, go out and retain Daley or Haskins? Would you give them some money of yours in trust?

For you to convict Charley Bonk on their testimony you will have to make a similar decision. You have got to be convinced that Mr. Bonk is guilty beyond a reasonable doubt to the level of belief that you use in making a decision in a really important matter in your life. You have got to be convinced.

> *How would you like to be sitting where Charley Bonk is on the basis of those two scum putting you into it? Nothing else. Just their scheme to make money from their clients, and then getting out of it by saying, "I didn't keep it; I gave it to Charley."*

In this case the government has failed totally to fulfill its duty, its burden. The government has just failed to prove him guilty beyond a reasonable doubt.

This case cries out reasonable doubt, reasonable doubt, reasonable doubt. Everybody in it who knew Haskins and Daley well, say they might have put that money in their own pockets. They *might* have. *And if they might have, Mr. Bonk is not guilty.*

Don't be afraid to bring in a verdict of not guilty. Thank you.

Appendix IV

IMMUNITY:
HOW IT WORKS IN REAL LIFE
BY
JUDGE WARREN D. WOLFSON
OF THE CIRCUIT COURT OF COOK COUNTY
from an article in
JOURNAL OF LAW AND CRIMINOLOGY
NORTHWESTERN UNIVERSITY SCHOOL OF LAW

(Judge Wolfson was formerly a prominent criminal defense attorney in Chicago, Illinois; Adjunct Professor in Trial Advocacy, Illinois Institute of Technology-Chicago Kent College of Law; Lecturer on Criminal Law, University of Chicago Law School and Northwestern University of Law, 1971-73. *The article that follows is reprinted by special permission of the Journal of Criminal Law and Criminology, Copyright © 1976 by Northwestern University School of Law Vol. 67 No. 2. All footnotes omitted.*)

A major issue confronting Americans today is the amount of power we want to give the federal government. That is, where do a purportedly free people draw the line between their government and their right to be let alone? The subject of immunity raises moral and philosophical questions that must be asked about a government's behavior toward its citizens. In each instance where immunity is granted to a witness, a change takes place in the power relationship between government and citizen. The line between them becomes blurred. The witness gives up something, his concerns change.

A practical analysis of this shift in power must concern itself with two kinds of immunity. By that, I do not mean "transactional" as against "use" immunity. While distinctions between the two are important, the inquiry is not begun until it separates voluntary from involuntary immunity. Some people seek immunity and some have it thrust upon them. Different questions should be asked in each instance.

It is not intellectually safe to conclude that whenever

a witness is granted immunity he must be guilty of a crime. An *involuntary* witness often receives immunity simply because a prosecutor wants to know what the witness knows. He is given use immunity, the only kind allowed by statute, but his lawyer will tell him, correctly, that he still may be indicted. The government might have a taint problem, and some United States Attorneys have a policy of not indicting immunized witnesses, but the possibility of indictment is real in terms of legal permissibility.

Voluntary witnesses are immunized pursuant to a strategic decision by the prosecutor. There is no statutory way to get immunity from *prosecution,* but friendly witnesses get it anyway when they, in person or through their lawyers, sit down and make a deal with the [federal] government.

> *The issue in either case is not the guilt of the witness. The decisive factor is the conclusion that has been reached by the prosecutor and the way he communicates that conclusion to the witness or to the witness's lawyer.* **For the witness, it is the prosecutor's belief and asserted position that create the crime. After all, the witness's real fear is the indictment itself. He knows what every prosecutor should know: that the power to indict is the power to destroy.** *The witness knows who holds the power; he reacts to what he is told, although what he is told is not necessarily a valid legal conclusion.*

What must be remembered is that the prosecutor alone decides who will receive immunity. He can do it by obtaining a formal court order, by writing a letter, or by making an oral commitment, but there is no one outside the Justice Department who has the power to review or overrule a prosecutor's decision to immunize.

The procedure for obtaining a court-ordered grant of immunity is the same for witnesses who are friendly or unfriendly to the prosecution. First, the local prosecutor decides he wants the testimony. Then he convinces his United States Attorney that he ought to begin the machinery for obtaining a court order. A request, signed by the United States Attorney, is sent to the Justice Department. The request is examined and almost always a form approval is sent back.

On September 22, 1975, I sent a letter to Attorney General Edward H. Levi asking among other things, whether the Justice Department has made any "meaningful review" of local requests for immunity. The answer, dated November 14, 1975, came from Deputy Chief Roger A. Pauley: "The standards for approving requests are being reviewed and modified at present." I take this to mean that at least until November of 1975 the Justice Department has been virtually without standards for approval of the requests. I hope the system will change. But the point remains valid: decisions that are basic to the existence of a free people cannot be left simply to the good faith and judgment of a man who holds an office at a particular time. Recent history has made that lesson clear.

When the local United States Attorney receives approval from Washington, he files a petition before the presiding judge. All he really has to do is tell the judge the witness has used or has threatened to use the fifth amendment. Then he indicates that it is his judgment as United States Attorney that the witness's testimony in regard to the investigation before the Grand Jury is necessary to the public interest. Defense lawyers in some instances have attempted to oppose these petitions, citing the lack of factual allegations. After all, the judge has not been told the specific area of inquiry or why the witness's testimony might be relevant to that inquiry. Whether the evidence could be obtained from other sources is immaterial. Judges are not eager to receive arguments that the prosecutor is not in good faith, that his motives are something other than a search for needed information.

> *In effect the judge is being asked to sign an order affecting basic rights without being given an opportunity to exercise judicial discretion. The witness is told: "Answer all questions or you will go to jail until you do. Your testimony cannot be used against you, unless you testify falsely." There is no other area in the law where a judge is told he must do so much to a person without pausing to determine if he should. The judge is, in reality, a rubber stamp for the prosecutor.*

When a defense lawyer is opposed to a grant of immunity, he should say so to the presiding judge, clearly stating his reasons. The law is against him, but the issue must be raised repeatedly. *The present system is unjust, and if change is to come about, rational opposition must be expressed at every opportunity.*

The Justice Department has kept count of the number of requests for court-ordered immunity it has received during the past five years. Some of the requests involve more than one witness.

About one-half of the authorizations actually were used in court during 1970 through 1973. Figures on actual use were not kept for 1974 and 1975. Emerging from the statistics, or more accurately the lack of them, is the clear impression that at least for the past five years the Justice Department really does not know what local prosecutors have been doing with their power to grant different kinds of immunity. Clearly, the power has been used. Any criminal defense lawyer who has practiced in the federal courts knows that. Anyone who has kept track of current history knows it, too. But only recently have we begun to hear any substantial expressions of· concern about the government's use of immunity powers. The murmurs of discontent coincide in time with immunity grants in cases involving lawyers, police officers, businessmen and public officials.

Few words of dissent were heard in the early 1970's when the Internal Security Division of the Department of Justice began a massive grand jury campaign against antiwar and leftist groups. The immunity grant was the chief weapon between 1970 and 1973, when the I.S.D. presented evidence to more than 100 grand juries in 36 states and 84 cities. More than a thousand witnesses were called. Many received little or no notice. They were required to travel hundreds and sometimes thousands of miles for their grand jury appearance.

Faced with grants of immunity, witnesses were compelled to answer questions about political ideas and associations, about conversations with friends and neighbors, and about relatives. In short, traditional first amendment rights were trampled upon by zealous prosecutors. The I.S.D. investigation was a shameful episode in American jurisprudence. It could not have happened without the unfettered power to obtain immunity grants.

Criminal defense lawyers who have practiced in the courts of the Northern District of Illinois have learned, painfully, that there are different categories of immunized witnesses. Within these categories there are degrees. Any attempt to deal with and understand immunized testimony must carefully take into account the kind of witness that has been created and the pressures used to make him that way.

THE WITNESS WHO IS VOLUNTARY ALL THE WAY

This witness is best characterized by his quickness; that is, an impressively short reaction time. He is alert to the danger that faces him and wastes no time before seeking legal advice. His lawyer weighs the odds, makes suggestions to his client or accepts some from him, and then visits the prosecutor's office. There, the lawyer learns more about his client's prospects. Usually, when a lawyer seeks a deal to avoid a charge against his client, he gives the prosecutor a fairly detailed idea of what the client would say should he become a witness. The prosecutor may or may not express deep interest the first time he hears the proposed testimony. Negotiations begin.

Of course, not every case is the same; nor is every defense lawyer and prosecutor. Each has a different way of dealing with the immunity question. The suggested scenario is one that haunts every lawyer who is concerned about the integrity of the fact-finding process in criminal cases. It could happen, and it probably has.

> *Assume, as part of a hypothetical fact situation, that a big-time real estate developer (Developer) has income tax problems. He has received cash that did not turn up on his return. An IRS special agent pays him a visit. The agent explains that he knows about the cash, but what he really is interested in is the place to which the cash went. Further questioning makes it clear that the agent is interested in the large new shopping center put up by Developer after obtaining a vital zoning change. It is at this point that Developer decides he had better talk to his lawyer. The agent is put off to another day.*
>
> *Since Developer has agreed to pay a handsome retainer, he decides to be frank and open with his lawyer. The cash, $50,000, was given to Developer's former lawyer, a self-avowed zoning expert (Expert), who had said he needed the cash to "take care of" the zoning commissioner (Commissioner). It was Commissioner who arranged for the change that allowed the shopping center to be built. Developer never met Commissioner, but shortly after the necessary zoning change was accomplished, the cash was paid to Expert.*

After talking to his client, Developer's lawyer contacts the IRS agent for the purpose of learning the name of the assistant United States Attorney handling the file. Then the lawyer makes an appointment with the prosecutor. They agree to hold an "off the record" conversation.

Lawyers have different ways of conducting these conferences. Some frame their proposals in the future conditional: "Suppose my client should say he gave the money to Expert as a bribe to Commissioner, what would his criminal liability be?" Some use the straightforward approach: "My client gave the money to Expert so he could bribe Commissioner. What are you going to do for my client?"

There are variations of the theme, but the result is the same. The prosecutor agrees that in return for Developer's testimony, as proposed, the government will not charge him with a crime. Developer is off the hook. The first-in, first-out theory, learned in law school, has been used successfully. Speed, not virtue, has been rewarded.

But this does not solve the prosecutor's problem. He has a fairly good case against Expert, but the target is, and always has been, Commissioner. At this point, the prosecutor has to make a decision. He can decide Expert fraudulently extracted the $50,000 from Developer by falsely claiming he was going to use the money to bribe Commissioner. After all, as an experienced zoning lawyer Expert probably knew he was entitled by law to the zoning change. He could have told Developer he needed the money for a bribe; then, when the zoning change went through in the ordinary course of proceedings, he collected the money and kept it. Or, the prosecutor could take the position that the money was paid to Commissioner as a bribe, since Commissioner did support and vote for the zoning change. The prosecutor makes the choice that has been made in so many other cases. Commissioner will be the target.

Word of what is going on must get to Expert. Perhaps Developer's lawyer tells him. The special agent might pay him a visit, or he might receive a grand jury subpoena. At any rate, Expert learns that Developer had told the government about their transaction. It is clear that Developer is in the government lineup and that what he has said to the prosecutor is accepted and believed.

Expert hires a lawyer, who quickly makes contact with the prosecutor. It is made clear to Expert that he is not the real target, that the government is much more interested in Commissioner. The signals are sent. We know, says the prosecutor, or the agent, that Expert received the $50,000 claiming it was to be a bribe to Commissioner, *and that the money was paid to Commissioner for his help in getting the zoning change.* That means that Expert and Commissioner must have met and discussed the bribe at least once before the zoning change took place. It is a well-known fact that the two men knew each other during the time the zoning change proposal was pending.

Expert is not a fool. He receives the signal and his lawyer delivers the response: "If Expert tells you how he bribed Commissioner to go along with

*the zoning change, what will you do for him?"
In some cases, the prosecutor will hold out for a
plea to a minor charge with a recommendation of
probation, but if he wants the "target" badly
enough, he will offer complete immunity in return
for the testimony.*

The case now takes shape. Developer and Expert will
testify against Commissioner. Developer will show how
he generated the cash by going to his safety deposit box.
An entry receipt at the vault will support his testimony.
Expert will testify to payoff conversations with Commissioner, the corroboration coming in the form of Expert's
diary entries showing the two men were scheduled to meet
on the dates of the conversations. The other evidence is
uncontested. Commissioner twice spoke in favor of the
zoning change. Commission minutes show he voted in
favor of the change. At trial, Commissioner will deny
talking about or receiving money from Expert. They did
meet, but the conversation consisted of Expert's attempts
to persuade him of the proposal's merit.

*It could be that just before Commissioner is in-
dicted he is subpoened to appear before the grand
jury. By then, his lawyer has learned that the
government has dealt for and accepted Expert's
evidence. He wisely advises Commissioner to refuse to testify. His grand jury testimony would
be nothing more than a discovery deposition taken
by the government, or an invitation to a false-
statement indictment.*

Other things happen before trial. Both Developer and
Expert receive court-ordered use immunity before appearing at the grand jury. Just before the trial begins
the trial judge, at the request of the government, again
grants use immunity to Developer and Expert.
One might wonder why the government bothered to
obtain use immunity grants when it was clear that the
decision not to prosecute the two men had been made and
communicated. The answer is that it is a strategic play
by the prosecutor which becomes apparent during preliminary questioning of the witnesses at trial.

*The following is an example of this line of questioning:
Q: On.................................., 19........, did you testify
before a Federal Grand Jury pursuant to a court
order granting you immunity but requiring that
you testify?
A: Yes, sir.*

Q: When was the immunity order entered?
A: About one week before I testified, by Judge
....

Q: Now, would you relate to the Court and Jury your understanding of the terms of the immunity order under which you testified before that Federal Grand Jury.
A: I was compelled to testify. Anything I testified to could not be used against me in a court of law, unless I perjured myself on the stand.
Q: You understood at that time that if you lied under oath you could still be prosecuted for perjury?
A: Yes, sir.
Q: Now are you also testifying here today pursuant to a court order granting you immunity?
A: Yes, sir.
Q: And that order was entered just a few hours ago by Judge ....[trial judge]?
A: Yes, sir.
Q: And do you understand that the terms of your immunity are the same, that your testimony cannot be used against you unless you give false testimony?
A: Yes, sir.
Q: In addition to the order entered under the statute granting you immunity, has any representative of the government made you any other promise?
A: Yes, sir.
Q: What is that promise and who made it?
A: Mr. ....[assistant United States Attorney] *told me I would not be prosecuted for anything that came during this investigation, in return for my truthful testimony.*

The impact on the jurors is substantial. *Twice* the witnesses have been ordered by a judge to testify truthfully. *The first judge and the grand jury must have believed them, because they were not prosecuted for perjury.* Obviously, the government believed them. Now the trial judge is adding his prestige to the picture the prosecutor seeks to create, that of a witness who has nothing to fear from telling the truth, who faces peril only if he tells a lie. The preliminary questions create the impression that the trial judge has reviewed and approved of the immunized testimony. The jurors cannot help but be impressed.

If the point somehow escapes them, they will be reminded by the prosecutor at final argument.

> *Developer and Expert had no reason to lie. They knew they could not be prosecuted if they told the truth. They had absolutely nothing to lose by telling the truth. Judge.............................'s order made it clear to them. They were told the only way they would be prosecuted was if they told a lie. And that is the same order they were given before they appeared before the grand jury that returned this indictment.*

In setting out this scenario, it is not contended that Expert is lying while Commissioner is truthful. *The point is that the case against Expert for obtaining and keeping the money was just as strong as, if not stronger than, the bribery case against Commissioner.* Expert was the witness and Commissioner the defendant because the prosecutor so decreed. Once the prosecution determined his priority, the pieces fell in place. The power of the prosecutor in this situation is immense.

Testimony such as Expert's is inherently unreliable. It is, in effect, purchased.

> *The government gives a reward and the seller-witness knows that. In return, he usually is smart enough to know what is expected of him, especially after conversations with an agent or prosecutor. There is no requirement in law or practice that the immunized witness be corroborated in matters material to his testimony This is not to say that agents and prosecutors tell a witness to lie. Most really believe what is told them by people like Expert. They want to believe, and that which fits the pre-ordained theory is accepted. That which is inconsistent with the theory is rejected.*

THE WITNESS WHO AT FIRST SAYS "NO" BUT LATER SAYS "YES"

Some people, for various reasons, resolutely set themselves against the idea of testifying on behalf of the government. But later, after the immunity power is felt, they have a change of heart. The best example of that occurred during the Chicago Avenue police investigation that eventually resulted in *United States v. Braasch.* The government had information that tavern owners in the district were making monthly payoffs to police officers as a kind of protection. Three of the officers who allegedly ran the "club" were subpoenaed to a grand jury. They refused to testify before and after being granted use immunity. Each went to the Cook County Jail for violating the order to testify, their term to be the life of the grand jury or to the moment when they decided to answer questions. Life in the County Jail took its toll. Each man struck a bargain: freedom, no prosecution, in return for being a government witness. The indictment resulted. They testified against fellow officers. With a few exceptions, the policemen who were convicted had played minor roles in the shakedown. Mostly they were in the "go-along" category. The three club-leaders went free.

The jury thought the testimony was reliable, but the machinery that brought it about must at least make one pause to consider. First, a prosecutor decided he needed the testimony. Then, the steps mandated by the statute were taken. The three men, after refusing to testify, ended up in the Cook County Jail, an unpleasant place by any standards. They were told, in effect, talk or stay there for 18 months.

Lawyers are trained to believe that beating people and coercing them psychologically in order to get statements violate the law and our sense of decency. Basic to our distaste for those kinds of tactics is that they result in unreliable evidence. The fact that the three Chicago Avenue witnesses were coerced by a court order does not change the nature of what happened to them. Court orders, like blackjacks, can be irrational and inhumane.

> *One of the most famous cases ever tried in the Northern District of Illinois involved a man who did not become the "star" government witness until after he was indicted. William Miller was named in the indictment with Otto Kerner and Theodore Isaacs. His negotiations with the government before indictment were unsuccessful. After he was charged the negotiations continued, and an agreement finally was reached: dismissal from the case in return for his "truthful" testimony. The agreement was contained in a letter from the United States Attorney.*
>
> *A reading of the trial transcript leads to the conclusion there was no case without Miller's testimony. If that is accurate, why then was the indictment returned? One might conclude, as I do, that the purpose was to recruit Miller as a government witness. If that was the strategy, it was successful.*

There are other ways witnesses can start out unfriendly to the prosecutor's theory, yet end up testifying for the government. For example, assume old friend Expert had made a statement to the IRS agent denying he received any cash from Developer. Or perhaps he made his denial under oath at the grand jury. In either case, the prosecutor makes it clear he is convinced Expert has made a false statement, since he already has Developer's testimony about the $50,000 payment. Expert is in a dilemma. He knows he faces prosecution for his denial. If he changes his story, to be consistent with that of Developer, nothing will happen to him. He will gain approval of the people who procure the indictments from grand juries. After obtaining a promise of immunity, Expert changes his story to fit that of Developer.

Expert's second story is not necessarily untrue. The point is that the change was brought about because the prosecutor had decreed the first version to be false. He was ready to support that decision with the tremendous prosecutorial strength of the government.

THE WITNESS WHO AT FIRST SAYS "NO" AND MEANS IT

Some people never do become government witnesses, no matter how hard the prosecutor tries. There is the case of Lennie Patrick, an alleged hoodlum. Over his objection, after immunity was imposed by court order, he testified at a grand jury. As a result, a Chicago police lieutenant was indicted on income tax charges. But, at trial, Patrick refused to testify, despite an immunity order from the trial judge. The lieutenant was acquitted, but Patrick was proceeded against pursuant to rule 42 (b) of the Federal Rules of Criminal Procedure. He received a four-year sentence for his refusal to testify. The case is on appeal at this writing.

Something else happened to Patrick before the lieutenant's trial. As a result of his three immunized grand jury appearances, the Internal Revenue Service made an $835,-558 jeopardy assessment against him for unpaid gambling taxes. His lawyers reminded the Court of Appeals for the Seventh Circuit that the Supreme Court in *Kastigar* had assured an immunized witness that his testimony could not be used against him. The court of appeals answered by holding that the immunity applies only to criminal proceedings. The assessment is civil. Patrick was stuck.

Rewards for friendly witnesses, however, have gone beyond promises of non-prosecution. The tavern owners who have testified in police cases such as the Chicago Avenue trial have received added protection. Their immunity orders extend to city or state license revocation proceedings. In a recent case, a lawyer-witness not only received immunity, but gained a court order stating that his compelled testimony could not "be used against him in any administrative proceeding, disciplinary committee, any bar association or state Supreme Court, in conjunction with any professional disciplinary proceeding or disbarment." In other words, a federal judge told the Illinois Supreme Court it could not use the lawyer's testimony in any disciplinary proceedings. At trial, the lawyer told how he bribed a county commissioner to obtain zoning changes.

At that same trial, the defense found a witness who had told the prosecution something that would have been helpful to the accused, but the witness told the defense lawyers he would invoke the fifth amendment. The government then was asked, but refused, to request the immunity for the defense witness. The government had made its choice. It would believe its own witnesses, and there would be no immunity for someone who contradicted them.

The government has another technique for using the immunity statute to pry testimony from unwilling witnesses. After a man is convicted of a crime and is sent to the penitentiary he is brought back, placed before a grand jury, and immunized. If he refuses to testify, he is in civil contempt and is sent to a local jail for the life of the grand jury. His original sentence is interrupted and does not begin to run again until he purges himself of the contempt or the grand jury is disbanded. This procedure was upheld in *Anglin v. Johnston*. There is an obvious cruelty involved in the sentence-interruption procedure. Consider the pressure that kind of technique puts on a man to conform his thoughts and words to the desires of his questioner. For those who resist and are subjected to longer incarceration, present law does not provide for any kind of meaningful judicial review.

HOW TO DEAL WITH AN IMMUNIZED WITNESS

The foregoing represents some of the ways people come into contact with the government's immunity powers. All prosecutors do not do all those things all of the time, and there is no intent to demean or attack the conduct of any specific United States Attorney. But prosecutors have the *power* to do these things. The point is that there are no real controls on their behavior, except self-restraint. That is not enough. One must consider, warily, the existence of power and its possible exercise.

THE THOMPSON INDICTMENT

> *Aside from the philosophical implications aris-*
> *ing from the immunity power, there is, for crimi-*
> *nal defense lawyers, the more immediate and prac-*
> *tical problem of how to deal with the immunized*
> *government witness at trial. The defense lawyer*
> *will have to make the jury understand the way in*
> *which the witness was created and the reasons*
> *why he therefore is unreliable. It should be noted*
> *at this point that it is easier to write about this*
> *task than it is to accomplish it in a real court-*
> *room.*

There is a theme to play for the jury. It begins in the
opening statement, continues through the cross-examination, and reaches a crescendo in the final argument. It is
that of a tainted witness with a good reason to lie. He
has done something wrong, and to extricate himself he
has sold a story to the government. Once the prosecution
indicated acceptance of the story, the wrongdoer-seller has
a vital interest in repeating that same story to the jury.
He knows that as long as he sticks with that version no
harm can befall him. After all, it is the prosecutor-buyer
who will determine the fate of his witness.

THE OPENING STATEMENT

The defense lawyer who knows he will be facing one or
more immunized witnesses never should waive opening
statement. Reasonable men will differ on how much to
tell the jury, but after extensive ordeals by fire I have
concluded that the immunity issue ought to be met head-on.
Consider the following:

> *The star government witness,.................................*
> *will tell you how he betrayed his trust, sold out*
> *his badge and the public, extorted money from*
> *small businessmen and told lies, all for his own*
> *personal gain, for his own selfish purposes. You*
> *will hear him say he passed some of that money*
> *along to my client .... The evi-*
> *dence will show that when the witness was*
> *threatened with indictment, realizing the danger*
> *he was faced with, he began bargaining with the*
> *government, again for his own personal gain, for*
> *his own selfish purpose. The evidence will show*
> *he concocted a story of how he paid money to my*
> *client . . . and the evidence will show he did that*
> *to get himself off the hook. You will see that he*
> *sold his false story to the prosecution, a story —*
> *the evidence will show — that includes meetings*

> *and conversations that never took place. You will*
> *hear that the witness has immunity from prosecu-*
> *tion, that he will not be charged with all the*
> *things he has done, but that he can be charged*
> *with perjury for testifying falsely. The evidence*
> *will show _____ has no fear of being*
> *charged with perjury, because he has sold his*
> *phony story to a willing listener, the prosecution.*
> *You will see the deal has been made, and all that*
> *_____ must do to save himself is*
> *to tell the same story to you.*

Of course, the defense lawyer who makes that statement must be prepared to back up his words. The jury should discern from the defense lawyer's opening statement just what he thinks of the government witness and the way in which the witness was created and nurtured.

Since the witness will testify to meetings and conversations, the jury should know in advance there will be evidence that those meetings and conversations never took place. The jury should not be allowed to hear the witness's testimony without first being made aware that its truth will be challenged. Finally, promising that a defendant will testify is not ordinarily a good idea. I hope a major portion of the defense lawyer's purpose can be reached during cross-examination.

CROSS-EXAMINATION

Many of these prosecution witnesses, before making their separate peace with the government, have made statements to agents or grand juries that are at odds with their trial testimony. But the defense lawyer must be wary of proving too much. There is a trap involved. For example, when the witness is forced to admit in great detail his prior lies or misconduct, he then might be able to convince the jury all of that took place before his personal reformation. He was bad, now he is good. He lied, but now he is telling the truth.

The trap is especially deadly when the defense lawyer goes into detail about a prior "false" statement that exculpated the defendant along with the witness. For example, if the witness told a grand jury he never paid money to the defendant, but now he says he did pay off, it is silly to take the position that all the first testimony was false. That would mean he is telling the truth at trial. The point to make for the jury is that his current story is false, that he is telling it for reasons of his own, and that he knows he never will be charged with perjury as long as he sticks with it.

A witness's motivation and expectations are legitimate areas of inquiry. Questions directed to these areas should be framed in a way that tightly controls the scope of answer. "Yes," "No," and "I don't know" are the desired answers. Unfortunately, witnesses do not always follow scripts, for the cross-examiner at least.

[Judge Wolfson goes on to cite a lengthy and typical cross-examination scenario, which is here omitted.]

FINAL ARGUMENT

Final argument is the defense lawyer's last opportunity to bring home to the jury the message he has been sending throughout the trial. Again, he must establish the buyer-seller relationship between the witness and the prosecution. There is a fine line to walk here because it is dangerous to accuse a prosecutor of knowingly using perjured testimony. Not only do you create a lifelong enemy, but since he has the last word before the jury he can remind the jurors of his dedication to decent law enforcement and to pursuit of truth and justice on behalf of the [federal] government.

> *The defense lawyer is better off emphatically stating to the jury that he is not, absolutely not, accusing the prosecutor of knowingly putting on false testimony. It is simply that the witness was so devious and so consumed by self-interest that he fooled the prosecutor just as he is attempting to fool the jury. The prosecutor, after all, was an eager buyer. The witness was selling, and he would say anything he thought the buyer wanted to hear to get himself off the hook.*

During one of his final arguments the prosecutor will say that he really regretted having to use someone like .... [his witness], but how else could he root out the cancer of corruption that is represented by the defendant? It is for that reason, the prosecutor will say, that his witness received immunity. He then will underline the indisputable fact that the witness's grant of immunity does not cover perjury.

The defense lawyer must anticipate that argument by tracing the way in which the witness was created. Consider the following suggestions:

> *The prosecutor argues he had to arrange immunity from prosecution for .... to take out a cancer. But what worse disease can there be than to use the word of a man like .... to unfairly and wrongfully convict*

*someone of a serious crime? The prosecutor says
he had no choice, that he had to take his witness
as he found him. That's not so. He had a choice.
He could have said, "We are not going to try to
destroy someone solely on the word of ....
........................." Well, in law as in life, you make
decisions. And one decision you have to make is
— how high a price do you pay for what you get?
If you force someone to give you something by
threatening him with indictment and jail, how
reliable is it? If you dangle a man's freedom in
front of him he will say anything he thinks you
want to hear. ....has learned
his lesson well. He doesn't want to be charged
and he doesn't want to go to jail so he tells the
prosecution a series of stories; when he finds one
that he knows they want to hear, and when it is
accepted by them, he comes here and repeats it to
you. Why not? He has everything to gain and
nothing to lose, because he knows that as long as
he sticks to the story he will not be charged. If
he did change it now the buyer would call off the
deal, and terrible things, such as indictments,
would happen to him. He has to keep selling.
Like any good salesman, ...knows
his customer. He knows what his customer is
looking for, and now he's trying to sell the product to you. Are you buying? If ....
came to your house to sell you something would
you risk 2¢ on his word knowing what you know
about him? You are being asked to risk much
more in this case.*

There are numerous possibilities and each lawyer will
have to decide for himself which approach to take. It is
my conviction that the immunized witness must be met
offensively and with indignation. By communicating that
indignation to the jury in a professional and responsible
manner, the lawyer will be performing a service for his
client.

SUGGESTIONS FOR CHANGE

I do not take the view that all immunity is wrong all
the time. There are occasions when immunity can be a
reasonable prosecutorial as well as defensive tool. But my
suggestion is that immunity is too powerful a weapon to
entrust to prosecutors and their sense of self-restraint.
Kastigar and its progeny make fruitless any attempt to

seek change in the courts. The remedy is in the Congress. Congress should establish binding guidelines for immunity grants. These guidelines would extend to trials, grand jury proceedings, and administrative and congressional hearings. The courts would be charged with the duty of enforcing them.

I can suggest at least some of the standards which should be imposed. The government, at a fact hearing, should be required to show the following:

(1) That the grant of immunity is in the public interest. That is, the government ought to make a showing that the one to be immunized is not more blameworthy or more culpable than the one he will talk about. I have mentioned the three Chicago Avenue club-leaders who went free while their go-along associates received jail sentences. The question is also raised in some of the extortion cases involving public officials. Who is more culpable: the millionaire industrialist who arranged for and paid relatively small bribes to make big money, or the salaried public official who cannot resist the temptation? Indicting the public official is easier and makes more headlines, but is it good policy? The question is important and merits serious debate.

For those who say immunity is the only way to obtain evidence against wrongdoers, a reading of the Watergate Special Prosecution Force Report is instructive. Not only did the Watergate prosecutors feel the witness who pleaded guilty was more credible to a jury than the immunized witness, but,

> *plea bargaining is probably a better basis than a grant of immunity for assuring that a witness does not fabricate information he thinks the prosecutors "want to hear" in his offer of proof, since he would expect the offer to result only in a negotiated guilty plea rather than in his freedom. Most important, it avoided the unfairness of permitting one guilty of serious misconduct to avoid all liability.*

The special prosecutors recognized that plea bargaining is more cumbersome than immunizing a witness and getting his immediate cooperation. "But the result of the practice was that no one whom the prosecutors could prove had major responsibility for criminal conduct was immunized on WSPF's initiative."

In the plea bargain, the man who does the corrupting of the official would make a public and legal admission of his criminal conduct. Here one might pause to consider whether the public is served by protecting the license of the lawyer who admits that on several occasions he paid bribes to a county commissioner. That is a very large reward to pay for a man's testimony. Such a witness has everything to gain from accommodating his testimony to the expectations of his protector. Beyond that, consider what happens to the public view of a profession that contains a self-confessed corruptor of public officials.

(2) That there is no countervailing legal interest. Here, one might inquire into whether the anticipated area of questioning violates first amendment rights. At least, the right to raise the issue would serve to deter the kind of prosecutor who used the immunity statutes to harass and terrorize alleged radicals and radical sympathizers in the early 1970's.

This is an appropriate place to consider the plight of Charles Bonk, the county commissioner who faced payoff charges in the Northern District of Illinois. Bonk was acquitted, despite the testimony of two immunized lawyers. He was then given a grand jury subpoena, immunized, and ordered to testify. A textbook issue arises: how should a government treat its citizens? The real impact on Bonk is one of harassment and continuing anxiety.

(3) That the grant is sought for the witness's information and not for some other purpose. Implicit in the seeking of a grant of immunity is the government's good faith. At a hearing, a witness whose testimony is sought ought to be given the chance to show that the government intends some other purpose. For instance:

(a) The government may be immunizing a potential defendant in order to obtain what is, in effect, a discovery deposition. Under present laws, there is nothing to stop a prosecutor from calling in a defendant in a pending case, putting him before the grand jury, immunizing him, and asking him questions about the transaction with which he already has been charged. That practice was approved in *United States v. Goldberg*, where the Court noted that the immunity statute made no exception for defendants in pending cases. The potential mischief is obvious.

(b) The immunity grant may really be a strategy move to impress the jury. There are some prosecutions where the facts are basically uncontested, where the issue really is whether, given those facts, a federal crime has been committed. In a recent case in the Northern District of Illinois, a Chicago alderman was charged with violating the mail fraud statute by voting on matters in which he held a concealed interest. Very little was in dispute. The defense claimed that the facts did not add up to a crime. The jury heard evidence from witnesses who had been granted immunity from prosecution. In effect, it received the impression that a judge believed a crime had been committed. Why else would he grant immunity? The message, admittedly, is less than clear, but *jurors are finely tuned to judicial signals*. A defendant in such a case ought to have the right to raise the issue.

(c) The immunity grant might be an effort to punish a witness for non-cooperation, or to set him up for a potential false-statement charge.

The other standards which are suggested are self-explanatory:

(4) There is a need for the testimony sought and no other reasonable way to get it.

(5) A statement should be made of the specific area of inquiry and the nature of the relevant questions to be asked in that area.

(6) The government should state what it expects the testimony to be and how it comes by that expectation.

> *In sum, the government must show it is engaged in a good-faith attempt to gain information, I would bar any attempt to immunize an imminent or present defendant against his will. For a voluntary witness, the kind who seeks immunity, I would require corroboration of material parts of his testimony before it could be used.*

Some proceeding ought to exist where the defense might establish to a judge's satisfaction that the interests of justice would be served by immunizing a potential defense witness. A defendant does not have the constitutional right to compel the government to seek immunity for a defense witness who has exercised his privilege against self-incrimination. The hearings, at which these standards would be litigated could be confidential, the record sealed until such time as secrecy would not be needed. The right to counsel must be applicable.

The list of guidelines is not exhaustive, but it is a beginning. Admittedly, the hearings suggested would make the prosecutor's task more laborious, but immunity without strict legislative and judicial control is wrong and dangerous. It imperils our traditional notions of individual dignity and freedom.

CONCLUSION

For purposes of analysis and inquiry, immunity grants were separated into two categories — voluntary and involuntary. My concern with *the voluntary witness*, the one who seeks governmental protection, is his impact on the integrity of the fact-finding process. To understand how he becomes a witness is to understand the danger he poses. This is not to say or even suggest that all witnesses who seek and obtain immunity are liars. But the possibility of false testimony must be considered.

The *involuntary witness* arouses different concerns although he, too, might be tempted to fit his coerced testimony to what he thinks his questioner wants to hear. He is the witness who has asserted his privilege against self-incrimination but must testify anyway. Although it is too late in the day to say that Congress cannot constitutionally require that testimony, we may still contemplate Mr. Justice Goldberg's view of the privilege:

> It reflects many of our fundamental values and most noble aspirations: our unwillingness to subject those suspected of crime to the cruel trilemma of self-accusation, perjury, or contempt; our preference for an accusatorial rather than an inquisitorial system of criminal justice; our fear that self-incriminating statements will be elicited by inhumane treatment and abuses; **our sense of fair play which dictates "a fair state-individual balance by requiring the government to leave the individual alone until good cause is shown for disturbing him and by requiring the government in its contest with the individual to shoulder the entire load,"** . . . our respect for the inviolability of the human personality and of the right of each individual "to a private enclave where he may lead a private life" . . . It is "an expression of the moral striving of the community . . . a reflection of our common conscience."

Appendix V

United States Department of Justice

THOMAS P. SULLIVAN

UNITED STATES ATTORNEY

NORTHERN DISTRICT OF ILLINOIS

(This is an internal memorandum issued on January 26, 1978, to all Assistant U.S. Attorneys by Thomas P. Sullivan, who succeeded James R. Thompson and Samuel K. Skinner as United States Attorney for the Northern District of Illinois. It represents a sharp departure from the Thompson-Skinner media relations practices.)

TO: All Assistant United States Attorneys

RE: RELATIONS WITH NEWS MEDIA

I have consulted at some length with representatives of the various news media, and with the supervisory lawyers in this office. We have done extensive research into the legal and ethical problems involved in the prosecutor's relationships with members of the news media. I have been told by many of the Assistants that they would find it helpful to have a written statement concerning office policy on this subject.

Accordingly, until further notice, the following are the guidelines (adopted by unanimous vote of the office supervisors) which govern our relations with members of the news media.

1. None of us should initiate contact with the news media relating to matters pending in this office, except in matters of courtesy, such as a change of date or time of hearing or sentence, a jury about to return, etc.

2. Inquiries from the news media regarding pending investigations (including whether or not we have a pending investigation) should be referred to the United States Attorney, the First Assistant, or the Executive Assistant. *The general policy of this office is to make no comment whatever — whether "on" or "off" the record — about a matter under investigation or as to whether or not a matter is within the office or is under investigation.*

There may be special reasons in some instances for our acknowledging or denying the existence of an investigation, or announcing a declination. For example, it may be appropriate to acknowledge the existence of an investigation involving a matter which has received publicity. But the making of exceptions to the general rule is the sole function of the United States Attorney.

3. *Statements at the time of indictment or the filing of pleadings in civil cases will be handled solely by written press release approved by the United States Attorney*, subject to the Attorney General's statement on the matter as set forth in the attached memorandum dated July 28, 1977. *With the approval of the United States Attorney, the press release may be read by an Assistant United States Attorney on radio or television, but no oral responses will be made to news media inquiries.* Clarification should be handled by supplemental written press release, unless it concerns a simple matter.

At the conclusion of a press release relating to an indictment, we will include the following:

> *Members of the public are reminded that the indictment is only a charge and is not evidence of guilt. The defendant is entitled to a fair trial in which it will be the government's burden to prove guilt beyond a reasonable doubt.*

4. After indictment or civil complaint or answer, no comments should be made about the case, except that Assistants may respond to inquiries regarding matters of record, for example, the date of a hearing or trial, the age or address of the defendant, name of defense counsel, potential penalties, sentence imposed, date of surrender to jail, and the like. When asked regarding the content of an order, opinion or testimony, or an exhibit in evidence the Assistant should if at all possible *refer the news media to the text or to the court reporter, or read from the text or transcript, rather than attempting to summarize.* No opinions should be given or comments made on orders, opinions or testimony. Use your common sense in responding to such inquiries. If in doubt, please talk to the First Assistant, Executive Assistant or me.

5. At the time of verdict or trial court ruling, or ruling by a reviewing court, unless expressly authorized by the United States Attorney, our comments will be limited to "We are pleased with the (court's ruling — jury's verdict)," or to "We accept the (court's ruling — jury's verdict)."

6. In the event you receive a request for an interview or discussion with news media personnel, or other matter not covered by this memorandum, please check with the First Assistant, Executive Assistant or me.

S/ Thomas P. Sullivan
United States Attorney
Northern District of Illinois